THE AGE OF

MELANCHOLY

THE AGE OF
MELANCHOLY

"MAJOR DEPRESSION"

AND ITS

SOCIAL ORIGINS

DAN G. BLAZER

Routledge
Taylor & Francis Group

NEW YORK AND HOVE

Published in 2005 by
Routledge
Taylor & Francis Group
270 Madison Avenue
New York, NY 10016

Published in Great Britain by
Routledge
Taylor & Francis Group
27 Church Road
Hove, East Sussex BN3 2FA

© 2005 by Taylor & Francis Group
Routledge is an imprint of the Taylor & Francis Group
Formerly a Brunner-Routledge title

Printed in the United States of America on acid-free paper
10 9 8 7 6 5 4 3 2 1

International Standard Book Number-10: 0-415-95188-7 (Hardcover)
International Standard Book Number-13: 978-0-415-95188-3 (Hardcover)

Library of Congress Cataloging-In-Publication data:

Blazer, Dan G. (Dan German), 1944-
    The age of melancholy : "major depression" and its social origins / Dan G. Blazer.
        p. cm.
    Includes biblographical references and index.
        ISBN 0-415-95188-7 (hardback : alk. paper) 1. Depression, Mental—Social aspects. 2. Depres-sion, Mental—History. 3. Social psychiatry—History. I. Title.

    RC537.B527 2005
    362.2'5—dc22

2005006824

Taylor & Francis Group
is the Academic Division of T&F Informa plc.

Visit the Taylor & Francis Web site at
http://www.taylorandfrancis.com

and the Routledge Web site at
http://www.routledgementalhealth.com

To Berton Kaplan, Ph.D.
Mentor, Colleague, Sometime Rabbi, Friend

Contents

Preface

Depression causes more disability than any other psychiatric disorder and challenges the public's health worldwide. Many now view the burden of depression as being of epidemic proportions. Perhaps the frequency of depression is increasing dramatically in Western societies. Perhaps we are just more aware of depression. Regardless, epidemics demand a name, such as an epidemic of tuberculosis or arteriosclerotic heart disease. The name psychiatry and society have chosen for this epidemic is *major depression*. Society-wide epidemics, however, are almost always caused by some change in the environment, not the body or mind. What is the cause of the current epidemic of depression? We don't know. Why don't we know? We haven't looked. We explore body and mind to understand our age of melancholy, not the environment, especially the social environment.

Even as depression has come to the public's attention more than ever before, the search for its social origins has all but ceased. The epidemic of depression has been "medicalized" as major depression. Medical scientists search for the locus of the problem solely within the individual, whether that locus is hypothesized to be biological vulnerability or inaccurate "depressogenic" perceptions of the environment. We are autonomous souls, alone in the crowd. If we are depressed, the problem must reside within us, uncoupled from wider social and economic forces. The diagnosis major depression, when viewed as a medical disease, affirms this uncoupling. If major depression is more frequent among young women, among the economically disadvantaged, and among people exposed to violence, we dare not explore the causal linkage between depression and discrimination, poverty, or fear. Or so it seems.

The rise of major depression (as the prototypic diagnosis of modern psychiatry) and the retreat of social psychiatry reflect the sea change in psychiatry over the past 40 years. In this book, I make an argument for connecting these two trends and suggest reasons for their rapid evolution and devolution, respectively. In addition, I propose that social psychiatry should be revived, albeit in a different form. We must explore the social causes of depression. Social psychiatry must not replace but rather complement current psychobiological and clinical research. *Complement* is too weak a term. Basic social psychiatric investigations will compel mental health investigators and practitioners to embed depression within the society from which it emerges.

The reader will notice a piece of the causal puzzle dramatically underrepresented in this book—the mind. Understanding cognitive processes, the nature of consciousness, and the influence of the unconscious, memory, and reasoning, to name but a few aspects of the mind, is, of course, critical to understanding the nature and origins of depression and its treatment. I have chosen to juxtapose the current focus on the biology of the brain and the disappearance of interest in social origins. Many propose that the mind is the mediator between body and society. Others view the mind as an epiphenomenon of the activity of the brain influenced by environmental stimuli. For the purpose of my argument, I see no reason to enter this debate. I do not propose a grand model of depression.

The reader will also note that I do not focus on the contributions of the disciplines of sociology and social psychology, though I refer frequently to studies that have been published by these disciplines. I purposefully have focused my comments on psychiatry. Psychiatry in many ways drives other disciplines, especially in the move to a biomedical model of emotional distress. In addition, only the medical profession at present widely prescribes medications, the most obvious manifestation of our changing views toward depression as a society. Fully 10% of the adult U.S. population takes antidepressant medications. I also have focused on the experience with depression and psychiatry primarily in the United States. Though similarities abound across Western countries, the United States has tracked a unique history in my view.

Each chapter contains a section titled "A Case in Point" that segues to the real world of psychiatrist, patient, and society. Some cases reflect real people. Even though names are changed or omitted, the events are described accurately while at the same time limited in description so that anonymity and confidentiality can be maintained. The essence of the cases accurately reflects the patients' experiences, though the patients would have great difficulty identifying themselves.

I wish to thank the Foundations Fund for Research in Psychiatry and the Center for Advanced Study in the Behavioral Sciences at Stanford, California, for providing me with the opportunity to pursue this argument. In addition, I wish to thank my home institution, Duke University School of Medicine, for extending a sabbatical year for these studies. The JP Gibbons Professorship in Psychiatry and Behavioral Sciences has been critical in support of this year as well. My thanks go out to many colleagues who have assisted me in this work, including Kathleen Much at the Center for Advanced Studies and George Zimmar and Dana Bliss at Routledge. Finally, I forever am grateful to my wife, Sherrill.

The Diagnosis of Depression

1

Introduction

The biological and the social are neither separable, nor antithetical, nor alternatives, but complementary. ... All human phenomena are simultaneously social and biological.

—Richard Lewontin, Stephen Rose, and Leon Kanin, *Not in Our Genes* (p. 1)[1]

We live in an age of melancholy.[2] Depression, the most frequent of the serious chronic mental illnesses, causes disability equal to if not greater than medical illnesses such as diabetes and hypertension. Epidemiologic studies have demonstrated that depression exerts the greatest societal burden of all the psychiatric disorders.[3-5] According to the World Health Organization, depression ranks 4th among the 10 leading causes of the global burden of disease and is expected to rise to 2nd within the next 20 years.[6] Psychiatry and society have chosen a name for this melancholic burden: *major depression*. The diagnosis and treatment of major depression dominates the practice of therapists from psychiatrists to pastoral counselors.

We are thankful that we do not live in an age of hopelessness, at least from the perspective of psychiatry. Major depression is a treatable disease. Indeed, 70% of those who take antidepressant drugs respond,[6, 7] and relapse following initial treatment can be significantly reduced with a combination of antidepressants and psychotherapy.[8]

Despite the good news—a better understanding of the brain, improved diagnostic capabilities, and the improvements in therapy—something in therapists' understanding and treatment of the disease is missing. W.H. Auden believed that society was adrift after World War I, leading to widespread anxiety, and he designated the era between the world wars of the 20th century the "age of anxiety."[9] He coupled the epidemic of anxiety with the unstable, "anxiogenic" social environment of Western Europe and America. The world was a threatening place in which to live. Uncertainty abounded. Given the world situation, anxiety was to be expected. Somehow, however, we seem to have lost sight of the connection between the way we feel and the world around us. How does the world around us currently contribute to our feelings of depression?

The Medicalization of Depression

Today, biological explanations of the burden predominate. Biological treatment is focused on the brain in the form of medications, and psychotherapy for depression emphasizes the need of the individual to adjust to the social environment. Psychiatrists rarely acknowledge that something is wrong with the social environment, and they encourage change in that environment even more rarely. In other words, despite the commonly accepted facts that major depression is prevalent in our society and that our social environment is rife with stressors that make us vulnerable, psychiatry does not link our melancholy with the society in which we live. Social psychiatry—the study of the social origins of psychiatric illness—has all but disappeared as a paradigm for investigating the origins of depression and, instead, has been replaced by biological explanations.

A CASE IN POINT

A few years ago, I worked with a group of valued colleagues to sketch a geriatric psychiatry research agenda for the future. We agreed that a focus on major depression made sense as a starting point. The umbrella term *major depression* encompasses quite a few types of inquiry. We added many research projects to the agenda, including brain imaging of severely depressed older adults and clinical trials of new, promising medications. I am a social epidemiologist and a geriatric psychiatrist. I also am a little older than these colleagues and well remember the heyday of social psychiatry in the United States. It seemed obvious for me to add items to the agenda from my research and clinical experience.

I suggested that we add the study of primary prevention for late-life depression to the agenda. The social stressors of late life, such as the lack of economic resources or the fear of crime, seemed obvious topics to study. In other words, I proposed that we research ways in which depression can be prevented in the first place. My colleagues turned to me in disbelief. One responded, "There is no primary prevention of major depression." I stared back in equal disbelief. Of course, no one had yet proved that changing the living conditions or the social context of an older adult would prevent late-life depression. But we were setting a research agenda for the future, not summarizing findings from the past. Could my colleagues believe that such an intervention was not even feasible? Could they totally discount the context of late-life depression and refuse to add explorations of the social origins of depression to the agenda? Yes, they could! I realized, to my dismay, that social psychiatry had all but disappeared from the view of most psychiatrists.

The Advance of Major Depression and the Retreat of Social Psychiatry

Social psychiatry, which thrived during the 1960s, is virtually moribund in the United States, whereas major depression, born during the late 1970s, has become an everyday label accepted by psychiatrists, their patients, and the public. The term *major depression* could scarcely be found in the psychiatric literature prior to the publication of the research diagnostic criteria in 1978 and their expansion in the third edition of the American Psychiatric Association's *Diagnostic and Statistical Manual of Mental Disorders–Third Edition* (DSM–III) in 1980.[10, 11] (John Feighner and other psychiatrists at Washington University developed the core operational construct of major depression as early as 1972 and applied the term *primary depression*.)[12] I believe the advance of major depression as a diagnosis and the retreat of social psychiatry are linked.

During the 1960s, clinically significant depression was divided into two categories: reactive and endogenous (or internal). The most common form of depression was diagnosed as depressive neurosis (a reaction). In contrast to the more severe endogenous depressions, such as manic-depressive illness, the much more frequent depressive neurosis was caused by an excessive reaction to internal (psychodynamic) and external stressors.[13] An external stressor was essential to the onset of reactive depression, whether that stressor was the loss of a loved one or a response to a dysfunctional social environment. Depression was a complex malady that required a comprehensive explanation.

In the past, psychiatrists expended many words describing the emotional suffering of their patients, for no one word conveyed from one psychiatrist to another the nature, context, and severity of the suffering. The advent of the new diagnostic system allowed psychiatrists to use one label, such as *major depression*, and another psychiatrist knew what the first had observed. The new nomenclature says, essentially, that "a person has major depression if the following criteria are met, such as a depressed mood and five additional symptoms lasting at least two weeks." Therefore, psychiatrists have become more reliable—that is, consistent—in their use of terms.

Unfortunately, though, much of the richness and context of the more lengthy discussions of the past have been lost. Psychiatrists, it seems, have come to believe that if they label the person with a diagnosis such as major depression, they have said it all. In other words, there is a "real disease" called major depression and, by attaching the label, the psychiatrist pronounces that the patient has this disease. (This process of making an idea real has been labeled "reification." To treat an abstraction as substantially existing is to reify the abstraction.) Reification numbs us to the possibility that depression can be more a signal of the emotionally toxic society in which we live than a thing in and of itself. And if the effects of this toxicity are initially expressed through depression, then depression should signal a need to better understand and improve society.

During the first 60 years of the 20th century, medicine in general and psychiatry in particular became increasingly concerned about social and cultural contributions to illness onset. There was widespread interest in the potential of community-wide interventions that might decrease the onset and persistence of those illnesses. Social medicine arose from general medicine as a separate entity, even a specialty (though never a large one). The research arm of social medicine was epidemiology, with a specific emphasis on social epidemiology.[14] In addition, the social sciences, especially anthropology[15] and sociology,[16] focused many of their efforts on health and illness. Of all the medical specialties, however, only psychiatry formalized a special relation to the social sciences by developing a subspecialty of social psychiatry—there was never a "social obstetrics" or a "social pediatrics."[17] Departments of social medicine were almost always separate from departments of internal medicine and were more aligned to schools of public health.

Following World War II, social psychiatry gained momentum in Europe and the United States. This momentum was fueled by the belief that social factors contributed more to emotional suffering than biological and individual psychological factors did. The 1960s saw an overarching optimism about the ability of social interventions to counter destructive social conditions. As a result of that optimism, the Community Mental Health Center (CMHC) movement was launched, with the goal of intervening in society's institutions, from families and schools to the federal government. Gerald Caplan, a prominent social psychiatrist in the 1960s, described the goal of the CMHC movement:

Primary prevention is a community concept. ... It does not seek to prevent a specific person from becoming sick. Instead, it seeks to reduce the risk for the whole population, so that, although some may become ill, their number will be reduced. ... A program of primary prevention will focus on identifying current harmful [environmental] influences ... [seeing] that harmful pressures will be reduced in intensity, [and] that people will be helped to find healthy ways of dealing with them.[18]

Society, not just the individual, was the patient. To treat depression, one must treat a depressogenic society. This focus on society was considered the most effective means of reducing the burden of depression.

Psychiatry and government, however, were inept at treating society and quickly retreated from the broad objectives of the CMHC movement. The retreat was almost universal, and psychiatrists turned their backs on the implications of a potentially noxious society. Social psychiatry, as it was known during the 1960s, had all but disappeared by the mid-1990s. The rapidly emerging medical model of depression within psychiatry facilitated the retreat of social psychiatry. Sam Guze summarized the medical model for psychiatry:

Scientific progress in psychiatry ... comprises two broad streams of investigation ... one epidemiological and the other neurobiological. ... Each requires, reinforces, and ultimately validates a classification of psychopathology. Classification is indispensable for thinking, studying, teaching, and communicating.[19]

In the move to sharpen classification, *depression* became *major depression*. Specifically defined cases of illness caused by identifiable neuropathology characterized the medical model in psychiatry. If you can define it, you can count it, and if you can count it, then you can search for neurobiological causes. Epidemiology counts—counts cases, that is.

The retreat of social psychiatry and the profession's wholehearted embrace of the medical model, however, can only partially be explained by the failure of the CMHC movement to influence society as a whole. Financial constraints (which, in large measure, scuttled Lyndon Johnson's Great Society) or the influence of the pharmaceutical industry, a popular target,[20] cannot be held responsible for the changes. Other social forces must be explored to explain changes in the view of depression and the virtual disappearance of social psychiatry during the past 30 years. In chapter 6, for example, I examine war syndromes, such as the Gulf War syndrome, which many people are inclined to attribute to specific physical toxins, such as oil well fires, excluding the stress of war. Although it should be noted that multiple factors can contribute to war syndromes, perhaps the most significant factors are ignored because they are not specific—that is, they are societal rather than physical.

Methodological Individualism and Its Limitations

A broad-based psychiatry must consider biological, psychological, and social origins of disease and dysfunction.[21] Psychiatry, however, has retreated into a narrow, "medicalized" view of depression, ignoring, for the most part, the connection between depression and society. Medicalized depression has focused etiological and interventional research on biological origins and person-specific treatments. The classic medical model insists that disease represents specific biological vulnerabilities interacting with specific environmental insults. For example, a family history of coronary heart disease coupled with a diet high in cholesterol and fat leads to a heart attack. Treatment consists of specific interventions to correct the individual genetic-environmental aberration, such as a change in diet. This medical model has been called methodological individualism.[22]

Recently, however, the limitations of methodological individualism for many of the most frequent chronic physical illnesses have been revealed. For example, the serving sizes and fat content of fast foods have increasingly come under attack. Indeed, there is a substantial literature suggesting that the influence of advertising fast foods has contributed significantly to the increase in our sedentary lifestyle and increased obesity.[23, 24] The intuitive answer to the problem of obesity—either that we, as individuals, are responsible for our weight or that there is something genetically wrong with us that leads to obesity regardless of our behavior—has been expanded to include social forces. In other words, the treatment and prevention of obesity must include intervention beyond the individual to the types and quantities of foods served by the restaurant industry.

Consider, also, exposure to another person's cigarette smoke—passive smoking. Because passive smoking is now thought to increase the risk of lung cancer, many hospitals and other public places have begun to prohibit smoking on the premises. The prevention of lung cancer extends beyond the individual's genetics and behavior. For example, people have known of the connection between smoking and lung cancer for years. Yet only when the government banned advertisement of cigarettes on TV and put bold warnings on tobacco products has there been a reduction in smoking.[24]

Depressive illness, likewise, should not be constrained by methodological individualism. As with cardiovascular disease, depression must be viewed as more than an interaction between a biologically vulnerable person and his or her behaviors toward a unique environment. Regardless of biological vulnerability, most first episodes of major depression are closely associated with a stressful life event, events often out of the control of the individual. During times of economic turndown, for example, the rate of depression goes up. When the economy is in recession or depression, people lose jobs or face other financial challenges. These social stressors clearly increase the frequency of depression.[25] Yet the individualistic approach maintains a strong hold on the way we think about depression.

All cultures place individual experiences into agreed-on social categories. Americans increasingly project the mood of depression onto biological processes, such as a chemical imbalance, and then turn to biology to validate that mood as natural and unique to the individual. Those in the United States are not alone in turning to biological processes and pharmaceutical answers. In Japan, where severe depression has long been recognized as a medical illness, less severe downturns in mood have been attributed to *ki*—a downturn in mood because one's vital energy was leaking—because that energy was sluggish.[26] *Ki* was a state of the soul. These downturns were not considered abnormal, for happiness was believed to be not the continued natural state but rather a fleeting experience. Therefore, seeking medical help for mild to moderately severe depression (what we might consider a less severe case of major depression or minor depression) was not an option.

In recent years, however, things have changed in Japan, in large part because of an advertising blitz by the pharmaceutical industry. *Kokoru no kaze* became a byword across the airwaves: Your *kokoru* was coming down with a cold and you could do something about it. What can be done? Take antidepressant medications. Though few would deny that romanticizing suffering is something to be avoided, nevertheless the loss of sadness as a signal to reflect and to assess the world around cannot bode well for any society.

How Medicalization Affects the Research of Depression

No one can reasonably deny that those suffering from depression deserve as much attention as those suffering from diabetes or lung cancer, and one cannot reasonably deny that relieving the burden of depressive symptoms is a central challenge for health care providers. Yet the boundaries of major depression are far more fuzzy than those of most established medical diagnoses.[27] Although we have tests to identify malignancy in tissue, we cannot diagnose depression by looking at it under a microscope. We have no way to know where the boundary lies between a depression that deserves clinical attention and the usual adaptations to the slings and arrows of everyday life, adaptations that lead people to moan and groan but from which they emerge as strong as before and perhaps a little wiser.[28]

This fuzziness renders the diagnosis major depression especially deceptive. Specifically, major depression as a medical diagnosis effectively shapes and limits the explorations of its causes. In other words, when clinicians make a diagnosis of major depression, they make a sharp distinction in a span of otherwise indistinct emotional suffering. Grouping so many sufferers under the medical diagnosis of major depression leads to two troublesome outcomes: First, the social forces that contribute to the person's symptoms are not considered, and, second, by ignoring social factors, the diagnosis limits the search for treatment and prevention to the individual.[29]

Do clinicians have evidence that the medicalization of major depression limits inquiry into its causes? According to the Depression and Bipolar Support Alliance,

> Depression is a treatable illness involving an imbalance of brain chemicals called neurotransmitters. It is not a character flaw or a sign of personal weakness. You can't make yourself well by trying to "snap out of it." Although it can run in families, you can't catch it from someone else. The direct causes of the illness are unclear, however it is known that body chemistry can bring on a depressive disorder.[30]

Personal weakness in our society is usually attributed to not being able to adapt to the social situation, to not being able to pick oneself up by one's bootstraps regardless of the circumstances. In other words, the stress (external) versus diathesis (constitutional predisposition) model that traditionally was the basis for investigations into the causes of depression has tipped sharply in favor of diathesis—in this case, biological vulnerability. Medicalization also leads to unambiguous assumptions regarding prevention and treatment. Because the assumption is that biological vulnerability is innate, the conclusion is that primary prevention (preventing the onset) of depression is virtually impossible to achieve (except through use of medications in high-risk populations). According to this model, treatment should focus on individuals, and the core treatment is biological (pharmacological).

These assumptions, in turn, shape the research agenda. Within this model, an appropriate research question is, "Does this antidepressant medication lead to greater symptom improvement than placebo does?" In contrast, an inappropriate question is, "Does reducing stress in the workplace reduce the frequency of depressive symptoms?" Of course, it is much easier, logistically, to conduct pharmaceutical trials than it is to carry out workplace interventions, but it is not the difficulty of intervention that should drive the research agenda. Rather, focus on the individual and, specifically, on the biology of the individual reflects a belief that the manifestation of depression signals pathogenic brains, not pathogenic social environments.

Beyond the Medical

The current views of depression can be attributed largely to the progressive uncovering of the biological etiology of depression and the development of new and improved medications, as well as to the influence of the pharmaceutical industry.[7, 31] Nevertheless, other factors beyond the influence of biological science and industry focus attention on the body rather than on society. For example, the advertising industry hammers home the message that, if we want to *feel* better, then we must lose weight, improve our complexion, or change our hair's style or color. In addition, we, as a society, face a paradox. Even though we seem to be gaining much more knowledge of and control over our bodies—the promise of gene therapy, for example—our increasingly complex society makes us, in reality, even less in control of our lives than we used to be. We are working far more hours in, probably, more stressful jobs than we were 40 years ago, but we see no way out of the increasing demands at work and home.[32] Therefore, when looking for answers to our disease, we tend to look in areas that appear to offer the simplest hope of success—improving our bodies and ourselves. But despite the specific success stories we so often hear about in the media (such as the discovery of a new therapy for cancer), the ability of the new biology to appreciably improve our quality of life in the face of today's societal ills is questionable. Nevertheless, the emphasis on the individual body and brain means that the social origins of depression (especially causes beyond personal control) are, today, of little interest to psychiatrists and, perhaps, the public.

This lack of interest in the social origins of depression reflects the tendency to attribute depression (and virtually all illnesses) to causes that can, in theory, be controlled by the individual or by interventions directed toward the individual. This person-specific, concrete approach undoubtedly reflects our highly individualistic society, coupled with a loss of confidence that we can effect society-wide social changes. Such social nihilism contrasts sharply with the vision during the 1960s, the zenith of social psychiatry, that society could be changed through aggressive policy in service of the common good.

Organization of the Argument

In chapter 2 I trace the origins of the diagnosis *major depression* and its rapid ascendance as the prototypical psychiatric diagnosis. If a mental health professional addresses a general audience, the chances are high that most of the audience will be familiar with the term *major depression*. From their exposure to the media, listeners will, most likely, already have formed ideas of what is meant by the term. *Major depression* conjures images of a severe but common emotional disturbance caused by a chemical imbalance. We do not bring major depression on ourselves; it "happens to us," just as a stroke happens. Such an image is in stark contrast to our views of depression earlier in the 20th century. Depression was a sign of psychological weakness or overwhelming life events, especially losses. Our minds and experiences, not our bodies and brains, caused depression.

In chapter 3 I describe the history of the belief that depression is a reaction to a toxic social environment. Prior to the 20th century, the depression of interest to psychiatrists was of the most grave variety: severe melancholia or manic-depressive insanity. Sigmund Freud's psychoanalysis centered psychiatry in the office, not the hospital. The depression of interest to Freud was widespread, the neurotic response to the loss of something valuable to a person. During and following World War II, psychiatry moved out of the office and into the community. Depression was mostly reactive depression, and depressives reacted to a toxic social environment.

Critics challenged psychiatrists' attraction during the 1960s to psychoanalysis and social psychiatry, encouraging the discipline to return to the fold of medicine. This return to the medical model provided the background for the birth of the diagnosis major depression, and, as a result, reactive depression disappeared. In this chapter I trace the rise and fall of depression as a reaction to problems in the world around us. In addition, I examine the criticisms of psychiatry during the latter half of the century. An antipsychiatry movement arose during the 1970s, largely in response to social psychiatry. In the early 21st century, psychiatry is facing another dilemma: psychiatry has found the brain but lost the person within his or her family and community. And critics are once again emerging.

In chapter 4 I trace the birth and growth of social psychiatry. Emotional suffering is a social and personal experience. We feel a range of emotions in large part because of our interactions with people around us. Our feelings of comfort or fear are frequently based on our perceptions of the safety of our neighborhoods or on the extent to which we feel that the world around us makes sense. The way in which we communicate our emotions depends on the standards society sets for expressing how we feel.

Social psychiatry—the study of our feelings and behaviors within the context of society—was virtually unknown prior to the 20th century. Psychiatrists grew more interested in society as they became more interested in psychoanalysis, and social psychiatry blossomed during the 1950s and 1960s in the United States, especially given the boost from President Kennedy's Mental Health Act. Social research soon gave way to social activism as the movement advanced in parallel with the establishment of community mental health centers. Community psychiatry has been labeled "social psychiatry in action."

I trace the roots of social psychiatry, roots that run much deeper than the social activism of the 1960s. Interest in the social causation of psychiatric disorders, such as depression, was expressed earlier in the 20th century by sociologists such as Emil Durkheim, psychiatrists such as Adolf Meyer and Harry Stack Sullivan, and organizations such as the U.S. Army during World War II. The flowering of the movement during the latter 1960s, in conjunction with President Johnson's Great Society, led many psychiatrists to proclaim that real psychiatry was *social* psychiatry.

In chapter 5 I propose that social psychiatry has been in fast retreat for many years. The field, which flowered during the 1960s, wilted quickly during the 1970s. Though the social origins of emotional suffering continue to be of marginal interest to psychiatrists, they have been dramatically eclipsed by the biological origins. Yet the retreat of social psychiatry cannot be attributed purely to psychiatrists' increased knowledge of neurobiology. Rather, the social psychiatry of the 1960s has all but disappeared primarily because interest in society in and of itself, as well as in how society affects its members, has vanished. Attention to social factors has been restricted to assessing individual social risk factors, such as stressful life events, or individual social outcomes of psychiatric disorders, such as loss of employment or disruption of the family.

I trace the retreat of social psychiatry over the past 30 years. I explore seeds of social psychiatry's demise that were evident long before its decline. How could the obvious role of society in the origin and development of emotional suffering recede so dramatically? What were the signs of the demise of social psychiatry during its halcyon years of the 1960s? Why are psychiatrists today so averse to exploring the social origins of major depression and other psychiatric disorders?

A front-page headline in the *San Francisco Chronicle*, June 18, 2003, proclaimed, "Help for Depression Lacking, Studies Find: 14 Million Americans Suffer Major Episode Annually." The reporter summarized findings from a recent national survey of more than 9,000 people to determine the frequency of major depression (and other psychiatric disorders) and the frequency of treatment (differentiating adequate and inadequate treatment).[33] The message from the authors of this study is clear: Major depression is a critical public health problem, and people are not being treated nearly as often as they should. In chapter 6 I explore how to assess the studies of the frequency of depression in our society.

Community studies of the burden of psychiatric disorders provide the key evidence for the declaration that depression will be the number two public health problem worldwide during the second decade of the 21st century. How should we interpret such news reports of these studies? Would these headlines have been different 50 years ago? Given the wide attention these studies of emotional suffering command, we first must understand the assumptions on which they are based.

I review the studies that support such startling headlines. The study of the burden of emotional suffering in the community has progressed through two waves during the past 50 years. I examine these two waves and the distinctly different assumptions of the investigators who led the studies. Remarkably, the estimation of the overall burden of emotional suffering—and the specific burden of depression—has, if anything, increased despite the movement from a view of depression as a natural reaction to social stressors to the acceptance of major depression as a disease.

Because our views of depression have changed dramatically during the past century, our views of other types of emotional suffering should also change. War syndromes provide an excellent example of changing views of emotional suffering through time, and in chapter 7 I survey war syndromes as responses to the stress of war. Although every war in our history has been stressful and has taken an emotional toll on the soldiers who fight, our interpretation of the emotional response to the trauma of war has changed dramatically since the Civil War. The symptoms associated with Gulf War syndrome and our interpretation of those symptoms provide a critical lesson in the study of the social origins of depression.

Each of the major military conflicts in which the United States has participated during the past 150 years has caused the participants physical and emotional problems that have not been easily categorized or explained by physical causes. During each conflict, however, a particular characterization of these problems has emerged. The names given them include "shellshock" during World War I, "combat exhaustion or fatigue" during World War II, "post-traumatic stress disorder" following the Vietnam War, and "Gulf War syndrome" following the Persian Gulf War.

When perceived as one specific disease with clear yet undiscovered causes in the physical environment, Gulf War syndrome, is, in part, an example of societal "framing" of nonspecific symptoms into an understandable entity. The names changed according to the conflict. I discuss Gulf War syndrome and how the history of the syndrome in part illustrates such framing. As with major depression, society has been loath to attribute Gulf War syndrome, even in part, to the stress of war.

Although the study of the social origins of depression might be an interesting intellectual pursuit, how might it change the relationship between doctor and patient? In what ways can the perspective of social psychiatry be brought into the therapeutic encounter? Should the psychiatrist be interested in the world in which his or her patients live beyond the accounts provided by that patient? Does therapeutic encouragement to discover ways to better adapt to the social environment always meet the needs of the patient? In chapter 8 I address these questions.

Western culture is in the middle of a fundamental transformation that has shaken the foundations of the way we think, feel, and behave. The old "sacred canopy" of modern progress has blown away and the biting chill of anomie now settles on city and state. In other words, the society that we believed we understood and in which we felt secure during the 1950s has become incomprehensible and threatening in the 21st century. Our level of trust of authority, from religion through medicine to politics, has declined dramatically (despite the passionate and dogmatic religious and political proclamation we hear). Though much of our trust in the past was misplaced, our more accurate view of society has lead to what some call "the gravest sort of anxiety." Such anxiety results from a sense that we have lost our foundations and that chaos reigns. Chaos and its resultant anxiety cannot be tolerated for long, and depression, a signal to withdraw, is perhaps a natural adaptation to these feelings. People living in such a society will naturally react to that society.

I suggest that depression is one expected response to current Western society. Much of the natural emotional response to Western society is a negative experience. Depression captures the essence of this experience of the negative, especially the sense of not being one's self and the loss of meaning and hope. If the therapist ignores the society that contributes to the experiences of the patient, the therapist cannot treat the patient effectively.

Something needs to change. Social psychiatry must be reborn. How? What are the next steps? In chapter 9 I review the rebirth of social psychiatry, evidence of which is already seen. Now is the time for psychiatry to take full advantage of the maturity of the social sciences and to create and develop a new wave of basic social psychiatric research. Social psychiatry needs young investigators grounded in the basic social sciences who can conduct interdisciplinary research, exploring the impact of social forces on the frequency and distribution of emotional suffering, especially depression. These psychiatric investigators must move upstream from the phenomenology of psychiatric disorders that has dominated diagnostic psychiatry and the neurobiologic aberrations that have dominated biological psychiatry; that is, investigators must seek the root origins of the depression epidemic.

To accomplish this task, psychiatry must take full advantage of the advances in the social sciences during the past 25 years, advances of which most psychiatrists are unaware. Young psychiatrists considering a career in research should be encouraged to consider the basic social sciences, such as anthropology, sociology, and social epidemiology, and the basic physical sciences, such as molecular biology and neuropsychopharmacology. I review two areas—depression in the workplace and the social ecology of depression—to illustrate how the basic social sciences can be applied to understanding the causes of depression. In other words, risk factors for depression should be considered that are not strictly tied to the individual.

A rebirth of interest in the social origins of depression cannot ignore the dramatic advances in the understanding of the biology of depression during the past 30 years. Social investigations cannot proceed isolated from biological investigations. How can the two be linked? I explore in chapter 10 the linkage between body and society through emotion.

The future study of body and brain within the context of society must be linked through concepts familiar to social psychiatry and biological psychiatry, such as emotion. Depression is, if nothing else, an emotion. An informed study of emotion is a key link between body and society, given its rich history in biology, psychology, sociology, and anthropology. The empirical study of emotion should buffer the tendency of the biological sciences toward reductionism and the social sciences toward social construction.

I review two examples where the link has become more clear—social zeitgebers and allostatic load. Social zeitgebers refer to those personal relationships, social demands, or tasks that serve to entrain biological rhythms, rhythms that are core to the psychobiology of depression. For example, our work schedule shapes the time we go to sleep and the time we awaken. Sleep disturbance is a key symptom of major depression. The interaction of the body's natural rhythms and society's demands, therefore, shapes a key component of depression—sleep.

The allostatic load theory links the psychosocial environment to depression by means of neuroendocrine pathways. Allostatic systems (*allo* meaning variable) are those systems that help keep the body stable—that is, adapt to changes in the environment—by being able to change (such as the change in hormone levels when the environment changes). The price paid by the body and brain to make these changes over time is wear and tear on the organism, such as an increased vulnerability to depression.

One consequence of the rise of major depression as a medical disease and the retreat of social psychiatry is the increasingly widespread use of antidepressant medications. Is this a problem? If the drugs work, why should we be concerned? Yet many today have expressed grave concerns about the use of the medications. In his 1932 novel *Brave New World*, Aldous Huxley anticipated the conflict over the use of such powerful drugs, describing the use of the fictional drug *soma* (used by the leaders of Huxley's dystopia to placate the people).[34] In chapter 11 I explore the problem with soma. Huxley specifically recognized the likelihood that antidepressant drugs would emerge and be very effective in his retrospective *Brave New World Revisited*.[35] His caution regarding their use is perhaps an even more critical message today than it was 70 years ago.

Psychiatrists today focus their own complaints about the profession almost totally onto managed care, cuts in federal and state support of mental health services, federal cutbacks in research and training dollars, and a lack of respect from medical colleagues and patients. Each of these external challenges to the specialty is very real. Even so, psychiatry is numbed to an intrinsic problem, similar to the problem Huxley described with soma in *Brave New World*. The problem with soma, put simply, was that it numbed Huxley's fictional society to its social problems.

Although we are far from the tyranny of Huxley's brave new world, we have become numbed to the social context from which mental illness (especially depression) emerges, and we have become numbed to those social forces that shape the specialty. We have lost our sociological imagination. The loss of this sociological imagination is my greatest concern for psychiatry in the 21st century.

The Birth and Growth of Major Depression

When I go musing all alone
Thinking of divers things fore-known,
When I build Castles in the air,
Void of sorrow and void of fear,
Pleasing my self with phantasms sweet,
Methinks the time runs very fleet.
All my joys to this are folly,
Naught so sweet as Melancholy...

I'll change my state with any wretch,
Thou canst from gaol or dunghill fetch.
My pain's past cure, another Hell,
I may not in this torment dwell,
Now desperate I hate my life,
Lend me a halter or a knife.
All my griefs to this are jolly,
Naught so damn'd as Melancholy.

—Robert Burton, *The Anatomy of Melancholy*, 1621 (pp. 8, 10)[1]

Depression is a disorder of mood, so mysteriously painful and elusive in the way it becomes known to the self—to the mediating intellect—as to verge close to being beyond description. It thus remains nearly incomprehensible to those who have not experienced it in its extreme mood, although the gloom, "the blues" which people go through occasionally and associate with the general hassle of everyday existence are of such prevalence that they do give many individuals a hint of the illness in its catastrophic form.

—William Styron, *Darkness Visible: A Memoir of Madness*, 1990 (p. 7)[2]

What is this confusing, ambivalent, yet encompassing "depression" that Robert Burton attempted to dissect in 1621 and that William Styron tried to shed light on some 350 years later? Depression is a ubiquitous emotion that transcends objective description and confounds us today as it did 300 years ago. It is the prototypic mental malady because it is so prevalent and because virtually all of us intuit the phenomenon despite our inability to describe it easily. Therefore, the language of the poet and novelist, not the scientist, might best capture the experience.

Though the periodic severe disorder Emil Kraepelin described as manic-depressive insanity afflicts only the few (such as Burton and Styron),[3] the experience of depression is a prevailing mood across early 21st-century Western society. The frequency of moderate to severe depression is about 6.5% in the community at any given time, and the lifetime frequency approaches 20%.[4] The current frequency of sadness is even higher.[5] For example, 22% of older adults in one community survey reported "feeling sad" most of the day every day during the preceding week.[5] More than 14% of the participants in this sample reported feeling lonely for most of the day every day of the preceding week. We live in an "age of melancholy."[6, 7]

Yet the mood that defines the age of melancholy has been sterilized by the emergence of the construct *major depression*. The rich texture and depth of emotional suffering has been replaced by an almost mechanical description of this very human experience. This view of major depression as a specific, circumscribed, and widespread disease has been confirmed in the popular press:

> Major depression is so widespread that it has been called the common cold of mental illness. Famous sufferers include U.S. presidents Lyndon Johnson and Richard Nixon. ... In terms of lifetime risk, it's estimated that up to 25 percent of women and 12 percent of men will experience one episode of major depression. About half of those will suffer a recurrence. (Montreal Gazette, October 7, 2002, final edition, p. D3)

> "Our findings show that the number of people affected by major depression will continue to grow exponentially" said Molly Varnau, director of strategic market reports, Front Line Strategic Consulting, Inc. "Major depression ... is the leading cause of disability in the United States." (Financial News, August 1, 2002)

A Case in Point

John, at the encouragement of his fellow employees, participated in Depression Screening Day at the Uniflex factory. On Heart Disease Day, 6 months before, the nurse had pricked his finger to determine his cholesterol level and taken his blood pressure. John knew that high cholesterol and high blood pressure increase the likelihood of heart disease. But he was confused about Depression Screening Day. His aunt had been severely depressed a few years back and received shock treatments, but she had always been a little crazy and had not worked for years. John had his own troubles. He was concerned about keeping his job with Uniflex, especially with recent layoffs. His wife was pregnant again, and the bills were piling up. Just getting through the day had been tough recently, but he was not like his aunt. Or was he?

After John completed a standard questionnaire used to diagnose major depression, the nurse told him that he probably had major depression and needed medical help. He visited his primary care doctor for an evaluation. After about 10 minutes of questioning, the doctor told John,

> You have a psychiatric problem. We call it major depression and it is very common. It's a disease. I'll bet one out of every five people who come in here have it. Thankfully, we have some excellent treatments available now. I can give you a medicine today and will refer you to a psychologist who will work with you for three or four months. Don't worry, this is not like the counseling you have heard about in the past. You don't have to tell everything about your childhood or anything like that. You see, people with major depression get into ways of thinking that are not healthy. She can help you think about things more clearly.

John protested: "Doc, I've had a lot going on recently, worrying about my job and finances. I'm sure it gets me down at times. Maybe this stuff is on my mind most of the time, but I don't think I am depressed." The doctor responded,

> John, this is not something to be ashamed of. It's a disease. Just like having an ulcer. We don't understand all the reasons some people get depressed, but we know it involves a chemical imbalance.

We also know stress in life can help cause it. When you have a disease, you get treatment. You'd be surprised at how many people are getting treated for major depression. I am so glad we picked it up early. If we get treatment started early, people do better in the long run.

John agreed to take the medicine but said that he did not have time for the counseling, and his doctor did not insist. Once he began the medicine, he felt a little better. Then he lost his job. He could not sleep, he could not eat, and he felt terrible. What was he going to do? Unemployment compensation did not kick in for a couple of months, and he was already in debt. His doctor referred him to a psychiatrist. The psychiatrist said that John needed his medication adjusted, and he increased the dose. He also strongly encouraged John to get counseling soon. John's insurance did not cover the counseling, so he decided to try the medicine alone. He felt a little better with the higher dose.

Three months following his visit to the psychiatrist, John learned that his company was hiring back. He was hired the next day. Not only did John love his new job but the company also increased his salary. The depression lifted. He could now sleep at night, and he gained back about 10 pounds. His wife joked that he was getting a little pudgy. "Joan," he said to his wife, "I don't think most people understand that major depression is a disease. I was feeling so terrible and now I feel great. Thank God that, in the future, when these feelings start coming on, I'll know what to do."

Was this a case of disease or "dis-ease"? Although John apparently received some benefit from antidepressant medication, he also seemed to get as much, if not more, relief from positive changes in his situation. Although John probably did experience some chemical imbalance, the stress in his life was a much more important contributor to his depression. Did the relief that the antidepressant medication gave John necessarily imply that he suffered from a medical disease rather than from social stress? Psychiatry today—along with the media's ever-present input—would have society choose the medical explanation over the social. This emphasis on major depression as a diagnosis might be causing psychiatry to ignore equally important—or, perhaps, *more* important—contributors to emotional distress.

Major Depression and the Medical Model

The diagnosis of major depression today implies a tangible disease, widespread and biologically driven, rather than reflecting the existential experience of the age of melancholy. This view of depression has substantially shaped the approach taken by psychiatric clinicians and investigators. Etiological and interventional research focuses on biological origins and person-specific treatments, using the classic medical model. According to this model, psychiatrists are physicians who specialize in the treatment of specific emotional or behavioral disorders that are analogous with, if not identical to, medical diseases such as type I diabetes.[8] The model assumes clearly delineated disease boundaries, and the role of the physician is functionally specific: a specialist who limits his or her attention to circumscribed areas involving these diseases. The patient either has major depression or does not have it. And, if the patient has major depression, then the physician treats major depression.

Individual genetic or other biological aberrations interact with specific environmental insults to cause major depression, according to the medical model. Treatment is focused on correcting the individual genetic-environmental aberration—a concept of disease and its treatment that also has been labeled *methodological individualism*, as I define in chapter 1. Most current investigation of depression in the community, therefore, is based on the notion that its distribution in populations can be explained exclusively by reference to the characteristics of individuals. For example, if major depression is becoming more frequent in adolescents, then researchers must look to the unique biology and psychology of these individual adolescents.[9]

Phenylketonuria (PKU) is the prototypic success story of the medical model and methodological individualism. A specific genetic mutation inhibits the ability of the body to metabolize—that is, break down—the amino acid phenylalanine, which is toxic to the brain if it is not broken down. The mutation, when combined with the specific environmental insult of phenylalanine in the child's diet, leads to abnormal excretions in the urine (phenylketones—hence the name of the disease) and mental retardation. To make a diagnosis, the doctor simply determines whether the child excretes phenylketones. Treatment consists of eliminating phenylalanine from the child's diet. In reality, the story of PKU is much more complex, but this approach to diagnosis and treatment does work.

Though psychiatrists' knowledge of major depression in no way approximates such specificity, the current paradigm within psychiatry firmly embraces this individualistic approach to determining the cause of a disease, diagnosis, and treatment. Psychiatrists identify individuals who exhibit certain agreed-on symptoms of major depression and then treat them accordingly. And it is psychiatrists who drive mental health care. Although psychiatry is not the largest discipline that provides mental health services, the broad array of services that psychiatrists can provide (including medications, hospitalization, and other physical therapies) render psychiatry central to ascribing cause to emotional distress and prescribing potential therapies to relieve it.

The ascription of much emotional suffering to major depression in our society has been driven by the specialty of psychiatry in the United States, a specialty that has firmly embraced the medical model. This embrace derives in part from the rise of managed care. Managed care has an affinity for crisp biological diagnoses and straightforward therapies. Diagnoses such as "adjustment disorder," a diagnosis that implies a maladaptive response or adjustment to a stressor (such as a disabling adjustment to a crime threat in one's neighborhood), usually would not qualify for reimbursement for counseling to assist the patient in developing an appropriate response to the stressor. In contrast, a medical diagnosis that calls for a medical therapy, such as medications, easily fits the managed care approach to diagnosis and therapy.

The medical model has served psychiatry and its depressed patients well in many respects. A diagnosis of major depression provides the sufferer with an explanation for his or her suffering and gives the malady a name—and naming the malady provides some semblance of control over it.[10] Reliable definitions of emotional suffering have spawned an impressive body of community studies documenting the burden of this suffering within a framework analogous to the classic community studies of physical illness.[11, 12] Despite criticism of the widespread use of pharmaceutical remedies,[13-15] antidepressant medications have proved effective. More patients treated for depression are treated with medications than previously, and they are more likely than before to receive third-party coverage for this therapy—as patients with ailments such as diabetes and cardiovascular disease routinely do.[16] In fact, the leading edge of the arguments for obtaining much-needed parity of insurance coverage for psychiatric disorders has been the identification of emotional distress as a medical illness.

The medical model also has highlighted a most important fact: Depression is bad for your health. As Peter Kramer described in the *New York Times*,

> Chronic depressives may have enlarged adrenal glands, brittle bones and a diminished ability to fight off infections. ... Evidence from a number of quarters is making depression appear more "medical"—the result and cause of concrete pathology in discrete parts

of the brain and then throughout the body. ... Depression may look ever more like a progressive, systemic disease.[17]

These adverse effects on health might reinforce the belief that depression is a biologically driven condition. However, though the *effects* are indeed physical, this in no way diminishes the possibility that depression has social *origins*.

Despite its advantages, the medical model stifles psychiatry and its patients by a reductionism. As Arthur Kleinman elaborated,

> *The key item for the biological approach has been "endogenous" psychiatric conditions such as depression, so called because they are believed to arise primarily from psychobiology of the person. ... [B]iology is the bedrock. ... Diagnosis becomes reductionism, the downward semiotic interpretation of the signs of the infrastructure of disease out of "the blooming, buzzing confusion" of illness and symptoms. (pp. 25, 73)*[18]

Problems with the Medical Model of Depression

The medical model does not apply to the majority of mood disturbances in our society.[19] First, depression, even a relatively severe episode, typically is transitory and experienced by most people at some point in their lives. Therefore, it is fair to ask the following: Can an almost universal experience qualify as an illness? In addition, depression can be a symptom of any number of more clearly defined psychiatric disorders, including schizophrenia and panic disorder. Perhaps the harshest critique of the medical model as applied to depression is that only the most severe expressions of depressive symptoms can universally be identified as diseases, such as a psychotic depression or bipolar disorder. The symptomatic boundaries of depression are fuzzy, and it is far from clear that even the core symptoms of depression are constant across cultures or societies.[19]

Given the ubiquitous nature of depressive symptoms, their expression is perhaps best viewed as an interaction between a depressed person and society.[20] The communication of emotional suffering reflects how individuals relate to society and how society shapes the expression of their emotional pain. How depression expresses itself in a society is profoundly influenced by that society. The medicalization of depression in our society is certainly related to our current sociocultural norms, structure, and relations. Milton Rosenberg suggested the idea of "framing" disease to describe this process:

> *Disease is at once a biological event, a generation specific*
> *repertoire of verbal constructs reflecting medicine's intellectual and*
> *institutional history; potential legitimization for public policy; an*
> *aspect of social role and individual intrapsychic identity; a sanc-*
> *tion for cultural values and a structuring element in doctor and*
> *patient interactions. In some ways disease does not exist until we*
> *have agreed that it does, by perceiving, naming and responding to*
> *it. (p. xiii)[21]*

This concept of legitimizing a disease is what I have called *reification* (see chapter 1).

It is usual for societies to project social categories, such as emotional suffering, onto nature and then to return to nature to validate these social categories as natural.[22] For example, consider a child in the neighborhood who is constantly getting into trouble. Neighbors say that the child "just comes from bad blood." Such thinking has, in part, stimulated us to seek the causes of misbehavior in children within their genes. Undoubtedly some misbehavior is caused by the hereditary makeup of children, yet seeking an answer in the genes might blunt investigations into social causes, such as parental abuse or neglect, poverty, and the influence of peers. Because we are living in an individualistic society, we tend to attribute emotional suffering to the individual (e.g., genes vs. social influences). We also avoid self-blame at virtually all costs.[23] And our culture praises a rugged individualism that overcomes whatever situational stress emerges. Given our societal norms, individual biological attribution is an attractive explanation for a persistent depressed mood that cannot be overcome by an act of will.

The medical model, though it easily fits our social norms, seriously limits our explorations of elements: (a) social factors that contribute to the burden of depression and (b) the social location (including social class and living arrangements) of the person, which can create the context for individual vulnerability to depression.[18] The very use of the term *major depression* has constrained our understanding of mood disturbances. According to Kleinman,

> *Where demoralization and despair are responses to actual condi-*
> *tions of chronic deprivation and persistent loss, where powerless-*
> *ness is not a cognitive distortion but an accurate mapping of one's*
> *place in an oppressive social system, and where moral, religious,*
> *and political configurations of such problems have coherence for*
> *the local population but psychiatric categories do not ... depres-*
> *sion can be a disease, a symptom, or a normal feeling. ... In*

making the distinction between distress and disorder, taxonomy
can become entangled in its own decision rules. (p. 1)[18]

In other words, even as the medicalization of depression has widened the influence
of psychiatry to advocate for the depressed, it has narrowed the focus of psychiatrists
in their search for its causes.

The Origin and Hegemony of Major Depression

The term *major depression* could scarcely be found in the psychiatric literature
until the publication of the research diagnostic criteria in 1978 and their expansion
in the *Diagnostic and Statistical Manual of Mental Disorders–Third Edition*
(*DSM–III*) in 1980.[24, 25] During the 1960s depression was dichotomized into exoge-
nous-reactive depression and endogenous depression. The most common form of
depression diagnosed was depressive neurosis, a reaction. Gutheil, writing in a
major textbook of psychiatry during this period, stated,

> *Reactive depression ... is not an illness but a reaction, a response*
> *to conditions of loss and disappointment. This response is highly*
> *subjective. ... [It] can be normal and transient [or] neurotic (one*
> *of the most frequent neurotic symptoms). For a neurotic depression,*
> *there may be an organic predisposition but [one] can always find*
> *also predisposing psychic factors involving loss. (p. 345)*[26]

This endogenous-reactive dichotomy, however, was gradually abandoned during the 1970s and eliminated from the third edition of the *DSM* in 1980.[25, 27] (I discuss in chapter 3 the evolution of the diagnosis of depression through the 20th
century.) At this point major depression began to exert its hegemony over the classification of mood disorders.

A review of the changes in terminology used to classify depression over the
past few decades gives us clues to changing concepts of depression. I performed a
Medline search for various terms since 1970. This search did not identify the use of
major depression until 1978 with the introduction of the research diagnostic
criteria by Spitzer et al.[24] Yet its ascendance over other diagnostic categories
in *DSM–III* and its successors since that time is most impressive, as shown in
Table 2.1.

In 1980, five mentions can be found, but since then the use of the term has
grown exponentially. *Primary depression,* introduced by Feighner in 1972,[28] was

Table 2.1 Mentions of Different Diagnoses Directly Connected with *DSM–III* and Its Successors, by Year

Year	Depressive Diagnoses			
	Major Depression	Minor Depression	Dysthymic Disorder	Unipolar Depression
1975	—	—	—	7
1980	5	1	2	13
1985	146	0	23	20
1990	282	16	28	28
1995	534	36	34	49
2000	1224	75	112	75

never well accepted, with no more than 16 mentions in any year since 1972 (and it never entered the *DSM*). *Unipolar depression* is closely associated with major depression. *Minor depression* (see following), for which criteria are provided in the appendix of the *DSM–IV–TR*,[29] has become a much more popular designate, especially after key epidemiologic studies codified the term in 1990.[30] A parallel diagnosis, *subsyndromal depression*,[31] was introduced to disaggregate further subthreshold depressive symptoms. It was not mentioned until the mid-1990s but received 15 mentions in 2000. *Dysthymic disorder* was introduced in the *DSM–III* as a less severe but more chronic variant of depression (reminiscent of depressive neuroses). *Clinical depression* (not found in the *DSM–III* or its successors), used mostly by nonpsychiatric physicians, was found 6 times in 1980, 32 times in 1990, and 156 times in 2000.

Older terms assuming an etiology for depression (though these terms might not have been applied specifically to indicate an etiology) have been rarely used since 1980 (see Table 2.2). Most of the mentions of *depressive reaction* were by nonpsychiatrists. The *DSM–IV–TR* diagnosis that implies a psychosocial etiology is *adjustment disorder with depressed mood*, which received 12 mentions in 2000 but no more than 4 in years prior (the term was created by the authors of the *DSM–III* so it does not appear before that time). *Exogenous depression* was mentioned a total of 7 times from 1970 to 2000. On the other hand, *endogenous depression* mentions persist. If terms implying an etiology of depression are used in the literature since 1980, they are much more likely to suggest a biological rather than a psychosocial etiology.

Since the 1980s, the popular and scientific press has referred to *depression* as *major depression*. This sentiment is illustrated by the following quote regarding subthreshold symptoms of depression. Lew Judd proposed that subthreshold

Table 2.2 Mentions of Depressive Diagnoses not Directly Associated with *DSM–III* and Its Successors, by Year

Year	Depressive Diagnoses		
	Depressive Neurosis	Depressive Reaction	Endogenous Depression
1975	3	2	115
1980	12	2	53
1985	7	1	75
1990	3	2	77
1995	4	3	26
2000	7	10	43

symptoms of depression deserve more attention,[31] yet his perspective on them is telling:

> The course of major depression is expressed by fluctuating symptoms that represent stages of the disorder ... depressive symptoms at the major, mild, dysthymic and subthreshold levels are all part of the long term clinical structure of major depression. ... Clinicians [should] treat all levels of symptoms in major depression.[32]

Major depression has become the bread and butter of psychiatry. In 1997, by far the most common conditions treated by psychiatrists were mood disorders (53.7%, with the vast majority being major depression), compared with 14.6% for schizophrenia and 9.3% for anxiety disorders. Patients received an average of two medications prescribed by psychiatrists, most commonly antidepressants (62.3%). Between 1985 and 1995, office-based psychiatry visits became shorter, fewer included psychotherapy, and more included a medication prescription.[33] In addition, the increase in antidepressant prescriptions after 1985 was for the less severely ill psychiatric patients.[16] Depression is major depression, major depression is a biological disorder, and biological disorders are treated with medications.

Psychiatrists and their patients experienced significant financial pressures during the past 20 years. Medications are less expensive than psychotherapy, further fueling the trend toward their increased use. And the move to medications appears to be effective. In one study, the incremental cost of successfully treating an episode of acute phase major depression fell during the 1991 to 1996 time period, about 1.5% to 2.5% per year.[34]

Major Depression, an Operational Diagnosis

Major depression is an *operational* diagnosis originally created to improve the reliability of epidemiologic and clinical research. The nature of operationalism is therefore critical to understanding how major depression became a real entity.

Operationalism was the 20th-century version of the standard empiricist account of classification and the meaning of classification as originated by John Locke.[35-37] For example, there is no real "temperature." Rather, a measure agreed on, perhaps the movement of a column of mercury a certain distance under standard circumstances, is the "operational" definition of a 10-degree (Fahrenheit) increase in temperature. One of the critiques of operationalism is that definitions change over time, and therefore a standard cannot be maintained indefinitely if science is to be advanced. Laboratory procedures for the measurement of temperature are routinely modified to improve their accuracy and even to provide for measurement of temperature under circumstances in which such measures were impossible previously (mercury is not an effective measure at exceedingly cold levels).[35]

Changes, albeit not dramatic ones, have continually shaped our operational definition (and measurement) of major depression since its appearance in 1978. Currently, to qualify for a diagnosis of major depression, a patient must experience a depressed mood or loss of interest or pleasure plus four additional symptoms (such as sleep disturbance). The symptoms must last for 2 weeks or more and cause clinically significant distress or impairment in social, occupational, or other important areas of functioning. The determination of what constitutes clinically significant impairment can vary widely. If a patient meets the criteria, then he or she is a case of major depression. If the patient does not meet the criteria, he or she is not a case. To meet criteria using the research diagnostic criteria,[24] one needs to experience the symptoms for only 1 week. More criteria symptoms, however, must be reported. The *DSM–III* increased the time requirement to 2 weeks, but only four symptoms plus a depressed mood were required.[25]

This evolution of the criteria for a diagnosis of major depression, however, has not been informed by theoretical considerations that change with new discoveries. Rather, the collective intuition of clinicians and clinical investigators effects the changes in our definitions. For example, melancholic depression (a subtype characterized by more physical symptoms such as loss of energy, agitation or retardation, and sleep disturbances) was a subtype of major depression in the *DSM–III*.[25, 27] It was removed from the *DSM–III–R*.[38] This removal is of interest especially because studies from Australia support a diagnostic, prognostic, and perhaps etiological distinction between melancholic and nonmelancholic symptoms. Melancholic symptoms, according to these investigators, reflect an underlying cause of depression different from that of the nonmelancholic symptoms.[39, 40]

Of more importance for this discussion, however, is that the boundaries of major depression are fuzzy, especially given the relatively wide reach of the operational definition of major depression.[41, 42] The symptom distributions in community and clinical populations do not easily fit the procrustean bed of our nomenclature, and people experiencing depressive symptoms do not clearly cluster in one symptom complex rather than another.

In a community study of psychiatric symptoms, my colleagues and I used a statistical classification technique to examine whether depressive symptoms and symptoms frequently associated with depressive disorders would cluster into recognizable syndromes that parallel traditional *DSM–III* psychiatric diagnoses.[42] The analysis identified five profiles of symptoms. One profile described a syndrome (that is, a group of symptoms that naturally cluster together) somewhat analogous to the *DSM–III* classification of major depression. Other profiles that emerged included a premenstrual dysphoric syndrome among younger women and a mixed anxiety-depression syndrome. The procedure also permitted us to determine where participants in the sample clustered. Most of the participants with depressive symptoms clustered on more than one of these profiles. Clearly people in this sample could not easily be fit discretely into the existing diagnostic categories, such as major depression.

In addition, it is far from clear that people who meet criteria for major depression in the community behave like people who seek medical care. In an unpublished study,[43] we identified 19 participants who met *Composite International Diagnostic Interview* (CIDI)[44] criteria for major depression during the National Comorbidity Study.[12] (See chapter 6 for a more detailed description of this study.) We assessed these individuals (identified initially by a questionnaire) using a clinical examination. Eighty percent met criteria for major depression. Participants were further evaluated for dysfunction and health service use. None reported work days missed during the episode or other significant physical or social impairment. All had recovered from the episode within 1 month. None sought professional consultation for the episode. These "cases" of major depression did not behave as one would expect people with a psychiatric disorder requiring treatment would behave.

Illness behavior, such as the behavior leading to a diagnosis of major depression, is a complex interaction of people's symptoms with the social and cultural environment in which those symptoms emerge. If depressive symptoms emerge in our society, physicians diagnose major depression, and patients welcome that diagnosis. People want their emotional distress to be named, and physicians accommodate their desire. Does this tell the entire story? One critic of the *DSM–III* concluded that the best evidence indicates that (a) depression does not fit the pattern of interrelationships with other disorders that would justify its identification as an independent psychiatric syndrome, and (b) depression reflects a common negative emotional state that marks the presence of most stressors and diseases.[45] What the *DSM* developers have identified as major depression could be a generalized response to situational stressors and a marker for a symptom pattern that reflects a specific independent syndrome. In other words, a depressed mood can also be a nonspecific signal of distress rather than a single specific disorder.

An operational approach, although improving the consistency of diagnosis from one clinician or investigator to another, explicitly ignores one of the essential skills of the psychiatrist—empathy. Does the observer interpret the mood or simply record an observable phenomenon and then apply the operational criteria to classify the phenomena he or she saw? Depression is an intuitive concept, and psychiatrists have traditionally used their empathy and intuition as well as their objective information skills to recognize it. Jurgen Ruesch, in his description of diagnostic and therapeutic communication, emphasized the centrality of empathy when assessing mood and feeling:

> In empathy ... the observer-therapist disregards his own feelings and puts himself into the other person's place to understand what is going on. ... Words seldom do justice to this process, and it is from the nonverbal sound cues that the supervisor gets the idea of the extent of his trainee's understanding ... every therapist has to constantly check whether his empathic understanding is agreed to by the patient. (pp. 326, 327)[46]

The operational approach emphasizes the study of events, either psychic or physical, without embellishing those events with explanation of cause or function. Yet psychiatrists necessarily go beyond simply recording a neutral observation. Psychiatrists attempt to observe and understand the psychic event or phenomenon, so that they can, as far as possible, empathize with the patient's experience.[47] Is it possible for a psychiatrist to observe phenomena without understanding them? Operational criteria might numb the psychiatrist to understanding patients even though they improve the communication between psychiatrists. For example, one psychiatrist can communicate to another that a patient has a diagnosis of major depression and the other will have a good idea of the symptoms observed by the first psychiatrist. On the other hand, the same psychiatrist can assume falsely that she actually understands the patient or is communicating empathically with the patient.

Have psychiatrists become less sensitive toward their patients even as they better understand basic neurobiological mechanisms and use medications more effectively? Gary Tucker thought so:

> We are caught between Scylla and Charybdis—we no longer want to say that each patient is a unique individual, nor can we honestly say that every case clearly fits diagnostic criteria. All of this apparent precision overlooks the fact that, as yet, we have no identified etiological agents for psychiatric disorders. Our diagnoses are nowhere near the precision of the diagnostic processes in the rest of medicine. ... Other issues have been created ... we have lost the patient and his or her story (the diagnosis, not the patient gets treated) ... the study of psychopathology is almost nonexistent and the strict focus on diagnosis has made the field boring. It may also color our perception of the patient's functioning. Roy-Byrne[48] showed that psychiatrists' global ratings of patients' functioning were totally unrelated to nurses' rating of the same patients but highly correlated with their own rating of symptom severity. We now tend to study how a patient fits a diagnostic category, not psychopathology ... [this] tends to force fit all patients into diagnostic categories. (p. 160)[49]

The medicalization of major depression has sterilized emotional suffering and could have contributed in part to the significant decline in the percentage of U.S. medical graduates seeking careers in psychiatry during the 1980s and mid-1990s, even at a time when the neurosciences were exploding.[50] Throughout the 1970s, fewer and fewer U.S. medical students chose psychiatry as a medical specialty (only 2% to 3% by the end of the decade). The trend has reversed during the past 5 years. The number of U.S. medical graduates who entered a residency program in psychiatry reached its trough in 1998 (with 428 matching to a program). Since then, the numbers have been increasing gradually each year. In 2003, 597 U.S. medical school graduates chose to enter a psychiatry residency.[51] (Other factors could have played a role in the decline and recovery of interest in psychiatry. First, interest in psychiatry reached its trough when other specialties were declining, yet psychiatry's decline began years before the decline in other specialties. The decline in many specialties in the early and mid-1990s was directly related to the push that primary care assumes a greater role in health care delivery. The recent increase might in part be due to the relative financial benefits of psychiatry practice coupled with lifestyle benefits compared to primary care.)

Psychiatrists have gained much in reliability by use of the current *DSM* nomenclature. When they use the term *major depression*, they much more likely will be understood by their colleagues. In addition, this reliability made possible new generation epidemiologic studies such as the Epidemiologic Catchment Area Study and the National Comorbidity Study, as I describe in chapter 6. Nevertheless, as George Vaillant suggested, have we sacrificed generations of clinical intuitive skills on the altar of reliability?[52] Reliability of an operational diagnosis, however, does not lead to lack of empathy and abandonment of clinical skills. Rather, when psychiatrists begin to trust the diagnoses more than the patient, they sacrifice the clinical art.

Major Depression Becomes a Medical Disease

The medical model, with its emphasis on delineating discrete diseases, has emerged with a vengeance well expressed by the "return to our medical roots" motto (p. 14).[18] Major depression for the 21st-century psychiatrist is a disease with specific pathological underpinnings. It has become a medical disease. No one can reasonably disagree that severe depression should be considered a medical problem deserving as much attention as other serious and chronic illnesses. No one can reasonably deny that relieving the burden of depressive symptoms is a central challenge to the public's health. And few would deny that the psychiatrists and their patients catch the attention of the public when they use disease-specific language. Yet using the operational diagnosis does not necessarily imply a need to reify the disease. Reification, according to Luhrman, is a natural tendency for physicians:

> It's rarely the case that a particular symptom is produced by one
> and only one disease. Physicians learn to diagnose from clusters of
> related symptoms. In the training of the psychiatrist, a central
> turning point is when the resident moves from memorizing criteria
> to recognizing prototypes (clusters of characteristics that constitute
> a "good example" of a class). ... The great advantage of prototype
> use is that it is fast and efficient. The cost is that the boundaries
> between categories become starker. ... The cumulative effect of the
> learning process is to imply that for each diagnosis there is an

underlying disease, a "stuff" the diagnosis names, and that the
stuff trumps the diagnosis. The process is through memorizing the
criteria and learning to prototype the categories. Psychiatrists talk
and act as if the disorders are there in the world [they are
reified]. ... If you name something mysterious ... you gain mastery
over it. (pp. 31–45)[53]

In reality, the etiologic (cause), diagnostic (classification), and prognostic (prediction) boundaries of major depression as defined in the *DSM–III* and its successors are not distinct, and this fuzziness renders the reification of major depression especially deceptive. Once psychiatrists construct major depression as a specific disease, that construction shapes and limits their explorations of its origins. In addition, when they make major depression a medical disease, they limit the range of interventions for treating and preventing of depression. Clinicians should be aware that diagnostic categories are simple concepts, justified only if they provide a useful framework for organizing and explaining the complexity of clinical experience to derive inferences about outcome and to guide decisions about treatment.[54] Yet once a concept has come into general use, it is likely to be reified; that is, people too easily assume that it is an entity of some kind that can be invoked to explain the person's symptoms. Validity need not be questioned.

The *DSM–IV* does not insist that a diagnostic category be discrete: "There is no assumption that each category of mental disorder is completely a discrete entity with absolute boundaries dividing it from other mental disorders or from no mental disorder" (p. xxii).[55] The approach taken to establish the validity of psychiatric disorders, however, assumes the entities are discrete. For example, finding an increased prevalence of the same disorder in relatives of a patient has been put forth as strong evidence that one is dealing with a valid discrete entity, such as unipolar major depression,[56] yet such a finding would be equally compatible with the existence of continuous variation of a syndrome such as depression.[54]

Though the *DSM–III*[25] and its successors[29, 38, 55] do not propose that the etiology of mood disorders contributes to the operational definitions (except for mood disorders secondary to general medical conditions and substance abuse), major depression is currently conceived of as a biological disease constructed around the medical model and treated by biological interventions.[45] Treatment guidelines rest on the implicit premise that depression has an underlying cause or common set of causes that can be recognized, diagnosed, and treated. The implied cause links depression to biochemical and neurological conditions (e.g., a chemical imbalance) that can be treated with a specific intervention.[57] The implied biological origin of major depression has at times led to unexpected outcomes. The *Psychiatric*

News reported in October 1999 that the designated mental health insurance carrier for Connecticut had drafted regulations that, among other things, proposed to deny coverage for the treatment of depression unless antidepressant medication was used.[58]

Etiologic studies have focused extensively on a genetic predisposition that leads to altered circadian rhythms and a dysfunctional chemical messenger system in the brain.[59, 60] Studies also have implicated structural changes, such as microinfarcts of the brain (ministrokes).[61] In other words, the stress-diathesis model, which has traditionally undergirded etiological investigations of depression, has tipped sharply in favor of diathesis. The diathesis of interest is biologic vulnerability, as captured by the title of a recent popular book about the origins of psychiatric disorders, *The Broken Brain*.[62]

The Impact of a Reified Major Depression on the Depressed

The medicalization and sterilization of depression has not gone unnoticed by patients. William Styron mourns his own ignorance of depression and criticizes the shallow, simplistic explanations and prescriptions by his physicians. "Many psychiatrists ... simply do not seem to be able to comprehend the nature and depth of the anguish their patients are undergoing" (p. 68).[2] He rejects the term *depression* as a descriptor of his suffering:

> *I felt the need ... to register a strong protest against the word "depression." ... "Melancholia" would still appear to be a far more apt and evocative word for the blacker forms of the disorder, but it was usurped by a noun with a bland tonality and lacking any magisterial presence, used indifferently to describe an economic decline or a rut in the ground, a true wimp of a word for such a major illness. (pp. 36, 37)[2]*

Despite his experience of being overwhelmed with a "darkness visible," Styron continued to search for explanations other than a broken brain to explain his suffering.

In summary, making major depression a medical disease affects future investigations of depression. In addition, the disease model has a profound effect on persons experiencing depressive symptoms. Symptoms that could result from chronic psychological stress or inactivity, such as fatigue, poor concentration, and lack of interest, are interpreted as signs of the ongoing disease major depression.[63]

Attributing depressive symptoms to an illness can lead to a perception of being overwhelmed by the disease and can resort to withdrawal and inactivity in an attempt to "cure" the symptom. Such behavior is similar to the way many patients with chronic fatigue syndrome have interpreted their symptoms and responded accordingly.[64] Current approaches in the psychotherapy of persons diagnosed with major depression encourage an active coping style to overcome the "emotional deconditioning" that results from the depressive symptoms,[65-67] yet by prescribing an antidepressant medication and psychotherapy, psychiatrists give a mixed message to their patients. On balance, the mixed message "works," yet the success in selected clinical trials that demonstrate the "efficacy" of interventions might not translate into true effectiveness in the real world.[68] A significant placebo effect found in these clinical trials complicates the interpretation of their findings.[69] Some have even suggested that the relative benefit of antidepressant medications to placebo is marginal, even if it is statistically significant.

Depression as a biological illness did not dominate the 20th-century views of the disorder. Depression as a reaction, often a normal reaction, to a stressful society and an abnormal reaction to stressful life events such as loss of a loved one dominated much psychiatric thought during the century. In chapter 3, I review the rise and fall of depression as a reaction.

3

The Evolution of Depression
as a Diagnosis

While the psychiatry of the major mental illnesses took the high road of the neurosciences in the 1970s, the psychiatry of everyday affliction has tended to lose its way. … Biology counts for little, culture and socialization for lot. … At the end of the twentieth century, a capital problem for psychiatry lay in a new tendency for people to psychologize distress.

—Edward Shorter, A *History of Psychiatry* (pp. 288, 289)[1]

If a man comes to my office and complains, "I am depressed," a natural question for me to ask is, "What has caused his depression?" In other words, I might view his depression as a reaction to some cause. Forty years ago psychiatrists were likely to assume that this patient's depression was a reaction to something bad going on in his life. Perhaps he was fired from his job or his wife had recently died. Psychiatrists are less likely to make such an assumption today. Rather, the man could be experiencing a disease, major depression, that designates something wrong in his body. If so, then depressive symptoms are a reaction to changes in the body. In this case, however, the idea of reaction does not quite fit. Better to view depressive symptoms as a manifestation of the disease the body is experiencing. Of course, even today some psychiatrists continue to view depression as a reaction to something bad in life. Psychiatry has grappled with the idea of depression as a reaction throughout its history. And psychiatry has changed its views dramatically during the past 40 years.

Before the 20th century, the melancholy of interest to psychiatrists was severe (generally captured by Emil Kraepelin's manic-depressive illness) and thought to be primarily of biological origin. Severe biological melancholy must be treated by biological methods. Mild and moderately severe dysphoric moods were the purview of spiritual counselors, family, and friends and were treated by right living, good health habits, and good mental hygiene. In this chapter I present a perspective on the history of depression as a disease in the United States during the 20th century. (A comprehensive and exemplary review of melancholia and depression can be found in Jackson's *Melancholia and Depression*.)[2]

During the 20th century, Freud and others brought psychiatry out of the hospital and into the office. The number of American psychiatrists in private practice rose from 8% in 1917 to 38% in 1941 to 66% in 1970 (p. 160).[1] The popularity of psychiatry was due not to psychiatry's social control but to its focus on a realm of everyday concerns (sex, marriage, worldly failure).[3] Psychopathology became the psychopathology of everyday life, and depression was seen as a reaction to stress and loss. Yet during the past 30 years, depression has once again become a biological disorder—though far from being a rare one. Nancy Andreasen proposed that psychiatrists who have a more biological orientation prefer to restrict the use of the term *depression* to more severe forms that are likely to respond to medication and view the depressed mood as a disease that is physically based.[4] Psychiatry in theory has returned to its late-19th-century perspective and is quite aware of this return. Even so, psychiatrists today cast their biological net far more widely than Kraepelin ever imagined.

A Case in Point

If the same patient were to seek care from a psychiatrist in 1963 and in the year 2003, the diagnostic formulation would be quite different.

1963: A 46-year-old woman is experiencing many symptoms of anxiety and depression, including loss of sleep, subjective anxiety, and loss of appetite. The symptoms worsen when she has contact with her husband, who divorced her 3 years ago. Though she has custody of their 16-year-old daughter and 14-year-old son, when the husband visits with the children on weekends she becomes more depressed. The patient's father abused her physically as a child and later left the family when she was a teenager. When her husband divorced her, the feelings of abandonment she felt when her father left the family returned. Though she realized that the frequent verbal battles she and her husband engaged in were not good for the children and that overall she and the children were functioning better since the divorce, the anxiety returned when her daughter was with her former husband. She feared (she admitted unrealistically) that her husband would abuse her daughter as her father had abused her. One of the attractions to her husband, she admitted, was that he reminded her of some of the more favorable characteristics of her father. She also admitted that she ignored signs early in the relationship with her husband that he could become very angry and take that anger out on her verbally. She is experiencing a reactive depression secondary to the breakup of her marriage and the conflicts that breakup aroused regarding unresolved issues with her father.

2003: This 46-year-old woman, divorced, meets criteria for a major depressive episode, recurrent. She also has experienced a dysthymic disorder for the past 3 years. During the clinical examination, she scored 20 on the *Hamilton Depression Rating Scale*. Symptoms include depressed mood, insomnia, loss of appetite, agitation, some memory problems, and loss of interest in many activities that interested her in the past. She is physically healthy. The divorce 3 years ago might contribute to some of her symptoms.

Axis I: Major depressive disorder, unipolar and recurrent
Axis II: No personality disorder
Axis III: No medical problems at present
Axis IV: Social problems (divorce from husband)
Axis V: 75 (obvious symptoms but continues to function)

Melancholia

Depression, a relative latecomer to the psychiatric nomenclature, was called "melancholia" before the 18th century and varied relatively little over the years from the original Hippocratic (460–357 BCE) assumptions about causes. Melancholia was the Latin transliteration of a Greek term meaning a mental disorder involving prolonged fear and sadness or depression. The symptoms also included aversion to food, sleeplessness, irritability and restlessness (p. 4).[2] Translated into English as "black bile" or "biliousness," a melancholic temperament was thought to be due to an excess of one of four humors (black bile, yellow bile, blood, and phlegm). Aretaeus of Cappadocia (circa 150 CE) captured this view:

> *If it [black bile] be determined upwards to the stomach and diaphragm, it forms melancholy, for it produces flatulence and eructations of the fetid and fishy nature, and it sends rumbling wind downwards and disturbs the understanding. (p. 298)[5]*

Though a theological view predominated as an explanation for melancholy in medieval Europe (see following), the parallel view that sadness and despair were caused by aberrant bodily functions persisted. Throughout the Renaissance, writings about the passions increased and gradually escaped the purview of the theologians. Fear and sadness were usually the central features. During the 17th and 18th centuries, the term *melancholia* seemed gradually to have become restricted to a disease, whereas *melancholy* remained a synonym for *melancholia* and a popular term (with breadth and diffuseness of use much as *depression* is used today).

Physiologic explanations were increasingly employed after the Renaissance to explain the more severe varieties of melancholia.[2] Despite his dualistic philosophy, Descartes (1596–1650) reaffirmed the traditional physiologic explanations for melancholia and introduced a mechanical etiologic theory. Specifically, he thought that the animal spirits of the nervous system moved and agitated the brain to cause melancholia.

During the 17th and 18th centuries, chemical and mechanical explanations vied for supremacy. For example, Richard Napier (1559–1634) dismissed the humoral theory for a wholehearted acceptance of alchemy as he developed an arsenal of chemical medicines (p. 109).[2] In contrast, Herman Hoerhaave (1668–1738) proposed that melancholia derived from sluggish flow of the blood and humors (p. 119).[2] Such mechanical theories did not hold sway, however, for they did little to change the existing approaches to therapy. The chemical theory was resurrected with a vengeance in the 20th century with the advent of effective chemicals (medications) to treat the symptoms of depression.

The 17th and 18th centuries produced two well-known popular authors who experienced recurrent episodes of depression. Robert Burton (1557–1640) first published *The Anatomy of Melancholy* in 1621.[6] For Burton, melancholy was primarily the disease melancholia, even though he waxed eloquent in many literary genres to describe his experience with the malady (p. 95).[2, 7] He suggested that the consensus definition was *"a kind of dotage without fever, having for his ordinary companions fear and sadness, without any apparent occasion"* (p. 148).[6] In his lengthy survey of the disorder, he believed the theory of humors to be central and an excess of black bile to be causative.

Burton was not unidimensional in his etiologic explanations. He developed a detailed description of a multicausal web that would do a 21st-century conceptual model proud. At the top of his hierarchy of causes he left sufficient (though not necessary) room for God and the devil to work their ways with the moods of men. In addition, he proposed more mundane contingent but not necessary life experiences to which persons might react with melancholia, including death of friends, loss of liberty, and poverty. He catalogued a host of biological causes, including external biological insults (such as a blow to the head) and internal bodily disorders (such as a "default of the spleen"). Burton thought heredity contributed to melancholy as well.

Health-related behaviors, such as eating a poor diet and sleeping too much, did not escape his attention. The irascible passions (shame, envy, malice) and concupiscible passions (desire of praise, pride, and love of learning) could also contribute. He was realistic and cautious regarding the difficulty in treating melancholy, though he prescribed social (e.g., be not solitary), psychological (e.g., confess grief to a friend), and physical (e.g., use leeches) therapies. Yet, as melancholia implies, "the name is imposed from the matter, and the disease denominated from the material cause" (p. 148).[6]

Samuel Johnson (1709–1784) felt "overwhelmed with an horrible melancholia with perpetual irritation, fretfulness, and impatience; and with a dejection, gloom, and despair, which made existence misery."[2, 8] He considered his problem a disease of the mind for which there was no relief save the company of his friends. He also believed that this disposition of mind was inherited from his father. Johnson feared the malady would drive him insane. He also viewed his malady as coming from within. Though he became frustrated with his inability to overcome melancholia, he did not blame the cause of his problems on his behavior or his thoughts. The fault lay in his body, not his will. Johnson was also among the first to use the term *depression* in the English language to describe his mood. He wrote in 1761 that he was "under great depression" (p. 126).[2, 9]

The French alienist Jean-Philipe Esquirol (1772–1840) recognized the more severe forms of melancholy, which were expressed through psychotic thoughts and melancholic affect (a monomania that he described as lypemania or sorrowful insanity).[2] His work set the stage for other European psychiatrists to propose less severe states of melancholia without delusions, which were eventually categorized as simple melancholias.[10] As these disorders were "affectively based," he set the stage for the Anglo-Saxon psychiatric term *affective disorder*.

An Interlude: Religious Melancholy

Despite physicians' focus on biological origins of melancholia from ancient times in Western civilization, another type of melancholia emerged within the Judeo-Christian world in parallel with "biliousness"; namely, "religious melancholia."[11] Depending in large part on the influence of the sacred in society, religious themes can be more or less dominant, yet among the religious the themes always have been present. For example, the centrality of religious melancholy was much greater in medieval Europe than during the Enlightenment.

Religious melancholy was prominent among the Puritans in America throughout the 18th century. That which renders religious melancholy of interest in this
discussion is the perspective that severe episodes of melancholia were "reactions"
to factors outside the body. The body was "visited" by a malignant spirit, often secondary to being abandoned by the supreme being for sinful behavior. Melancholy
has been closely associated with spiritual life in many religious traditions;[2, 12]
I focus on the Judeo-Christian tradition because it has had the strongest influence
in Europe and North America.

The cause of religious melancholy might be direct from God as punishment
for sin, direct from God for self-improvement as a purge of sins, or abandonment
by God to the devil or demons.[2, 11] Each of these causes is implicit in the Hebrew
Bible though it is difficult to read through our modern conceptions of depression
without bias to accurately interpret the symptoms and causes of depression in scripture. King Saul experienced violent swings in his mood:

> Now the Spirit of the Lord had departed from Saul, and an evil
> spirit from the Lord tormented him. Saul's attendants said to him,
> "See, an evil spirit from God is tormenting you. Let our lord com-
> mand his servants here to search for someone who can play the
> harp. He will play when the evil spirit from God comes upon you,
> and you will feel better." (I Samuel 16:14–16, New International
> Version)

David, the harp player and later adversary of Saul, did little to assuage his
mood swings. Saul eventually committed suicide. Given these symptoms and outcome, readers of the accounts of Saul for hundreds of years have interpreted his
malady as manic-depressive illness,[6, 13] yet the writer of the scripture clearly identifies the origin of his malady as the actions of God. According to Richard Burton, in
the *Anatomy of Melancholy* (1661), "that God himself is a cause [of melancholy],
for the punishment of sin, and satisfaction of justice, many examples & testimonies
of holy Scriptures make evident unto us" (p. 156).[6]

King David experienced depression while being pursued by Saul. He cried out
to God,

> Be merciful to me, O Lord, for I am in distress; my eyes grow weak
> with sorrow, my soul and my body with grief. My life is consumed
> by anguish and my years by groaning; my strength fails because of
> my affliction, and my bones grow weak. Because of all my enemies,
> I am the utter contempt of my neighbors; I am a dread to my

friends—those who see me on the street flee from me. I am forgot-
ten by them as though I were dead; I have become like broken pot-
tery. For I hear the slander of many; there is terror on every side;
they conspire against me and plot to take my life. (Psalms 31:9–13,
New International Version)

Unlike Saul, David viewed his emotional suffering as resulting from the perils secondary to his service to God, perhaps contributing to his spiritual growth. He found
hope toward the end of the psalm, despite his melancholy.

Job experienced severe despair, to the point of gladly receiving death if it were
offered (though he refused to commit suicide):

May the day of my birth perish, and the night it was said, "A boy is
born!" That day may it turn to darkness; may God above not care
about it; may no light shine upon it. May darkness and deep
shadow claim it once more; may a cloud settle over it; may black-
ness overwhelm its light. That night may thick darkness seize it;
may it not be included among the days of the year nor be entered
in any of the months. May that night be barren; may no shout of
joy be heard in it. (Job 3:3–7, New International Version)

The writer clearly viewed melancholia as external to Job. Though the reason
for his anguish was (and remains) unknown, the theme of God's abandoning Job is
implicit throughout the narrative. Saul's, David's, and Job's melancholy all derived
from a reaction to external circumstances.

Burton developed the theme of religious melancholy (and devoted a chapter
to the topic).[6] His experience with melancholia during the late Renaissance was
compatible with the concept of the malady as a visitation on a person because he
or she has wandered from the ways of God.[6] Belief in God and the practice of religion were not the causes of melancholy. Religion was the fabric from which the
lives of people in the 17th century were woven. Religion provided meaning
through faith, a worldview that in turn provided answers to a set of ultimate and
grounding questions. Rather, religious melancholy derived from religious excess or
defect. In other words, religious aberration, such as deviation from the faith of
one's community, could cause severe depression. Despite Burton's interest in the
humors, he could not ignore the social context of depression, especially the religious context.

Religious melancholy was an especially important phenomenon among protestant evangelicals. J.H. Rubin suggested that the "system of theology and practice

of piety [in early American Protestant culture] led to distinctly pathological consequences for believers who struggled to forge a life in precise conformity with these
ultimate religious values" (p. 10).[11] Given that one could never ultimately know
God's plan, "doubt, despair, times of spiritual dryness, and 'dark nights of the soul'
assailed believers" (p. 35). Escape from these episodes of despair through revival
sermons and the revival itself became a social movement of awakening to a new
light of religious enthusiasm that helped shape and drive the Protestant ethic and
its resultant industry and productivity.

By the beginning of the 20th century, however, religious melancholy was a
phenomenon of the past. Pastoral care (which focused on moral management during the 19th century) had failed to cure religious melancholy (p. 182).[11] Freud
expanded the psychoanalytic viewpoint to the community, even the religious community, despite his professed atheism.[14] Religious experiences were no longer considered the cause of the more severe forms of mental illness. Conservative
Protestants, by the mid-20th century, had rejoined the mainstream of American
culture.[15] Perhaps of most importance, the American religion of the 20th century
emphasized the freedom of the individual. The sense of control and punishment
by God, much less the control of a religious community, virtually disappeared.[16]

Depression as a reaction to an act of God or the religious community therefore
faded quickly, except for a few isolated examples. Eaton and Weil performed an
epidemiologic study among the Hutterites in northwestern North America at mid-
20th century.[17] This isolated group of religious pacifists valued simplicity, communal ownership of property, and government consensus, in marked contrast to the
individualistic and increasingly secular lifestyle around them. Their social system
was quite stable, yet the value of this stability was purchased at the cost of social
conformity among its members. The protective social structure of the Hutterite
community was associated with a high frequency of depression (both mild and
severe) and feelings of guilt among those who feared that they might not live up to
group expectations (p. 190).[17, 18] On the other hand, character pathology was rare.

Religious melancholy, a reactive melancholy, flourished before the Enlightenment, persisted in many religious communities well into the 19th century, but virtually disappeared in the 20th century. Melancholy as a reaction did not die so
quickly, for the theories of Freud were theories of a reactive depression. Even so,
the biologic theme, as associated with the more severe depressions, gained new
energy in Europe during the early 20th century, and 50 years later came to have a
profound impact on late-20th-century American psychiatry.

Manic-Depressive Insanity

A physical-biological view of severe depression and all nervous conditions dominated 19th-century European psychiatry. Maudsley described this view:

> *That which ... has its foundations in a definite physical cause must have its cure in the production of a definite physical change. No culture of the mind, however careful, no effort of will, however strong, will avail to prevent irregular and convulsive action when a certain degree of instability of nervous element has, from one cause or another, been produced in the spinal cells. It would be equally absurd to preach control of the spasms of chorea, or restraint to the convulsions of epilepsy, as to preach moderation to the east wind, or gentleness to the hurricane. (p. 83)*[19]

This biological reductionism and focus on the most severe of nervous maladies, however, did not hold. Psychiatry at the turn of the 20th century began to show interest in the least severe forms of depression, and the increased use of the term *depression* was in part a reflection of this broader interest. Derived from Latin, meaning pressed down, *depression* was used initially in English to describe a "depression of spirits." The term did not become extensively used in psychiatry until the early 20th century. One of Emil Kraepelin's (1856–1926) three "depressive states" was "simple retardation":

> *Onset is generally gradual ... a sort of mental sluggishness; thought becomes difficult; the patients find difficulty in coming to a decision and in expressing themselves. ... They fail to find the usual interest in their surroundings ... poverty of thought ... hard to remember the most commonplace things ... feel tired and exhausted ... patient sees only the dark side of life ... they are unsuited to their environment; are a failure in their profession; have lost religious faith ... insight is frequently present, the patients appreciating keenly that they are mentally ill ... improvement is gradual. (pp. 299–300)*[20, 2]

At the same time, psychiatry did not ignore or abandon the more severe forms of depression, as described by William James:

*There is a pitch of unhappiness so great that the goods of nature
may be entirely forgotten, and all sentiment of their existence van-
ish from the mental field. For this extremity of pessimism to be
reached, something more is needed than observation of life and
reflection upon death. The individual must in his own person
become the prey of pathological melancholy. ... Such sensitiveness
and susceptibility to mental pain is a rare occurrence where the nervous constitution is entirely normal; one seldom finds it in a healthy
subject even where he is the victim of the most atrocious cruelties of
outward fortune ... it is positive and active anguish, a sort of psy-
chical neuralgia wholly unknown to healthy life. (p. 192)[21]*

The severe mood disturbances described by James were categorized as manic-
depressive insanity, which became a synonym for and eventually replaced
melancholia as a designation for severe depression. Kraepelin considered all severe
depression circular (p. 191):[22]

*Manic-depressive insanity ... includes on the one hand the whole
domain of so-called periodic and circular insanity, on the other
hand simple mania, the greater part of the morbid states termed
melancholia and also not inconsiderable number of cases of amen-
tia [confusion or delirious insanity]. Lastly, we include here certain
slight and slightest colourings of mood, some of them periodic,
some continuously morbid, which on the one hand are to be
regarded as the rudiment of more severe disorders, on the other
hand pass over without sharp boundary into the domain of personal predisposition. ... I have become more and more convinced
that all the above-mentioned states only represent manifestations
of a single process. (p. 1)[23]*

Though Kraepelin recognized the occurrence of psychogenic states of depression caused by situational misfortunes, he believed that heredity was at the base of
manic-depressive illness and the circular (or bipolar) character of manic-depressive
illness explained much of the terrain covered by the term *depression*.[10] Manic-
depressive illness was functional in that brain function was considered to be altered
physiologically (though the specific nature of this altered physiology was not
known). Kraepelin was especially interested in the more severe biologically driven
types of depression.

The depression that Kraepelin identified as part of manic-depressive insanity is quite similar to the definitions of major depression in the *Diagnostic and Statistical Manual of Mental Disorders–Fourth Edition* (DSM–IV). The disorder was characterized by apathy, loss of energy, and retardation of thinking and activity, as well as intense feelings of gloominess, despair, and suicidal ideation. Kraepelin described a diurnal variation in mood and focused on the vegetative symptoms of depression, such as poor sleep and loss of appetite. These symptoms are difficult to explain without assuming a biological problem, the same biological assumption that underlay the melancholic subtype of major depression in the *DSM–III*.[23, 24] Yet this focus on the biological (and the severe) was soon to be challenged.

Depression as a Reaction

Adolf Meyer introduced the depressive neuroses as distinct from melancholia, a depression of mental energies. *Neurosis* was a late-18th-century term that referred to a presumed disorder of the nerves. Meyer emphasized rather the importance of the lifelong history of the person in understanding his or her unique experience of a disease. He challenged Kraepelin's discrete disease entities and instead proposed that psychiatric disorders were maladaptive reaction patterns that depended on constitution and life experiences. Life experiences and a supportive social environment were critical to the etiology and treatment of all depressions.

Meyer went on to outline the most common symptom-complexes: constitutional depression (a pessimistic temperament), simple melancholia proper (excessive, altogether unjustified depression), and other forms characterized by prolonged "neurasthenic" malaise. Affective reaction is one of his six reactive types. In contrast to the pessimistic view derived from the idea of hereditary predisposition, Meyer emphasized a search of the reactive picture for points of modifiability.

Meyer also distinguished a constitutional depression (pessimistic temperament), simple melancholia (much like our major depression) and other forms characterized by neurasthenic malaise, and hypochondriacal complaints from the reactive type.[2] Perhaps of more importance, he challenged Kraepelin's reliance on outcome as a diagnostic criterion. He argued for a less complex approach involving situation, reaction, and final adjustment. In other words, he focused on reactions of the depressed as "part of an adjustment, a response to a demand" (p. 598).[25] He went further. Kraepelin implied that diagnosis is prognosis; that is, categorizing the patient correctly predicted the outcome for that patient. Meyer, in contrast, recommended replacing the term *manic-depressive* with *affective reactive group* (p. 198).[2]

The adjustment of the patient to the social milieu predicted outcome. This shift opened the door for Freud and his followers. It also broadened the horizon of psychiatry.

Freud's psychoanalysis was a discipline of the everyday (p. 47).[3] In the early years of the 20th century, American psychiatry was fundamentally transformed. Nineteenth-century psychiatry focused on insanity and the asylum. Psychoanalysis focused on normal, everyday problems — sex, marriage, womanhood, manhood, work, ambition, worldly failure, habits, and desires — as proper subjects of psychiatry. This transformation was labeled the second psychiatric revolution following the development of humane methods for treating the insane (p. 474).[26] The vulnerable individual was acutely sensitive to the social environment around. According to Edward Bibring,

> One may roughly distinguish three groups of ... persisting aspirations of the person: (1) the wish to be worthy, to be loved, to be appreciated ...; (2) the wish to be strong, superior, great, secure ...; and (3) the wish to be good, to be loving. ... It is exactly from the tension between these ... aspirations on the one hand, and the ego's acute awareness of its (real and imaginary) helplessness ... that depression results. (pp. 24–26)[2, 27]

Endogenous and Reactive Depression

From the competing views of depression as originating in the body and brain and the view that depression was due to a reaction, a proposal arose, especially in Europe during the latter part of the 19th century, that depression was binary. The binary model posited two principal types of depression: endogenous-psychotic and neurotic-reactive.[28] Initially the exogenous concept was directed to physical trauma, toxins, and other specific agents. Kraepelin accepted the endogenous-exogenous distinction but noted that "compared to innate predisposition external influences only play a very subordinate part in the causation of manic-depressive insanity" (p. 177).[23] He included alcohol, syphilis, and bodily illnesses such as typhoid and pregnancy among the exogenous causes. "Psychic influences," such as loss of a close relative and interpersonal conflict, also could contribute. Kraepelin did not propose that exogenous strictly meant an exogenous biological cause.

Robert Gillespie, in 1929, expanded the concept by distinguishing two main groups of depressions, autonomous and reactive.[2, 29] His autonomous group was similar to Kraepelin's endogenous group, yet his reactive group implied a significant role for precipitating circumstances. Other dichotomous pairings followed, such as endogenous-neurotic. According to Aubrey Lewis, while British and American psychiatrists were disputing if depression could be divided into endogenous and exogenous forms, German psychiatrists were taking for granted an endogenous, cyclothymic variety and a psychogenic, reactive variety.[30] Eugen Bleuler, however, had little to say about reactive depressions and probably represented the interest among psychiatrists in Germany and Switzerland during the first half of the 20th century. "Reactive depressions, which become aggravated to a mental disease, are quite rare" (p. 537).[31]

In Europe, the binary distinction was challenged by Edward Mapother (1926).[28, 32] He proposed that the more severe and less severe depressions fell along a continuum (there is only one type of depression that varies by severity). Lewis failed to find any clear demarcation between endogenous and reactive depression in clinical observation and suggested that a differentiation was not based on empirical data.[33] As a prelude to the DSM–III, Robins and Guze suggested that this distinction be abandoned for a more atheoretical approach based on chronology; namely, primary and secondary depression.[34] Secondary depressions were mood disorders that followed other disorders, such as an anxiety disorder.

Herman Van Praag, in 1970, distinguished vital depression (occurred without apparent reason and characterized by retardation, difficulties thinking, and loss of appetite) and personal depression (a depression that could be explained by environmental stress).[35] Personal depression would be of much less interest to psychiatrists because it would not necessitate medical treatment. Joseph Mendels and colleagues (1968) further elaborated the importance of the endogenous for psychiatrists by noting,

> The ... endogenous factor might represent the core depressive symptomatology, whereas the clinical features of the reactive factor may represent phenomenological manifestations of psychiatric disorders other than depression which "contaminate" the depressive syndrome. (p. 10),[36] (p. 213)[2]

In other words, depression at its core was endogenous. Reactive depression was a concept that was dying fast during the early 1970s. Much of the desire among biological psychiatrists to eliminate reactive depression in part derives from the false dichotomy between endogenous and reactive. Most episodes of moderate to severe depression derive to a biological predisposition to depression coupled with the stress associated with the social environment, such as a loss or threat (or perhaps ongoing hassles of daily life). Even the biological predisposition undoubtedly is conditioned over years.[37] In addition, under enough stress, most people will experience some type of emotional suffering, and many of these will express that suffering through symptoms of depression. Virtually all depression is at once exogenous and endogenous.

Reactive Depression, Major Depression, and the Role of Medications

Why did reactive depression disappear? Why did major depression come roaring to the forefront? Peter Kramer suggested the change is due to the success of lithium in treating manic depression but not schizophrenia, suggesting that psychiatric problems did not all derive from a common etiology—anxiety—as the psychoanalysts would have us believe.[38] Medications help us split patients into diagnostic categories. If medications are the splitters, then once a person responds to an antidepressant medication, the depression is "endogenous"; that is, biological in origin and substance. The "antidepressant era" over the past 30 years eliminated the construct of a reactive depression. (Of course such logic does not hold for other medications used in general medicine. The relief of pain with aspirin does not assume that the cause of the pain is biological in origin even though it does assume a biological substrate.)

The disappearance of depression as a reaction among psychiatrists was not necessarily accepted by the public at large. According to Edward Shorter,

> While the psychiatry of the major mental illnesses took the high road of the neurosciences in the 1970s, the psychiatry of everyday affliction has tended to lose its way ... [for most people]. Biology counts for little, culture and socialization for lot. ... At the end of the twentieth century, a capital problem for psychiatry lay in a new tendency for people to psychologize distress ... counseling tended to become defined in psychological terms, meaning that people believe their difficulties capable of resolution through nonmedical psychotherapy. ... Hence psychiatry, an arm of medicine, lost out to nonmedical forms of counseling such as psychology and social work. ... On a lifetime basis, more than a quarter of America's adult population would seek help from professional counselors of all descriptions. (pp. 288, 289)[1]

The public response was ambiguous, however, and from the perspective of the scientist, irrational. Though the symptoms of depression are not very different from those of past ages, sufferers today are more sensitive to these physical and psychological signals and are more ready to assign their symptoms to a given "attribution," a fixed diagnosis, a particular disease.[39] It is not at all clear, however, that these sufferers necessarily attribute the cause to the body (as noted previously). Nevertheless they readily accept the use of medications to seek relief.

The emergence of effective antidepressant medications changed psychiatry dramatically. The ability of the new biological psychiatry to make people feel better further opened the division within psychiatry between the "tough headed" types, with a predilection for medical models, organic explanations of illness, and pharmacotherapy, and "soft headed" types who invoked psychosocial models explaining symptoms as the result of problems of living and inclined to psychotherapy and family therapy (p. 288).[39] Perhaps psychiatrists, even during the heyday of the social psychiatry movement, were uncomfortable with their departure from mainstream medicine.

Even near the zenith of the social psychiatry movement, a poll of psychiatrists (not well designed but probably representative) found that they thought the most significant development in psychiatry during the 1950s and 1960s was the drug revolution. The rise of community and social psychiatry (along with ego psychology) was considered a distant second as a development.[40] A British psychiatrist, William Sargant, predicted in 1967 that within 25 years nearly all psychiatric patients will be readily cured with simple drugs mostly prescribed by general physicians.[41] Shorter, writing years later, went so far as to suggest that patients would view physicians as mere conduits to the new antidepressants (cosmetic pharmacology) (p. 341).[1] Depressed people would view the consulting physicians mainly as a way of getting a prescription for the antidepressants that they, the patients, had determined they needed (similar to what happened with Miltown and Valium). Drugs were an answer regardless of the perceived etiology of the problem (just as aspirin relieved the tension headache caused by a family quarrel).

Michael Norden, in *Beyond Prozac*, perhaps with some hyperbole and perhaps not, explicated what has in many ways been implicit for the past few years.[42] He suggested that we are experiencing a worldwide epidemic of depression caused by the serotonin-depleting times we live in. In other words, the introduction of Prozac and its sister drugs eliminates the distinction between reactive and endogenous depression. Modern living and hereditary predisposition (it makes no difference) have led to our current state of affairs. As the world we live in has changed drastically over centuries and millennia, the human body and brain have remained virtually the same. We have yet to develop the necessary coping mechanisms to deal with the alarming stresses of our modern technological era. The result is an epidemic of depression, among other disorders. Our inability to cope is the reason we medicate, using everything from caffeine to Prozac. Modern living, from stress on the job to the air we breathe, has led to depletion of the brain's serotonin. The stress of life makes us, as Norden put it, Prozac deficient. The Prozac-like drugs were designed to bolster our weakened neurochemical "stress shield" by increasing the serotonin levels in the brain.

Though Norden stopped short of proposing that Prozac is either necessary or sufficient to correct these problems, he closed even further the door to recognizing depression as a signal of an adverse physical and social environment that should be explored. Rather than address the stress, we should focus instead on bolstering our individual defenses. Of course, strengthening our defenses, whether through medications or developing better psychological methods of coping, is inherently appealing. Nevertheless, our approach must not stop with the individual. We must seek to understand the noxious stimuli in the environment as well.

Shorter proposed that inserting Prozac into the history of psychiatry required untangling good science from scientism:

> Good science lay behind the discovery of fluoxetine as a much safer and quicker second generation antidepressant than imipramine. ... Scientism lay behind converting a whole host of human difficulties into the depression scale, and making all treatable with a wonder drug ... millions of people ... craved the new compound because it lightened the burden of self-consciousness while making it possible for them to stay slim. ... Yet the Prozac episode produced one massive benefit ... it helped psychiatric conditions begin to seem acceptable in the eyes of the public. (p. 324)[1]

The Reaction to the Disappearance of Reactive Depression

The focus on medications coupled with a relative indifference to the psychosocial causes of depression has lead to considerable criticism of modern psychiatry, though most of the criticism has not reached the public mainstream. Breggin, in *Toxic Psychiatry*, suggested that people who are depressed sometimes feel "defective," as if their "brain is slowed down; it isn't working right" (p. 140).[43] This feeling makes patients susceptible to psychiatric pronouncements about chemical imbalances in their brains and encourages reliance on psychiatric authority.

Whatever the scientific basis for a biology of depression, according to Breggin, psychopharmacology is good for the business of psychiatry. Treatments for physical diseases are reimbursed by insurance companies much more generously than those for mental illness. He went on, like others, to criticize the close connection between psychiatry and the pharmaceutical industry:

> *Psychiatry is the political center of a multi-billion-dollar psycho-pharmaceutical complex that pushes biological and genetic theories as well as drugs on the society. Its diagnoses carry enormous legal weight and have vast political implications. (p. 408)*

Ross and Pam criticized the theory and methods of biological psychiatry:

> *Biological psychiatry is dominated by a reductionist ideology that distorts and misrepresents much of its research. According to its tenets, the individuals with behavior problems must suffer in some way from defective protoplasm (no one is accountable for his or her behavior). Human choice and values are negated and the sociocultural status quo remains intact. Since Freud, symptoms have been understood as a nonverbal protest—a symptom conveys the bitter message that developmental needs have not been met, resulting in unmistakable signs of suffering ... dispensing a pill can reinforce a pseudoscientific biological determinism that covers over or distorts the patient's actual social situation. (pp. 1–4)[44]*

Healy, in *The Antidepressant Era*, believed that the patient who stops at the pharmacy to pick up his or her Prozac is buying into a disease and a drug.[23] He further emphasized that the previously "rare" melancholia has become the most common of disorders—major depression. Major depression, in turn, has become a booming business.

The disappearance of the concept of depression as a reaction (not the designation *depressive reaction*) is an unfortunate constriction of psychiatric thought. Depression is at once body, mind, and environment. Depression is at once endogenous and exogenous. The interaction of the person with the social environment elicits and shapes what comes to be labeled a psychiatric disorder, such as major depression. Rarely can it be effectively argued that a depressed mood emerges in pure form as the phenotype of a genetic vulnerability and runs its course free of the social and historical events that encompass the person experiencing depression at a given point in time. In the next chapter, I review an episode in the history of

American psychiatry—the social and community psychiatry movement, which focused on the social environment and the social context of psychiatric disorders. Depression for the social psychiatrist was very much a reaction to social stress and the absence of a supportive family and community.

Social Psychiatry

4

The Birth and Growth of Social Psychiatry

Social psychiatry ... presumes that every individual is valuable and that most persons possess potentialities that are never fully realized because of personal emotional or social interferences. Social psychiatry is etiological in its aim, but its point of attack is the whole social framework of contemporary living.

—Thomas A.C. Rennie, *International Journal of Social Psychiatry* (p. 5)[1]

During most of the 19th century, psychiatrists practiced primarily in asylums, isolated from the rest of society. Their patients were isolated as well,[2] perhaps being relegated to actual "ships of fools" floating in the canals of Europe if they were not housed in asylums. At the dawn of the 20th century, psychiatry moved from the hospital to the office of the psychotherapist. It even became fashionable to seek help from a psychiatrist, perhaps through psychoanalysis. Yet psychoanalysis was almost as isolated as the asylum, at least during the time spent by the patient with the analyst. Analysis, among other benefits, granted patients the opportunity to escape, for a time, from the present and from the press of everyday matters to the sanctity of the couch and recollections of a distant past. With time, however, psychiatry ventured out of the office and into the community. By the 1960s, many psychiatrists joined the fray in the battle to improve society, correct injustices, and ensure community care of the mentally ill. And thus social psychiatry and its siblings, community psychiatry and cultural psychiatry, were born.

Social psychiatry is concerned with the effects of the social environment on the mental health of the individual, and with the effects of the mentally ill person on his or her social environment.[3] It usually refers to the theoretic and research field that investigates the role of social factors in the origin, treatment, and prevention of psychiatric disorders and the promotion of mental health. The focus of social psychiatric investigation is the person within the context of society, whether that society is the family or a larger community.[4]

Community psychiatry (more broadly community mental health) is the applied field. It is concerned with the delivery of mental health services to individuals, families, and social groups within their communities. Given the social psychiatric underpinnings of community psychiatry, the association between the two is at times seamless. The principles of community psychiatry were laid out by Leona Bachrach (though she labeled these as principles of social psychiatry) and include geographical responsibility, humanization of services and equal access to care, comprehensive service and continuity of care, primary prevention (preventing mental illness before it ever develops) and rehabilitation, and clinical egalitarianism.[5]

Cultural psychiatry is also closely associated with social psychiatry, yet there is a clear conceptual difference. A society, according to Leighton and Murphy, is a group of human beings who live together in a social relationship.[6] In contrast, a culture is an abstract concept that describes the entire way of living for a group of people; that is, shared patterns of belief, feeling, and knowledge that ultimately guides everyone's conduct and definition of reality. In a diverse society, such as the United States, one might encounter multiple cultures within a relatively small geographic area. Those cultures, however, might spread to many different geographic areas.

A CASE IN POINT

Massive screening of recruits during World War II exposed an unexpected high level of mental health impairment among the young men recruited for the war. Eleven percent of those screened were turned down as mentally unfit to serve. This high rejection rate (the rate was less than 2% during World War I) surprised the medical profession and policy makers, which hitherto had assumed mental health impairment was more or less limited to those severely disturbed people who were admitted to psychiatric hospitals. Even with the high rejection rate, 12% of those men who served experienced significant mental health problems.[7] If the frequency of psychiatric disorder was soaring among young men recruited for the military, could it be even higher among in the community at large? To answer this question, psychiatrists and sociologists surveyed the community at large for mental health impairment and its causes. They found the frequency of impairment to be shockingly high, perhaps 20% to 30% of the overall population. What was to be done with such a burden of emotional suffering and behavioral disturbances?

The culmination of these surveys and discussions led to the following conclusion. Institutional psychiatric care was outdated and inadequate to the task. The Joint Commission on Mental Illness and Health, created by Congress in 1955, recommended in 1961 that mental hospitals must be reorganized.

> *The objective of modern treatment of persons with major mental illness is to enable the patient to maintain himself in the community in a normal manner. To do so, it is necessary (1) to save the patient from the debilitating effects of institutionalization as much as possible, (2) if the patient requires hospitalization, to return him to home and community life as soon as possible, and (3) thereafter to maintain him in the community as long as possible. (p. xvii)*[8]

President John F. Kennedy backed the recommendations, and Congress passed the Mental Retardation Facilities and Community Mental Health Centers Act (Public Law 88-164) was passed in 1963. Social science research provided the foundation for a society-wide program of intervention in the service of community mental health. Social psychiatry was alive and well.

The Origins of Social Psychiatry

The social psychiatry movement gained momentum following World War II but has 20th-century roots in Freud's psychoanalysis and Durkheim's sociology. The movement is based historically in the age-old belief that mental illness is a product of civilization.[9] The importance of understanding society and context as they relate to the treatment of the mentally ill dates from the enlightenment and industrial revolution.[10] For Freud, society and the psyche were in conflict, and the ultimate outcome of the battle was the neuroses.[11, 12] A neurosis, such as melancholia, arose because of anger originally directed outward toward a lost object of social support; for example, a dead spouse. Expressed anger toward a lost object is not tolerated by society (and the internalized representation of society—the superego). Anger is thus directed inward, leading to melancholia.[13] The conflict between the innate drives and society is inevitable, for civilization requires the sublimation, suppression, or repression of fundamental human drives. As summarized by Freud,

> *The inclination to aggression is an original, self-subsisting intellec-*
> *tual disposition in man, and I return to the view that it constitutes*
> *the greatest impediment to civilization. (p. 57)[11]*

For Durkheim, the ultimate tragedy of emotional suffering was suicide. Suicide reflects the relationship between individuals and society. Anomic suicide occurs when a person senses that the group norms are weakened; that is, the person loses the security that group norms can provide. Suicide rates are lower in societies that are more integrated and in societies where the individual is more integrated into the society's religions and politics.[14] Egoistic suicide, in contrast, results from excessive individualism; that is, weak attachments to society. A lack of family and social ties increases the risk of suicide. Altruistic suicide results from an excessive integration of the individual within society. For example, the perceived need to benefit society at the expense of the individual might lead to suicide, such as the suicide of frail older men.

The interests of Freud and Durkheim in the interactions between persons and the social environment, however, were eclipsed by greater focus on the ills of society. Social psychiatry is, according to Havens, the "movement outward."[15] Social psychiatry should concentrate on identifying the elements of a more effective society and supporting them. With this focus, social psychiatry gained momentum during the middle of the 20th century. At its heart, social psychiatry arose out of a new humanism in psychiatry, a humanism that moves beyond not only the biological theories of Kraepelin I describe in chapter 2 but also the reductionistic psychodynamic theories of Freud. Walker Percy, in 1957 at the threshold of the social psychiatry movement, expressed this humanistic core:

> *The question, then, is no longer whether the ... sciences, given suf-*
> *ficient time ... may succeed in applying the biological method to*
> *man, but whether the very attempt to do so has not in fact wors-*
> *ened man's predicament in the world. The pursuit of physics does*
> *not change the physical world; it is all the same to the most sub-*
> *atomic particles whether there is or is not a science of physics. But*
> *if Western man's sense of homelessness and loss of community is in*
> *part due to the fact that he feels himself a stranger to the method*
> *and data of his sciences, and especially to himself construed as a*
> *datum, then the issue is no longer academic. ... The suspicion is*
> *beginning to arise that American psychiatry with its predomi-*
> *nantly functional orientation ... is unable to take account of the*
> *predicament of modern man. (p. 252)[16]*

For Percy, the predicament was a loss of focus on the whole person, a loss that can be appreciated only by placing humankind in the context of society:

> We all know perfectly well that the man who lives out his life as a consumer, as sexual partner, as "other-directed" executive; who avoids boredom and anxiety by consuming tons of newsprint, miles of movie film, years of TV time; that such a man has somehow betrayed his destiny as a human being. (p. 257)[16]

Social psychiatry initially emerged from this humanistic, socially conscious perspective and then evolved into a discipline closely allied initially with social epidemiology and later also with the Community Mental Health movement. The research and the practical arms of social psychiatry were necessary.

Warren Dunham crystallized the importance for the research efforts of such a society-wide perspective. He proposed

> that a total conjoint force operating during the past half century to produce tremendous changes in our social organization is found in the linkage of science, technology, and federal power. This trilogy has been successful in introducing elements into our community life which have been productive of vast changes ... some of which are crucial to ... the interpretation of epidemiological studies of mental disorder. (p. 8)[17, 18]

The Rise of Social Psychiatry

Social psychiatry as a designation was not employed before 1904 in Germany (Illbeg).[19, 20] Fischer, in 1919, described a program of social psychiatry in Germany that emphasized the importance of investigating social causes of mental illness and posited public health interventions as preventive measures.[21] Sartorius proposed a reason for the rise of social psychiatry and critiqued this reason from the perspective of psychiatry near the end of the 20th century:

> The 18th and 19th centuries were the triumphant era of simplification. The technological revolution was based on shedding complexity, dichotomizing and disregarding uncertainty (mind and body were dichotomized and the mindless were given to the alienists, search for a single cause, treatment relied on physical means) ...

*over time medicine became more fragmented … concerns became
the domain of social psychiatry such as patients in their social context, data about mental health in a social framework, social policies regarding mental illness and health. We need more precise
means of describing such constructs as community and family, for
these words are used as blunderbuss descriptions for a multiple of
complex relationships (such as contextual variables related to
social and geographical location). (p. 342)[22]*

Social psychiatry in Europe during the 20th century had three connotations:
an area of theoretical and empirical science, a political movement, and a way to
practice mental health care. Social psychiatry as a discipline continues to be practiced in Europe, though it varies from one country to another.[19] For example, in
Germany the field has become a political movement, whereas in the United Kingdom the focus has been on the science. In the United States, as I describe next,
the second and third connotations have all but disappeared from psychiatry.
The first connotation has disappeared from mainstream psychiatry, though social
scientists continue to use concepts and methods of their disciplines to investigate
social factors influencing the occurrence, expression, course, and care of mental
disorders.[23]

Schwab et al., in 1970, suggested that the research endeavors of social psychiatry are based on the following: (a) epidemiology's attention to the relationship
between psychiatric disorders and differences in populations and living conditions,
(b) psychiatry's concern with understanding human motivation within the context
of society, and (c) the social sciences' focus on how social organizations and cultural attributes influence the definition of illness, the setting in which it arises, and
provisions of care.[9] In the United States, these endeavors persist largely within the
social sciences and at the margins of psychiatry.

In the United States, Southard, in 1913, set the stage for social psychiatry,
claiming psychiatry's science was underdeveloped and derivative.[24] He believed
pronouncements of psychiatrists were mere elaborations of the obvious and that
the specialty was "unduly neurologized." He argued that psychiatrists had attended
too little to the intrinsic normality of the structures—the brain, the nervous system—that produced mental diseases, and he proclaimed that it was altogether possible that the causes of mental disease lay not in the nervous system but elsewhere
in the body, even "conceivably in the environment."[25] He was perhaps the first
American psychiatrist to use the term *social psychiatry* (in 1917).[26]

Early in the 20th century, psychiatrists became more cognizant of society's
evils such as crime and poverty (p. 63).[25] According to Luhrman,

In the mid to late 19th century America, marital difficulties, finan-
cial misfortunes, and anxiety were not the domain of professionals
whose job it was to remove them. By the end of the 19th century,
Americans apparently began to believe that rapid social change
was creating an epidemic of "nerves" ... though psychoanalysis
was not responsible for the shift in attention from the "alien" to the
everyday, it became a powerful theory that justified psychiatrists'
treatment of ordinary people. (p. 212)[27]

Psychiatrists were initially reticent to become involved with social issues
despite the move from the asylum to the community. They bristled at the excesses
of the social reformers, especially at their faith that social forces, not individual
drives and endowments, molded behavior, and the conviction that planning
healthy environments (housing, parks) would produce better citizens. The emerging (and deceptive) science of studying human intelligence appeared to prove that
persons were at birth and throughout life unequally endowed. Therefore environmental approaches to social problems, which rested on a belief in human perfect-
ibility, were at worst naively misguided and at best merely beyond the psychiatrist's
purview. The psychiatrist as physician was a born individualist and thus concerned
less with improving the social environment than with controlling (or at least toning
down) the undesirable citizen.[28] Inequality was natural. The individualistic
approach, however, did not prevail for long.

Psychiatrists focused more and more on society and the community during the
next few decades. They promoted an asylum that must reach out to the community.[29] By the 1950s, social psychiatry had embraced an even broader horizon.
Shorter noted,

The term social psychiatry thrived in the US during the 1950s and
1960s, in the sense of large surveys of the mental health of the pop-
ulation such as the Midtown Manhattan Study. ... And the Amer-
ican definition of social psychiatry was broad enough to encompass
every influence imaginable on the patient's life: childhood, friends,
social class, poverty, and the like. (p. 237)[29]

Social psychiatry early bore the stamp of social activism, yet its origins were in
the social sciences (the force behind the surveys to which Shorter referred and to
which I return in chapter 6), specifically social epidemiology.[30-33] Social epidemiology is the study of the distribution and determinants of an illness or pathological
condition within the social structure. After World War II, the World Psychiatric

Association manifested the tie of social psychiatry to social epidemiology by creating a Section on Social Psychiatry and Epidemiology.[4] Many social scientists that participated in epidemiologic research of that period were interested in demonstrating the role of social factors in mental illness, such as social stress, social class, poverty, and urbanization.[31, 32, 34] Investigators in Chicago fielded an early social epidemiologic study of psychiatric disorders during the 1930s. They found that the highest rates of first admissions for schizophrenia were concentrated in the central city (an area characterized by social disorganization and social isolation), whereas manic-depressive illness admissions were evenly distributed throughout the city.[32]

Adolf Meyer (1866–1950) and Harry Stack Sullivan (1892–1949) were the most influential U.S. psychiatrists prior to 1950 in the social psychiatry movement.[35, 36] Meyer was primarily a clinician, not an investigator. He began his clinical inquiries with the person in the context of society. After observing the psychiatric problems of many people, he concluded that these problems resulted from the people's groping with the world (p. 180).[36] He went to great lengths in an attempt to demonstrate the power of social data to explain psychiatric disorders. For example, he explored by neighborhood the distribution of cases referred to a child guidance clinic (p. 340).[37] The patient no longer was the sole subject of treatment. Treatment should be directed to adjusting the environment and adjusting to the environment (p. 180).[36]

Sullivan was equally influential. According to Gordon Allport, "During his productive lifetime, Sullivan, perhaps more than any other person, labored to bring about the fusion of psychiatry and social science" (p. 135).[38] Sullivan was suspicious of the psychiatrist who rigidly classified patients, as did Kraepelin. Instead, he emphasized the importance of the psychiatrist as a participant-observer in the therapeutic process (hence he developed *interpersonal psychotherapy*). His theory clarified how the forces of society affected the person and how expressions of the person (such as anxiety) were manifested in the problems of society.[35] Sullivan challenged the central role of infantile sexuality proposed by Freud. As an alternative, he emphasized the role of culture and society as the primary determinants of personality development and psychopathology. Sullivan did not hesitate to speak out against societal ills. For example, in 1962, he wrote, "If we are to develop ... a national solidarity, we must ... cultivate a humanistic, rather than a paternalistic, and exploiting, or indifferent attitude to these numerous citizens" (p. 107).[35, 39] From the roots of Meyer and Sullivan, social psychiatry blossomed at midcentury.

The social psychiatry of the 1950s and 1960s was driven by two objectives. On one hand, it was a field of scientific theories about social forces in the origin, treatment, and prevention of emotional suffering. Social psychiatry was theory driven.

On the other hand, social psychiatry was social activism. The theories of social psychiatry derived from an amalgamation of virtually all the social and psychological sciences.[30, 40, 41]

Murphy and Langner described the subject matter for study.[31, 42] The study of the sources of mental disturbance was the primary goal of social psychiatry. Social psychiatry concerned itself primarily with the forces in the social environment that affect a person's ability to adapt, to adjust, or to change himself or herself and the environment.[31] Social psychiatry should therefore be concerned with impairment in social functioning and disease.[9] This impairment is not always related to a specific disease process but could include uncomfortable feelings and maladaptive behaviors. Alexander Leighton suggested that social psychiatry asks,

> What are the situational factors which evoke certain patterns of feeling and behavior to such an extent that they are disturbing to the person, the social group around him or both? (p. 929)[43]

The noxious or potentially noxious social factors were designated *stress* (or stressors), and the reaction to the stress was designated *strain*.[31, 44] Social stressors included culture; acculturation; economic position; residence (urban residence was considered more stressful than rural residence); alienation; family stress such as marital instability, labeling, and stigmatizing; and behavior settings. Behavior settings, such as religious worship services and community meetings, exert pressure to participate and can be a factor in promoting mental health. Some settings can be inherently stressful, such as a totalitarian state. Others can be stressful because they are "redundancy" settings; that is, settings that exert minimal force in stimulating and using human resources. For example, in a large school, students are more likely to be onlookers, and the role of onlooker rather than participant can increase stress because people need to be included.[42]

Disease and distress are multicausal, and these causes are interrelated.[9, 45] Mora reflected on this multicausal view of psychopathology in 1959, at the threshold of the social psychiatry movement (p. 24):[46]

> Psychiatry required a number of concepts toward integration of various fields such as Engel's study of homeostasis,[47] Rado's formulations on adaptational psychodynamics,[48] Leighton's study of social integration,[30] Wiener's cybernetics,[49] and Bertalanffy's open and closed systems.[50]

Social psychiatry was riding an even larger wave. As Mora noted,

> The psychiatrist ... extends his investigations to the subjective
> world of the individual and must include, in all of its aspects, the
> drama of man ... the psychiatrist searches areas which were, until
> recently, reserved to the intuition of the poet and the artist and to
> the speculation of the philosopher. With this increased responsibil-
> ity psychiatry's horizons are larger and richer. (p. 20)[46]

Freud had moved psychiatry from the asylum to the office and psychopathology from insanity to everyday life. This shift set the stage for a vision that included
room for virtually all social sciences. Alexander and Selesnick, psychoanalysts who
authored a widely read history of psychiatry during the 1960s, explicated this
expanding sociological point of view:

> We live in an era of collaboration and integration. The solitary
> man of the 19th century with his impregnable self-sufficient system
> of values is rapidly yielding his place to the communal, the so-
> called other-directed person with a soul, searching vainly for his
> own identity. The imprint of this cultural shift upon psychiatry
> manifests itself in the growing interest in group dynamics and its
> sociological aspects ... psychiatry ... [is] no longer trying to solve
> the great mystery of human behavior from one single restricted
> point of view. This need for integration is the latest in the great
> chain of needs that has marked the evolution of psychiatry through
> the ages. (p. 495)[51]

Karl Menninger echoed these views.[52] He suggested that all psychiatric disorders could be reduced to the failure of the suffering person to adapt to his or her
environment. Psychiatric illnesses were not discrete and discontinuous but rather
differed only in severity. Treatment required understanding the underlying meaning of the symptom and that meaning derived from the social environment as
much as from the psyche and the body.

As social psychiatry flourished, the National Institutes of Health followed
suit.[53] Stanley Yolles, who became the director of the National Institute of Mental
Health (NIMH) in 1964, initiated support for psychiatry and behavioral sciences in
schools of public health. During the early years following the Community Mental
Health Act (see following), overall research dollars were flat though funds
increased dramatically for service. Research accounted for 40% to 50% of the

NIMH budget, and many of these dollars were targeted toward social issues. In 1972, 43% of the research monies were allocated to studies of psychiatric disorders; 35% to basic biological, psychological, and sociocultural research; and 19% to mental health aspects of broad social problems. During the late 1960s and early 1970s, many public officials looked to psychiatric research for answers to pressing social problems. Centers were created at the NIMH on crime and delinquency, urban mental health, minority group mental health, and the prevention and control of rape. Nonmedical influences on behavior were the focus of these centers. Given its high-profile role in research on social problems, the NIMH was separated from the National Institutes on Health in 1967.

Textbooks of social psychiatry were written by Alexander Leighton,[34] Ari Kiev,[54] Richard Rabkin,[55] and Jules Masserman and John Schwab,[56] among others. In addition, numerous review articles appeared in major journals.[57, 1, 9, 43, 58] During the 1970s the field moved toward disciplinary status. According to Schwab and Schwab, the field was coalescing, evolving, striving to accumulate facts, formulate theories, and delineate fields of activity for its investigative, diagnostic and therapeutic endeavors.[18] Organizations were established to bring more visibility to the field and to solidify its status. Social psychiatry, along with psychoanalysis and biological psychiatry, was accepted by some as one of the three major disciplines within the field.

Social Psychiatry and Social Activism

Social psychiatry in the 1950s and 1960s was a movement to change society (and to study society) to lessen emotional suffering. Social activism by social psychiatrists was rooted in psychoanalysis and the social sciences. Erich Fromm (1900–1980), a psychoanalyst (though not medically trained), reframed Freud's theories, saying that a great struggle for the person is individuation from society.[59] People, however, tended to yield to society because of the universal human yearning for fusion, safety, and security. Facing aloneness and challenging society leads to freedom and a productive life. Given Fromm's Marxist orientation, he pushed for the development of a utopian society but did not believe that such a society was the only one in which persons could develop their genuine selves. Yet four basic needs must be met to achieve individuation: a feeling of relating to others, transcendence (rising above basic instincts), identity (the feeling of acceptance by others coupled with uniqueness), and the discovery of a frame of orientation (such as a constructive religion).

In 1970, Raymond Waggoner, the president of the American Psychiatric Association, announced that "for too long we as psychiatrists have focused on the mental health of the individual." It was time, he went on, for psychiatry to turn its attention to pollution, overpopulation, racism, and nuclear war.[60] Dorner's hyperbole was perhaps not out of touch with mainstream psychiatry when he wrote that "psychiatry is social psychiatry or it is no psychiatry" (p. 18).[61] By the end of the 1960s, some social psychiatrists believed that social activism had already revolutionized (and would continue to revolutionize) psychiatry.[62] Proposals that were anticipated to emerge from this activism ranged from more effective communal and family life to the establishment more effective delivery of psychiatric services.

The model for activism dated at least from the Group for Advancement of Psychiatry report of 1950.[63, 64] The report encouraged the application of psychiatric principles to all problems related to family welfare, child rearing, child and adult education, or social and economic factors that influence the community status of individuals and families, intergroup tensions, civil rights, and personal liberty. The model implies that a psychiatrist concerned about preventive psychiatry must become involved in the political process.

Social activism in psychiatry rode the wave of Johnson's Great Society, which stimulated an extraordinary growth in federal social programs.[65] In rapid succession Congress enacted laws intended to diminish economic inequalities, stop racial discrimination, and ensure that all Americans would have access to medical care (e.g., Medicare). Mental health rhetoric and ideology paralleled the rhetoric of the Great Society and emerged from the belief that social programs could improve a deficient environment. The emphasis on community mental health services responded to that belief by stressing the empowerment of individuals and small groups at the local level. Their involvement in all decisions that affected the lives of the mentally ill should greatly improve their condition.[65] The demand for social justice was coupled with a demand to destroy any and all barriers to individuals in reaching their full potential.

In addition, the 1960s was a decade of rapid social change, and interest in social psychiatry was thought to accompany rapid social change.[18] (This view of social psychiatry as gaining strength from a society in flux has not held. We live in an era of ever more rapid social change and, as I describe in chapter 8, the social psychiatry of the 1960s has virtually disappeared. I discuss explanations for this retreat at a time when many would predict a resurgence of interest, in the latter portions of this book.)

Socially active psychiatry was embedded in the theories that pervaded social psychiatry (but unfortunately not on a secure empirical foundation). Social psychiatry had evolved from various propositions concerning the onset and evolution of emotional suffering.

A brief review of Leighton's theories demonstrates the intuitive connection between theory and action, which were characteristic and central to the proposed programs.[30, 34, 66] All human beings exist in a state of psychological striving that contributes to the maintenance of an essential psychophysiological condition. Interference with the striving of the person by social forces leads to a disturbance of this essential condition.[67] Because human society is composed of functioning self-integrated units—persons—who develop from integrated patterns of interpersonal relationships in society (including communications, symbols, and strivings), it follows that a disintegrated social environment will foster emotional suffering (p. 11).[67]

Recognizing that hereditary, biological, psychological, and social factors contribute to an integrated self and a disintegrated self (the self experiencing a psychiatric disorder), social psychiatry should focus attention on the interrelationship between the person and her or his social environment (p. 19),[54] (p. 15).[18] The identification of the problems that characterize a dysfunctional society should therefore naturally lead to solutions for those problems. A socially active psychiatry was an intuitive psychiatry.[68]

Key to social advocacy was the concept of primary prevention in psychiatry. Primary prevention in public health is preventing the onset of a disease, in contrast to secondary prevention (preventing an early onset disease from progressing to a more chronic status) and tertiary prevention (rehabilitation of a chronic disease). Primary prevention segues from social psychiatry as a science to social psychiatry as social activism manifested primarily through the Community Mental Health movement. Gerald Caplan's views were widely held among psychiatrists during the 1960s:

> *Primary prevention [in psychiatry] is that preventive effort which is concerned with studying the population-wide patterns of forces influencing the lives of people in order to learn how to reduce the risk of mental disorder ... [it] involves studying the provision of resources in a population and attempting to improve the situation when necessary—usually by modifying community-wide practices through changing laws, regulations, administrative patterns, or widespread values and attitudes [e.g., Operation Head Start].*
> *(p. 26)[69]*

In other words, preventive community psychiatry was to be concerned with developing the adaptive potential and psychosocial life skills of all people (not just the severely mentally ill) and decreasing the pathology in society as a whole. Leighton asked as the basic question for social psychiatry, "How can life be made better for more people?"[34]

The Community Mental Health movement was the most visible evidence of the activist arm of social psychiatry, and despite the protests of some social scientists working in psychiatry, community mental health centers perhaps were inherent in the social psychiatric theories. To maintain an integrated social environment, Leighton suggested certain "functional prerequisites of a society" (p. 16).[67] These prerequisites included family formation and perpetuation; indoctrination of new community members; patterns of leadership, fellowship, and association; meeting emotional needs during life's crises and day-to-day hassles; maintenance of communication; protection against weather, disease, and disaster; and systems providing economic stability and equitable distribution of money. Implicit within this list of functional prerequisites were two hypotheses: (a) integrated social environments contribute to mental health, and (b) more effective social arrangements in the community at large can be effected by professional and community leadership. Professionals interested in prevention should consider society and the patient as a target for intervention. Leighton took his theories to the community by establishing a community mental health center to effect social action.[66] Therefore, social science merged into social activism through the Community Mental Health movement.

The Community Mental Health Movement

Community psychiatry has been labeled "social psychiatry in action."[70] Social psychiatry stimulated the Community Mental Health movement during the 1960s, yet the roots of community psychiatry, like those of social psychiatry, extend back to the early 20th century. Adolf Meyer proposed a visionary comprehensive community mental health approach that included geographically congruent service boundaries and cooperation among psychiatrists, police officers, teachers, and social workers.

> I am anxious to emphasize the need of attacking the work in small enough units of communities and neighborhoods, of making the attack at the sources, by community organization in addition to legislation. ... Preventive work must have its places of attack; and the first places are the families. (pp. 298, 299)[71]

An equally important factor was the role of psychotherapy, which moved psychiatry from the asylum to the community. Ambulatory psychotherapy, as popularized by the followers of Freud in the United States, became one of the most widely acclaimed interventions of the postwar World War II era. Wartime practices of brief psychotherapy to speed the return of soldiers to the front seemed to confirm its effectiveness. Its popularity grew out of a combination of additional circumstances: the rise of private and community practice in psychiatry; the general receptivity toward psychological explanations; and economic prosperity.[72] The psychodynamic orientation aroused interest in other forms of environmental therapies capable of being applied in institutional and community settings. "Milieu therapy" was one such therapy, expanded by Maxwell Jones (see following).

These forces culminated in the passage of comprehensive mental health legislation in 1963 to fund the construction of mental health centers throughout the United States (the Community Mental Health Construction Act; Public Law 89-105) (p. 237ff).[29] The centers were required to ensure that a range of services would be provided, including inpatient, outpatient, partial hospitalization, and emergency services, as well as community consultation and education to a defined catchment area of 75,000 to 200,000 persons. The goal was to establish 1,500 centers.[53] By the late 1970s, more than one half of the NIMH budget supported the community mental health centers.

Though these centers were doomed in their larger goals from the beginning (see chapter 5), their services continued to expand for nearly 20 years. In 1975, the centers were required to provide additional services, including services for children and older persons, treatment of alcoholism and drug abuse, screening before state hospital admission, follow-up care for patients discharged from institutions, and transitional housing. The number and reach of the centers continued to expand until 1981, when 758 community mental health centers served 52% of the country's population.

The most obvious task for the centers was community care for people discharged from state mental hospitals, yet the centers did not embrace this role at their creation. The centers focused not on persons experiencing schizophrenia and severe depressive disorders but rather on the "socially maladjusted" or even those without a clear psychiatric disorder[73] (p. 319).[53] One reason the centers did not embrace the severely and chronically mentally ill was that the move to deinstitutionalized patients was not directly connected to the goals of the centers, despite their obvious relation. Deinstitutionalization was more a civil rights goal than a psychiatric goal. State psychiatric beds decreased from 560,000 in 1955 to fewer than 88,000 in 1993, even though community services were sorely lacking. Many of the deinstitutionalized were simply moved to nursing homes and board-and-care facilities. Private, freestanding psychiatric beds likewise declined. They peaked at 79,000 (in addition to 26,000 Veterans Administration beds) in 1988, declining sharply to 43,000 beds in 1993.[53]

Efforts somewhat analogous to the Community Mental Health movement occurred in other countries. In Europe, however, the idea of community mental health was closely tied to the therapeutic community and humane treatment of the mentally ill within institutions. This emphasis began with James Tuke in England and Emil Pinel in France during the 19th century.[74] In England, following the lead of Maxwell Jones during the 1950s, therapeutic communities designated the milieu within the hospital. The goal was to change the social perceptions of the patients, not change the milieu in which the patients resided.[75] Patients gained insights about themselves, and psychiatrists were taught to speak the patient's language. Jones reported that it was possible to alter social attitudes in desocialized institutional patients. These changes, however, assumed a functional milieu; that is, a functional social environment within and without the hospital. By "therapeutic communities," Americans understood mainly mental hospitals with open door policies (very different from the hospitals in England).[29] The community ranged from the hospital to the family and workplace. Community psychiatry was therefore a much broader concept in the United States than in England.

Bloom described a number of dimensions of community mental health in the United States.[76] The movement emphasizes practice *in the community*. Community mental health focuses on the total defined population (such as a catchment area). Preventive services are paramount. Indirect services, such as consultation to teachers and clergy, take precedence over direct services. When individual intervention strategies are used, ones that have the potential for meeting the mental health needs of large numbers of people (such as brief psychotherapy) are selected. Paraprofessionals are key to the workings of community mental health. A community mental health center can thus partner with other community representatives in planning for services and interventions. The movement also searches for sources of stress within the community. It views the community as having certain counterproductive stress-inducing properties, rather than assuming that psychopathology is exclusively within the skin of the individual. The translation of this theory of care to actual services met with virtually insurmountable challenges, as much theoretical as practical.

These dimensions, however, did not arise from whole cloth. Given the strong influence of psychoanalysis in American psychiatry, it is not surprising that the foundations of psychiatry practiced in community mental health centers during the 1960s and 1970s derived in part from psychoanalysis. As I noted previously, the conflict between the drives of the individual and the constraints of society were viewed as the seedbed of the neuroses. To some extent, the limitations of the community mental health centers can be blamed on their psychoanalytic roots, for the spirit of psychoanalysis emphasized the one-to-one relationship of doctor and patient despite the communal and preventive orientation of the centers. Though concern for community prompted community intervention in theory, community intervention and social activism felt strange to mental health professionals. In addition, psychiatrists and other mental health workers had gained their experience within the doctor-patient framework. Their training did not produce the skills needed for community intervention.

The community mental health model not only included a continuum of psychiatric care but also emphasized community consultation and education by mental health specialists to promote social integration. Optimism regarding the community mental health center movement was pervasive, and the comprehensive, cooperative approach was thought to provide the blueprint for enhancing emotional well-being throughout society. Leighton well summarized the optimism in his description of a mental health center he helped establish in Nova Scotia:

> My colleagues and I founded the Centre in 1951, planning to show that the great majority of people with mental illnesses could best be treated in their own communities, that preventing mental illnesses and promoting mental health were feasible goals, and that the involvement of community members in such a program would not only strengthen the program but would also increase the ability of the community to recognize and cope more effectively with many of its psychological and social problems. (p. 1)[66]

In retrospect, he recognized that his goals were unrealistic:

> The results suggest not so much that the theories were wrong ... as that they were insufficient and did not take into account many factors of major importance. ... The number of persons ... with complaints and disabilities of the kinds commonly treated by psychiatrists ... was far greater than was first supposed; also, the local management of community affairs was far more compromised, because of transcommunity networks of often competing powers and special interests. (p. 1)[66]

Leighton, reflecting on the failure of theory to be translated into effective social action in a small Canadian community, captured the failure and retreat of social psychiatry overall. The theory was deficient, the empirical data scanty, and the optimism not warranted. Nevertheless, social psychiatry in the United States was a powerful force in shaping psychiatry during the 1960s, though it is scarcely remembered today.

5

The Retreat of Social Psychiatry

The speculations of social psychiatry have contributed a great deal to the development of the community aspects, leading psychiatry to address such areas as poverty, racial prejudice, war and mass migrations. Unfortunately, social psychiatry's efforts were swallowed up by the magnitude of the problems addressed, with little or no impact.

—John Elpers, *Comprehensive Textbook of Psychiatry* (p. 3185)[1]

For all practical purposes social psychiatry has disappeared from the scene of American psychiatry. Though some social factors continue to be of interest to psychiatrists, they have been eclipsed by biological factors. Yet the retreat of social psychiatry cannot be accounted for purely by our increased knowledge of neurobiology. Rather, the social psychiatry of the 1960s has all but disappeared primarily because interest in social context has vanished. Attention to social factors has been restricted to assessing individual social risk factors, such as stressful life events, or individual social outcomes of psychiatric disorders, such as loss of employment or disruption of the family.

The fate of social psychiatry is no better demonstrated than by tracing the trend of the core science of the field, social epidemiology. During the past 30 years, social epidemiology has been increasingly important (though not central) in the study of the etiology of many chronic medical illnesses, such as hypertension, diabetes, and cardiovascular disease, by internists and primary care physicians.[2, 3] During this same era, social epidemiology has lost its importance for the study of the etiology of psychiatric disorders by psychiatrists.

A Case in Point

Jenny consulted with her local doctor. She was depressed, and she was gaining weight. In fact, she had gained 40 pounds during the 6 months preceding her consultation. "I don't know what is wrong with me," she informed her doctor. "I have a good job, but when I get off work, or even during the day, I just feel I have to eat. There is a hamburger joint just across the street. I go there in a flash, ordering French fries or a shake as soon as quitting time comes." Jenny went on to discuss her trouble sleeping at night, adding that her energy was almost gone and that she seemed nervous almost all the time. "I just seem to be on edge. I can't sit still, and I feel exhausted at the same time."

The doctor asked Jenny more about her work. She held a good and fairly demanding job with a local software company. She was considered one of their better employees and had been given raises about every 6 months since she was employed 3 years ago. In addition, she had received a nice bonus at the end of the year. For the first time, she was in a position to buy a house, and she put a down payment on a very nice house. She admitted that the mortgage was a stretch, but if she continued to receive raises like the ones she had received, she would have nothing to worry about financially. On further inquiry, she told the doctor that she and other employees had heard that the company was about to be sold to a larger firm and the local office might be closed. In addition, some recent contracts had fallen through, and her boss had hinted that bonuses would not be coming this year.

Jenny told her doctor that she thought she was depressed primarily because of her weight. If she could lose some weight, she would feel better about herself. But those fast food restaurants were so tempting. In fact, she could not believe how they could saturate her evenings watching television with all those ads. Small- and medium-sized orders could not be found on the menu. She could buy only large and extra large. She and some of the women in her office had been talking about the pervasive advertising on television and how the ever-larger portions of food in these restaurants were contributing to weight problems among young women. Nearly all the young women she worked with were gaining weight. A number of them were stressed about their weight, and Jenny suspected she was not the only woman at the office who was depressed. Jenny had heard that some of the new drugs for depression, such as Prozac, also helped people lose weight. Could she have a prescription? She was in a downward cycle, and she hoped the drug could help break it.

When the doctor suggested that Jenny also was stressed because of the job, she replied, "I have a great job. I never dreamed that I could earn so much money." When he asked about the potential of a layoff, she said, "I think a lot about that, but we don't talk about it. After all, what can I do about it? If I lose my job, I lose my job. I'll have to find something else. OK, the pressure is a little greater since I bought the house. But I think if I can get my weight down, I'll feel much better. Those fast food chains. They're a plague on society!"

Jenny experienced many symptoms of major depression. She believed the problem was a chemical imbalance, but she also thought she would feel better about herself if she could lose weight. She had great difficulty making a connection between her depression and the uncertainty at her job. The problem with depression was more downstream from stress in the workplace; downstream to the point that she could control the problem with medication or a change in her personal behavior. The problem was in the body, and the answer was in correcting the body's problem by taking medications and losing weight. On the other hand, she and her colleagues had no difficulty attributing part of their weight problems to external social forces, specifically the fast food chains. At the beginning of the 21st century, Americans, paradoxically, are more likely to attribute physical problems than emotional problems to social forces.[4]

Evidence for the Retreat of Social Psychiatry

In one of the major current textbooks of psychiatry, the *Textbook of Clinical Psychiatry*, "social psychiatry" cannot be found in the index, though topics related to social psychiatry, such as violence, the homeless, and poverty, are given some mention.[5] These topics are explored almost exclusively as outcomes of psychiatric disorders, not causes. The text does contain a chapter on anthropology and psychiatry and a chapter on cultural psychiatry. These chapters explore the subcultural contexts of psychiatry, such as psychiatry among Native Americans, and not the overall social context.

In another recent textbook of general psychiatry,[6] the author of a chapter titled "Public Psychiatry and Prevention" distanced current public psychiatry from the social and community psychiatry of the 1960s:

> *Public psychiatry today is far different from the much publicized and much criticized community psychiatry of the 1960s. This changing role has given rise to the need for a new term—hence the widespread and increasing use of the term public psychiatry. Community psychiatry of the 1960s generally neglected the chronically and severely mentally ill and instead focused on less sick patients (the healthy but unhappy, or the "worried well") ... primary prevention (which little evidence that such efforts were effective), and community activism in efforts to change the basic fabric of society. ... Modern day public psychiatry generally recognizes that chronically and severely mentally ill persons should be given the highest priority in mental health efforts. (p. 1535)[7]*

This goal is worthy, and those in the entire specialty must attend to these most severely ill patients they treat. The focus of psychiatry, however, knows no such limits, as I describe in chapter 2. Subsyndromal conditions have become increasingly important, especially minor depression.[8–10] The "worried well" (or at least persons not counted among the chronically and severely mentally ill) have become an important (though not the central) focus of psychiatry practiced in private ambulatory settings. Yet psychiatry's interest in subsyndromal conditions does not include interest in social or cultural causes and does not consider societal interventions among its cures.

A review of the principle journals in American psychiatry verifies the virtual disappearance of 1960s- vintage social psychiatry. Table 5.1 presents the results of a search of the *American Journal of Psychiatry* from 1966 to 1972 and 1996 to 2002. Note in these comparisons that the average number of articles in the journal has increased significantly during this 40-year span.

Sparse mentions of current issues of social interest, such as unemployment and poverty, can be found in either the titles or the abstracts of articles in the *American Journal of Psychiatry* during 1998 to 2002. I found only one mention of either neighborhoods or stress in the workplace. Socioeconomic status is mentioned more frequently (10 times), but 80% of the instances mention it as a control variable, usually in psychobiological studies. In contrast, two variables have become of much greater interest; namely, stressful life events and social support

Table 5.1 Mentions of Terms Relevant to Social Psychiatry in the *American Journal of Psychiatry* from 1966 to 1972 and 1996 to 2002

Term	*American Journal of Psychiatry*	
	1966 to 1972	1996 to 2002
Primary prevention	10	1
Social psychiatry	4	0
Social changes	5	0
Social factors	11	2
Social support	0	9
Stressful life events	0	14
Social control	2	0

(see Table 5.1). These variables tap the social environment through the perception of individuals rather than more objectively assessing society.

Harold Pincus and colleagues, in a review of the *American Journal of Psychiatry* and the *Archives of General Psychiatry*, 1969 to 1990, confirmed this shift in emphasis.[11] They found that during this 21-year period the number and percentage of research articles increased and case reports and opinion papers decreased. Emphasis on biological studies, especially those in clinical psychobiology, increased, and attention moved sharply away from general categories to a more disorder-specific orientation. The authors described the 1965 era as concentrated on drug trials, particularly of antidepressants in outpatients, constitution and personality, mental health of "normal" people in the community, and behavioral therapy. They described the 1995 era as drug trials involving atypical antipsychotics, post-traumatic stress disorder, sexual abuse, and chronic fatigue. Models of community care, including discussion of patient satisfaction and economic evaluation, can be found, but these discussions are of traditional care in communities. Though social psychiatry never dominated the major psychiatric journals in the United States, the shift in focus is clear.

In contrast, Moncrieff tracked articles in the *British Journal of Psychiatry* throughout the 20th century and found very little change in emphasis.[12] (His review might be misleading, for he groups social psychiatry and psychiatric epidemiology together. Many articles, for example, in the *American Journal of Psychiatry* and the *Archives of General Psychiatry* from 1998 to 2002 reported the frequency of psychiatric disorders estimated from community surveys.) Moncrieff found that from 1965 to 1995, the percentage of articles focused on social psychiatry–psychiatric epidemiology ranged from 7% to 12% of the total. Social psychiatry in the United Kingdom never expanded as it did in the 1960s and did not contract as it did in the United States. Dinesh Bhugra and Julian Leff, in the preface of the British-authored *Principles of Social Psychiatry*, proclaimed, "This book is a celebration of the coming of age of social psychiatry" (p. ix).[13] This optimism can nowhere be found in American psychiatry.

Henderson and Burrows, in their edited *Handbook of Social Psychiatry*, applauded this change in focus. They noted that the focus on the individual has permitted much better instrument development (such as instruments to assess stressful life events) and has facilitated the development of methods for rigorous testing of the dominant hypotheses on social etiology, such as longitudinal design:

> We believe that an impediment to the progress of knowledge of social psychiatry has been rigid confinement to an exclusively social paradigm. Such rigidity is far from the views of early contributors to the field, such as Adolf Meyer, where constitutional factors were embraced alongside life experiences. (p. xviii)[14]

One can scarcely argue with Henderson and Burrows; focus on individual risk probably saved social variables from the trash heap during the emergence of diagnostic psychiatry and the remedicalization of psychiatry during the 1970s. The major epidemiologic surveys that derived from *Diagnostic and Statistical Manual of Mental Disorders–Third Edition* (DSM–III) and its successors, the Epidemiologic Catchment Area Study[15] and the National Comorbidity Study,[16] were tailor-made for assessing the individual risk for "caseness" (such as being a case of major depression) secondary to person-specific stressful experiences or impaired social networks.

Yet this retreat from the larger social context also potentially killed social psychiatry as a unique paradigm. In Henderson and Burrows's *Handbook*, Norman Sartorius wrote,

> Social psychiatry will disappear and it is likely that the world will be a slightly better place without it. It will not go alone: epidemiological, biological and dynamic psychiatry will vanish with it. Clinical psychiatry—the use of medical and other measures to help a person suffering from mental illness—will assume the place which it deserves: that of a branch of medicine acquiring and applying knowledge about mental disorder and promoting the use of such knowledge within the body of medicine as a whole. The concerns of social psychiatry today, however, will not lose their importance and will therefore be handled in the broader context of

efforts to promote public health. There is no social dermatology …
yet the social issues are not neglected. They are a core part of pub-
lic health planning. … Social psychiatry arose while psychiatric
disorders were still considered a "thing apart," not diseases like oth-
ers but a special aberration, and psychiatry a discipline which did
not belong to medicine but in equal parts to social engineering,
police work, judicial preoccupations, rehabilitation of those
impaired in their cognitive or affective capacities, and a number of
other social pursuits. … It should now fade into the background.
(p. 345)[17]

Social Psychiatry and Cultural Psychiatry

Cultural psychiatry (and culture as a concept) has been closely associated with
social psychiatry during the past 50 years.[18] Cultural psychiatry is primarily concerned with cultural aspects of human behavior, psychopathology, and treatment
(including access to treatment and differential responses to treatment).[19] Culture
can be conceptualized as the behavior patterns and lifestyle shared by a group of
people, which are unique and different from those of other groups. Culture typically encompasses shared knowledge, customs, habits, beliefs, and values. In contrast (though the contrast is not sharp), social psychiatry can be considered the
impingement of social phenomena on the genesis and manifestations of psychiatric
disorders and the use of social forces in the treatment and prevention of psychiatric
disorders.[20] To illustrate this distinction, the social psychiatric surveys of the 1960s
assessed broad social constructs, such as the strain of living in metropolitan areas or
socially disintegrated communities, as I describe in chapter 6.[21, 22] The communities studied included multiple cultures.

Entire textbooks have been devoted to cultural psychiatry in recent years.[19, 23]
The focus of these texts has been cultural sensitivity, recognition of cultural
differences (including culture-specific syndromes), and to some extent the cultural
contributions to psychopathology (such as migration and difficulty with acculturation).[24] These efforts are worthy contributions to the field, though they are at the
periphery of the current focus in American psychiatry. The collection of empirical
data from a cultural perspective has been less frequent but not absent, as demonstrated by studies of Native Americans.[25, 26]

The *Comprehensive Textbook of Psychiatry* devoted one section of four
chapters to the contributions of the sociocultural sciences.[27] Two contributions

from this section reveal the present relationship of the social sciences to psychiatry. In one chapter, Becker and Kleinman challenged usual current practices.[28] (Kleinman has been an articulate critic of current American psychiatry elsewhere.)[29] They covered the usual topics, such as culture-bound syndromes, and specifically explored how the explanatory model for a psychiatric disorder is firmly based in culture.

In particular, Becker and Kleinman noted that psychiatric disorders always unfold in a particular social and cultural context. They encouraged a cultural formulation as the key to any psychiatric assessment, referring to the appendix of *DSM–IV*, which provides an outline for developing such a formulation (pp. 843–844).[30] What is striking about the chapter is that two anthropologists (Becker and Kleinman are each trained in both disciplines) spoke virtually as outsiders back to mainstream psychiatry, pleading with psychiatrists to consider cultural issues.

In contrast, Ron Kessler (a sociologist who has worked extensively as a psychiatric epidemiologist) spoke from the center of mainstream psychiatric epidemiology in his chapter on sociology and psychiatry.[31] Regarding social origins of psychiatric disorders, he focused almost exclusively on stressful life events (including daily hassles and childhood adversity) and social support. He explored other factors such as school failure, job instability, marital instability, and financial adversity that are the social consequences of psychiatric disorders. Finally, he reviewed in some detail the community responses to the mentally ill. Social origins (and therefore social causation, which is key to sociology) have virtually disappeared from this textbook. They have disappeared as an interest of psychiatrists. Cultural psychiatry, in contrast, continues to speak with a distinct though peripheral voice.

Why Did Social Psychiatry Retreat?

The blossoming of social psychiatry during the 1960s was in large part predicated on the ability of psychiatry to change society. The potential of social psychiatry to actually transform society, however, was questioned from within even before the activism of the 1960s emerged. H Warren Dunham, coinvestigator in the landmark Chicago study,[32] as I describe in chapter 3, did not believe social psychiatrists had unique skills in the techniques of social action (p. 249),[33, 34] and he was not impressed with the concept of prevention. In fact, he believed that social psychiatry was in its infancy. Psychiatrists had not adequately delineated social causes of psychiatric disorders. He was equally critical of the rush to treat people with mild emotional disorders that followed the rise of office psychiatry and frustration with the difficulties of treating the severely mentally ill. Community psychiatry, he insisted, mirrored the cherished American belief that all problems were solvable "if we can just discover the key by means of the scientific methodology at our disposal" (p. 311).

Nearly 35 years later, Flaherty and Astrachan, in a review of social psychiatry, affirmed,

> *Psychiatry has improved its image both within and outside the profession of medicine through rejection of the expansive and utopian promise of offering solutions to all social ills and by realigning with medicine to concentrate on nosological reliability, treatment of disease, and etiological and pathophysiological studies in neurosciences and molecular biology. (p. 39)*[35]

Psychiatry rejoining the mainstream of medicine has undoubtedly benefited the field in the short run. But has the abandonment of social psychiatry actually strengthened the field in the long run?

Yet another reason for the retreat of social psychiatry is that the initial positive findings that supported social origins of psychiatric disorders and their consequences have been challenged. For example, statistical data from Australia did not support Durkheim's theories about the three types of suicide—altruistic, egoistic, and anomic.[36] The early studies that associated the frequency of schizophrenia with lower socioeconomic status[32, 37] were challenged by studies suggesting that the socioeconomic status of parents of schizophrenic patients was identical to that of the general population.[38, 39] The concept of social drift among the psychiatrically impaired emerged, for the schizophrenic patients appeared to drift down the socioeconomic ladder rather than to develop the disorder secondary to lower status.

Urban living has been associated with increased risk of psychiatric disorder,[40, 41] yet other studies do not show such a relationship.[42] The classic Stirling County study (see chapter 6 for a more complete description) explored small communities with tight social contacts and a more or less uniform culture. In contrast, the constructs of social integration and social disintegration just do not hold in the diverse and multilayered societies found in large cities.[22, 43]

Though the evidence in many cases tilts strongly toward social factors as causative of some psychiatric disorders, the conflicting data from other studies coupled with alternate theories have undermined the view that easily identifiable and measurable social factors have a significant influence on the causes of psychiatric disorders.[38] The biological vulnerability of the mentally ill can be reflected in social characteristics, such as lower socioeconomic status, rather than lower socioeconomic status leading to an increased risk of mental illness. Regardless of the intuitive appeal of social causation, the evidence accumulated to date has been modest. The paucity of empirical evidence compared with theory was accompanied by a decline in the skills of the psychiatrist to treat the individual patient in favor of social activism. Mel Sabshin captured this problem in his reflection on psychiatry in the 1960s:

> The combination of psychiatry's boundary expansion, the predominance of ideology over science, and the field's demedicalization began to produce a vulnerability. Many decision makers became skeptical about psychiatrists' capacity to diagnose and treat patients. (p. 1270)[44]

Perhaps the most damaging blow from the investigative wing of the social psychiatry movement has been the virtual absence of evidence that primary prevention is possible and that manipulation of the social environment is beneficial, especially for the severely and chronically mentally ill (not to mention the difficulty in implementing social therapies at either the individual or the collective level). The assertiveness community training program for such patients and their families is an exception.[35, 45] The goal of assertiveness community training was to provide services, in part through "natural helpers," that would maintain patients' social adjustment and minimize the burden to families and cost to providers. The services were provided by a team that was available when the patient was in need, yet such a program requires up-front resources. Although the empirical evidence that such a program can be effective was emerging, governments slashed funds for community mental health centers (the logical site to provide such care).

Some have questioned if the investigation of the social origins of depression and other psychiatric conditions is discouraged at the federal level.[29] First, social risk factors are difficult to operationalize in research, and social therapies are difficult to implement in practical programs. Second, clinical trials of social interventions could prove threatening to the payers of psychiatric care, because proven efficacy implies that more expensive social programs should be implemented in lieu of drugs and psychotherapy.[46] Third, there is no effective national lobby for social research and social therapies. In contrast, the drug companies and psychotherapists derive major economic gain from the treatment of depression and therefore lobby actively for their interests. Finally, the gravitation of the media to the latest scientific breakthroughs ensures that biological rather than social issues will receive attention. Poverty just does not sell.

Yet another reason for the retreat of social psychiatry was the association by Roy Grinker in 1964 of social psychiatry with a "psychiatry [that] rides madly in all directions," just when social psychiatry was riding the crest of its wave.[47] He defined psychiatry as a specialty of medicine that consists of the medical practice or applied science of treating and preventing mental diseases or disorders of the mind. Others had broadened that definition to include the study of the variations and vicissitudes of human behavior, with optimal personal and social functioning as the goal. The specialty had become a heterogeneous collection of sciences and practices without a unified goal. Psychiatry appeared to range from basic biology to philosophy. Psychiatry, according to Grinker, had become the study of life!

The social psychiatry of the 1950s and 1960s should have been recognized as one of a number of perspectives, including biological psychiatry and psychodynamic psychiatry, from which emotional suffering and its causes and therapy can be viewed.[48, 49] Instead, social psychiatry competed with biological psychiatry, and many social psychiatrists believed that hiving off a separate discipline would best serve their cause. Social psychiatry was never best served by a subgroup of social activists championing social theories that had not received adequate empirical study. It therefore never gained a firm foundation as a subspecialty within psychiatry.

The rise of social psychiatry propelled it to the middle of psychiatry's search for an identity. According to Ransom Arthur,

> It is probable that the Zeitgeist of the last decade [the 1960s], which emphasized awareness of social phenomena, disillusionment with human institutions, and political activism, has enormously enhanced the expansion of social psychiatric thinking. ... Social psychiatry and the intellectual climate that gave rise to its flowering have struck with hurricane force. The past few years have witnessed a crisis within psychiatry and the growth of a feeling of nihilism, particularly marked among younger psychiatrists. ... Part of the motive behind this feeling of negation has been the experience of community in which the psychiatrist's claim to expert knowledge and skill has been severely questioned. ... In addition, the belief that progress in preventive psychiatry can come only through political action to alter society has cast further doubt on the appropriateness and value of professional skills. (p. 846)[20]

Psychiatry's identity crisis during the 1960s set the stage for the remedicalization of psychiatry, as I describe in chapters 2 and 3. The excesses of social psychiatry placed it in a poor position to challenge the biological paradigm. At best, social psychiatry should have been (and should be) a recognition of and reflection on the origins, perturbations, and treatment of emotional suffering by all mental health professionals from a societal perspective. The new paradigm should give societal influences prominence so mental health professionals can begin to sort through the mountains of empirical data that have arisen from the investigation of depression (and other disorders) during the past 50 years. We should adopt and adapt current social theories, as I describe in chapter 9, for the social sciences have progressed in many notable areas.

If social psychiatry had been honestly viewed by its adherents as a paradigm and not a subspecialty during the 1960s, if social psychiatrists had been more realistic about the empirical basis for social psychiatry's recommendations, and if the practitioners had practiced good science rather than "running wild in all directions," its history might have followed a different course. But instead, the excesses of social psychiatry opened the door for the neurosciences to crowd it out altogether.[50]

At the same time the public was losing interest in social interventions. The liberalism of the 1960s gave way to a new conservatism that emphasized individual initiative and abandoned the doctrine that government could effect widespread and meaningful social change. The public placed more confidence in the market. Still, a far more pervasive public influence hastened the retreat of social psychiatry: the attraction of the public to the medical (more specifically the genetic) model of illness in general.[51]

The genetic model assumes a specific etiology of illness and looks at the internal environment (not an imbalance between a sick person and his or her environment). Rene Dubos anticipated this viewpoint in his review of the all-too-ready acceptance of germ theory as the final explanation of most illnesses.[52] The popular press says, "one gene, one disease."[51] A gene for depression is more significant than the social origins of melancholy.[53] Of course, the "one gene, one disease" theory scarcely holds for psychiatric disorders (Huntington's disease is the sole exception to date). Nevertheless, genes have become the blueprint for the body as a machine (DNA builds the building, it does not just set the scaffolding).

Too many complexities confuse communication about illness among the public. Attractions of genetic explanations include the allure of specificity and the ease of communicating specific causes.[51] In addition, the genetic model appeals to existing Western ideas of individuality. The responsibility for illness shifts to individuals (specifically to their biological makeup) and away from environments and social structures.[54] Given the public acceptance of the new genetics and the virtual "gene a week" reports in the media, the virtual social contract between the public and biomedical research is self-perpetuating. Scientists must continue to publish new biomedical discoveries, whether those discoveries will be refuted 6 months later or not. On the other hand, reports that major depression is more prevalent in urban than in rural areas are at best old news and at worst irrelevant news.

The National Institute of Mental Health and Social Psychiatry

The budget of the National Institute of Mental Health (NIMH) reflects the retreat of social psychiatry. By the late 1970s, more than 50% of the institute's budget supported community mental health centers.[55] Yet evidence of the remedicalization of psychiatry was already apparent. In 1980, an advisory panel recommended that the NIMH increase its extramural research commitment to neuroscience and related brain and behavior research. In addition, clinical treatment studies (as opposed to community intervention) became its central focus. A new epidemiology (see chapter 6) was to emerge. Service should focus on the severely mentally ill.

Direct federal support for the community mental health centers ceased during the 1980s.[55] President Ronald Reagan instituted block grants to the states, a portion of which could be used to support community mental health centers. The research budget of the NIMH therefore shifted dramatically to basic biological research and doubled during the 1980s. In addition, the NIMH was directed to stop supporting "social problems research" in 1982.[3] Thereafter the institute attended increasingly to research activities more directly relevant to specific mental disorders and biological origins.

The shift to biomedical research did not entirely stifle public advocacy. Advocacy, however, took a different face.[55] In 1988, the NIMH mounted the public education phase of the first large U.S. public health prevention program targeted to a specific group of mental disorders. The NIMH D/ART (Depression Awareness, Recognition, and Treatment) program was launched to encourage better public understanding of depression, screening programs, and awareness of available treatments.[56] Under the direction of Lewis Judd, director of the institute, the 1990s were proclaimed the "decade of the brain" by then President George H.W. Bush.[57] These shifts at the NIMH were further institutionalized as the institute rejoined the National Institutes of Health in 1992.

In 2002, the NIMH published *The Strategic Plan for the Mood Disorders Research*.[58] This plan clearly reflected the current priorities of the institute in general and for mood disorders in particular. Social science is conspicuous by its absence. The plan targets brain science (neuroimaging), genetics (applications of the Human Genome Project), behavior (more specific phenotypic expressions of gene structure and function), treatment (behavioral and pharmacological treatments), prevention (identifying people who might be genetically predisposed to depression, and specific environmental triggers that might be corrected by behavioral, educational, and pharmacological methods), service systems, and the delivery of treatment (improving access and decreasing disparities in access).

The authors of this plan should not be criticized for omitting the social sciences. They reflected current mental health research agendas. Potential areas for social science research do emerge in recognizing particular needs of special segments of the population such as women or children. These explorations, however, are to concentrate on biological issues. For example, the focus on race, ethnicity, and culture is to ensure a racially and ethnically diverse scientific workforce and to include full racial and ethnic diversity within studies. Prevention is to be focused on persons who already experience an illness; that is, secondary (early intervention) and tertiary (avoiding chronicity) prevention. If race (because it is associated with other psychosocial risk factors such as poverty) is associated with an increased risk for depression, study of this increased risk does not fall within the plan.

The Decline of the Community Mental Health Movement

When *Action for Mental Health* was released to the public in early 1961, the political climate for introducing big changes in mental health policy was favorable.[59] President Kennedy was a strong advocate. Yet caution was noted from the outset. Even as the pervasive social activism associated with community psychiatry led the American Psychiatric Association to reorganize its structure to become a more effective vehicle for social change, Harold Modlin, in 1966, warned,

> The community mental health movement is at present handicapped by overenthusiasm, partly because of much childishly gullible fascination with the new and adolescent rejection of the old. We have been through these phases many times before [could the current era be similar?]. (p. 249)[60]

American community mental health was an almost unmitigated failure from the beginning (as I describe in chapter 4), despite the noble intentions and hard work of its many advocates. Thousands of severely and chronically mentally ill individuals were discharged from the state mental hospitals (though the trend of discharge had begun during the 1950s). The mental health centers were not prepared to treat the most severely mentally ill patients, and the patients gravitated to the streets. One of the prime causes of homelessness today is the persistent trend to deinstitutionalize patients who had lived many years in institutions, with little in the way of services in the community to assist them.

The rise of homelessness can be explained in part by the lack of community-based services for the mentally ill.[61] On any given night about 700,000 persons in the United States are homeless. Approximately 20% to 25% of the single adult homeless population suffers from some form of severe and persistent mental illness.[62] The streets, not a welcoming society or a comprehensive mental health program, became the receptacle for the mentally ill. Following the service orientation of psychoanalysis, the mental health centers found it easier to provide psychotherapy to middle-class neurotics than to provide community-based comprehensive care to psychotic patients.

The absence of any clear alternative to a psychoanalytic approach in the community mental health centers opened the door to psychopharmacology much wider in the United States than in Europe. Psychopharmacology and social interventions are not incompatible. In fact, the wide use of chlorpromazine was a key factor in emptying the state mental hospitals, and medications could (and should) be combined with community-based care. What happened, however, was that social psychiatry failed and the hegemony of psychopharmacology (and diagnostic psychiatry) emerged. The social psychiatry movement spectacularly failed to treat the severely mentally ill, as I describe in chapter 4.[63]

Critiques of Social Psychiatry and the Antipsychiatry Movement

Critics of psychiatry were marginal but quite vocal during the 1960s and 1970s, often classified as "the antipsychiatry movement." These negative portrayals of psychiatry are in large part criticisms of the assumptions and enthusiasms of social psychiatry. The best-known challenge internationally came from Michel Foucault in *Madness and Civilization*.[64] He argued that the idea of mental illness was a social and cultural invention of the Enlightenment.[65] What the mentally ill actually do is not what makes them "mentally ill" but rather how the culture categorizes their behavior. Therefore the social activism of psychiatry was actually social control.[66] Thomas Scheff continued this theme in his sociological study *Being Mentally Ill*.[67] Psychiatric symptoms, according to Scheff, were better categorized as "residual rule breaking"; that is, behaviors that violate established norms but lack clear cultural labels. Lacking any other way to understand the behaviors, people classified them as the result of mental illness. If the social psy-chiatric goal was to socialize the mentally ill to society, then it supported existing norms.

In *The Myth of Mental Illness*, Thomas Szasz, an especially strident critic, proposed that mental illness was in fact a myth that described people who actually experienced problems of living.[68] He believed that the psychiatric concepts of health and disease were value judgments. The argument is most relevant to social psychiatry, for as psychiatry became more active as an advocate for the mentally ill, psychiatrists also became advocates for labeling persons as mentally ill.[66] In other words, as psychiatry became more influential, it also became less benign.[69] The antipsychiatry movement did not topple psychiatry or eliminate the preeminence of psychiatric diagnosis criticized by Szasz. Yet the movement certainly contributed to the decline of psychoanalysis and social psychiatry and to the emergence of a more scientific (and medicalized) psychiatry. If a disorder fell under the umbrella of medical disease, buttressed by empirical data, then that disorder would be diffi-cult to conceive of as a myth.

In 1974, Torrey published *The Death of Psychiatry*.[70] Most people treated by psychiatrists, he argued, experienced problems of living and did not need to be treated by people with medical training (the very direction taken by the community mental health centers). The others had brain disease and ought to be given back to the neurologists. In addition, the medical model is a kind of contract between patient and society—one of the clauses says that the patient is not responsible for getting the disease (p. 97).[70] Torrey praised the emergence of a scientific psychiatry that removed the burden of responsibility from psychiatrists in training. These young trainees were determinedly trying to cure their sickest patients through car-ing, only to find that, despite their good intentions and hard work, they made no impact (and they received covert blame from their supervisors).

The evidence of caring but not curing is no better seen than in a pivotal legal case during the late 1970s. The Osheroff case in 1979 might have sealed the fate of psychoanalysis as a powerful force in psychiatry and social psychiatry at the same time.[71] Dr. Rafael Osheroff filed suit against Chestnut Lodge for negligence, specif-ically because the institution had failed to provide drug therapy to him when he became severely depressed. During inpatient and outpatient care, he received only psychotherapy. Imipramine had been introduced as an effective treatment 20 years previously.[72] Later Osheroff was admitted to a different institution, received drug therapy, and improved within 3 weeks. Gerald Klerman, a prominent epidemiologist and pharmacologist who testified in the case, argued that there was no scientific evidence for the value of psychodynamically oriented intensive individual psychotherapy in a severely depressed person.[48] The same could be said for social therapies. Empirical studies became the foundation of psychiatric therapies following Osheroff. Social psychiatric therapies could provide no empirical base.

The Frequency of Depression and a Lesson from War and Society

6

Interpreting the Burden of Depression

> *"Depression is more prevalent, causes more suffering, and has a more devastating impact on individual functioning and societal welfare than the public, policymakers, and even many health professionals realize."*
>
> —K. Wells, A. Stewart, and R. Hays, *Journal of the American Medical Association* (p. 1)[1]

A front-page headline from the *San Francisco Chronicle*, June 18, 2003, proclaimed, "Help for Depression Lacking, Studies Find: 14 Million Americans Suffer Major Episode Annually."[2] The reporter summarized findings from a recent national survey of more than 9,000 people to determine the frequency of major depression (and other psychiatric disorders) and the frequency of treatment (differentiating adequate and inadequate treatment).[3] The investigators estimated that more than 16% of Americans had suffered from major depression at some time in their lives, and 6.6% suffered major depression at some time during the previous year. If so, the disease major depression is perhaps the most common serious disease experienced by the U.S. populace. Adequate treatment, according to these investigators, consisted of either four visits to a physician for drug therapy or six visits to a mental health professional for psychotherapy, or both. Even though more than one half of the participants were receiving some type of treatment, just more than 20% were receiving adequate treatment. The message from the authors of this study is clear: Major depression is a critical public health problem and people are not being treated nearly as often as they should. Let us take a closer look at the studies that support such startling headlines.

A review of community-based epidemiologic studies of psychiatric disorders during the past 50 years charts much of the change in American psychiatry. Community-based studies of psychiatric disorder emerged in two waves. The first wave was fielded during the 1950s, and the results were published predominantly during the early 1960s. These studies fueled and defined the social psychiatry movement of the 1960s. The Stirling County and the Midtown Manhattan studies

97

were the prototypes of the first wave.[4–7] Both studies focused on overall mental health impairment and the social ecology that contributes to it.

John and Mary Schwab proposed that social psychiatry is a three-legged creature with one foot in psychiatry, one in the social sciences, and one in epidemiology.[8] The first-wave epidemiologic studies of the burden of mental health impairment in the community rested on all three legs. Psychiatrists trained in psychoanalysis and the social psychiatry of Adolf Meyer primarily directed these studies. The investigators were firmly grounded in the social sciences, especially sociology and anthropology, and they employed classic community-based epidemiologic methods.

The second wave of studies emerged during the 1980s and 1990s. The findings reinforced the new psychiatric nomenclature. Prototypical studies were the Epidemiologic Catchment Area (ECA) study and the National Comorbidity Survey (NCS).[3, 9–11] The principle goal of the second-wave studies was to determine the prevalence and distribution of specific *Diagnostic and Statistical Manual of Mental Disorders–Third Edition* (DSM–III) (and DSM–III–R) psychiatric disorders (see chapter 2). These studies, in turn, contributed to the reification of the DSM psychiatric diagnoses, such as major depression. Sampling focused on obtaining responses from individuals who would be representative of the U.S. population as a whole, not of a particular social context (and therefore a specific social vulnerability). Though individual social risk and protective factors were assessed, social ecology was all but ignored.

I look mainly at these four studies, for they clearly demonstrate the rise of diagnostic psychiatry (and therefore the rise of major depression as a diagnosis). They also reflect the decline of the 1960s variety of social psychiatry. Nevertheless, many other studies were fielded before and during this era. For example, Faris and Dunham compared the location of residence with the diagnosis of either schizophrenia or manic-depressive disorder.[12] Eaton and colleagues studied mental illness among an enclave of the Hutterites;[13] Hollingshead and Redlich[14] and the Dohrenwends[15] studied the frequency of diagnosed psychiatric disorder as it was associated with social class. Duke University investigators studied the frequency of clinically significant depressive symptoms among the elderly,[16] and studies similar to the ECA studies were fielded in other countries.[17] Yet these four studies fully demonstrate the retreat of social psychiatric epidemiology and the rise of the new epidemiology. The new epidemiology estimated major depression to extend far and wide across the United States.

A Case in Point

In the midst of my residency in psychiatry during the early 1970s at Duke University, many of my fellow residents traveled to the University of North Carolina (UNC) (10 miles away) for psychoanalysis. UNC residents, in turn, would travel to Duke. Faculty at a university might be in conflict if they treated the same residents whom they taught and supervised, and the reciprocal relations worked well.

I had little interest in psychoanalysis, yet I made frequent pilgrimages to UNC. Dorothea Leighton, a pioneer in social psychiatric epidemiology and coinvestigator with the Stirling County study, was nearing the end of her active career. She had some flexibility in her time and was most willing to take on an informal student. I read the classics of psychiatric epidemiology, such as *My Name Is Legion*,[4] *The Character of Danger*,[5] *Mental Health in the Metropolis*,[7] *Culture and Mental Disorders*,[13] and *Psychiatric Disorders Among the Yoruba*.[18] Each week we would discuss my readings. From those readings and discussions, I committed my career to psychiatric epidemiology.

At that time, psychiatric epidemiologists studied the burden of mental illness in the context of society. I also developed an interest in cultural psychiatry, as I had spent 2 years as a medical missionary in Africa before I entered my psychiatric residency. I applied to the National Institute of Mental Health for a grant to study the burden of mental illness among older people in Africa, in retrospect a presumptuous effort. While in Africa, I had observed that older people were mentally healthy, on average perhaps more than their counterparts in the United States. I hypothesized that the respect and status given the elderly in Africa might contribute to this difference. The grant was not funded (it would have been unwise for the institute to fund the grant and disastrous to my research career—I was not prepared to undertake such a study). As a follow-up, however, I received a career development award that enabled me to return to school for training in epidemiology.

Three years later, Linda George (a sociologist) and I applied for Duke to be one of the sites for the ECA study.[9, 10] From the time that I began studying with Dr. Leighton to the time Dr. George and I submitted our application, I fully believed that my concepts and approach to social psychiatric epidemiology had been refined but not substantially changed. As we awaited the results of our application, I met with a well-known psychiatric epidemiologist. I asked him if he was applying for the ECA as well. I will never forget his answer: "I am not applying. The ECA represents a sea change in psychiatric epidemiology. Much of the progress we have made in the psychosocial study of mental illness will be thwarted by the ECA. The bottom line is that I do not agree with the conceptual orientation of the ECA and therefore will not take part in the effort."

Perhaps other well-known psychiatric epidemiologists from the 1960s and 1970s chose not to participate. Regardless, two unknown investigators from Duke received the grant to be one of the five ECA sites. *And the comment about a sea change in epidemiology was prescient.*

The Social Epidemiology of Psychiatric Disorders During the 1960s

The Stirling County Study

The Stirling County study was perhaps the most theoretically rich study of the social origins of psychiatric disorders to be published during the 1960s. Alexander Leighton, the director of the project, had studied at the Phipps Clinic in Baltimore with Adolf Meyer (p. 14).[8] The study therefore derived from theories developed earlier in the century, and that heritage continued into the studies fielded during the latter part of the 20th century, although with a significant twist, as I describe next.

Stirling County is the name applied by the investigators to a rural county in Atlantic Canada (population of 19,989 in 1950).[4, 5, 8, 19] The county contained one small urban center and a number of villages. Investigators surveyed two small rural villages (one fishing village with English-speaking inhabitants and one French Acadian village that derived its income from logging), the urban area, and rows of housing that were not well defined as communities. The basic hypothesis of the study, which captures the essence of the ecological approach to social psychiatry, was that a community's degree of integration or disintegration is related to the mental health of its inhabitants. (An ecological approach associates overall environmental factors, such as air pollution, to overall burden of a disease in the population. A one-to-one association is not assessed.)

The bridge between mental health and the sociocultural environment, according to Leighton, was sentiments:

> Sentiments are the predominant ideas that are colored with emo-
> tion and feeling, that occur and recur more or less consistently,

*which govern acts and give a sense of knowing what to expect …
each sentiment a union, or intersection, of cognitive and affective
processes and as having duration along the life-arc. … Personality
can be represented economically through a statement of its most
outstanding and pervasive sentiments. … Sentiments therefore provide a framework in terms of which personalities may be characterized descriptively and then salient points explored and analyzed
with reference to origins and determinants. … People are anchored
in [a sense of] place and time. (pp. 26, 27)[4]*

The essential striving sentiments, according to Leighton, were physical security, sexual expression, the giving and receiving of love, spontaneity, a sense of orientation in relation to society, inclusion in a moral order, and inclusion in and of a system of values. Sociocultural situations foster psychiatric illness if they interfere with the development and functioning of these striving sentiments (pp. 148, 158).[4]

Psychiatric illness was assessed by three methods: hospital records, general practitioner records, and self-report by the participant.[5, 20] Although the hospital records were sparse, the investigators interviewed physicians at length about the psychiatric status of their patients. Of the 1,010 individuals surveyed, only 49 were unknown to the physicians interviewed. To obtain self-reports of psychiatric symptoms, the investigators used a structured interview administered by lay interviewers. Clinicians reviewed their reports. The core instrument administered during the interview was the *Health Opinion Survey*, a 24-item symptom inventory developed from the Cornell Medical Index.[21, 22]

The Stirling County investigators categorized psychiatric illness into three interrelated forms. First, they determined the probability (see following) of a person being diagnosed as clinically ill if examined by a psychiatrist who applied *DSM–I* criteria.[23, 24] Each respondent also was rated for the degree of impairment produced by the psychiatric disorder, as shown in Table 6.1. Then participants were classified loosely into the symptom patterns of the *DSM–I*, such as depression (7.2%), personality disorders (6.0%), anxiety (10%), psychophysiologic disorders (59%), and psychoses (0.9%).

Table 6.1 Distribution of Psychiatric Impairment in the Stirling County Study

Level of Impairment	Percentage Rating
Unimpaired	69.9
Mild impairment	28.7
Moderate impairment	2.3
Severe impairment	0.1

The communities in Stirling County were placed on an integration-disintegration continuum. Communities were considered likely to be disintegrated if they experienced one or more of the following: a recent history of disaster, widespread ill health, extensive poverty, cultural confusion (a community containing two or more cultures without a stable and ordered relationship between the cultures), widespread secularization (i.e., the relative absence of religious sentiments), extensive migration, and rapid social change. Communities that were socially disintegrated were likely to exhibit a high frequency of broken homes, few and weak associations, few and weak leaders, few patterns of recreation, high frequency of hostility, high frequency of crime and delinquency, and weak and fragmented networks of communication (pp. 318–322).[4] Social scientists who worked in the field made the final categorization of the communities as integrated or disintegrated.[19]

The guiding hypotheses were ecological. For example, a community's degree of disintegration was associated with (and causative of) the psychiatric illness among its members.[4, 8] Social integration, in contrast, fostered mental health. As I noted previously, thwarted sentiments were viewed as the mechanism by which people living in socially disintegrated areas were more likely to experience psychiatric disorder. Such communities interfered with the striving sentiments. The investigators found a relationship between the probability of psychiatric disorder and the degree of social disintegration. They employed a unique method of calculating the probability of the individual's being a psychiatric case: the ridit—an index relative to an identified distribution, ranging from 0 to 1 with a mean of 0.5 (p. 248).[5] The ridit for a group was interpreted as the probability that an individual selected at random from the group was "worse off" than another individual selected at random from the reference population. The mental health status of the two integrated communities was 0.43 and 0.52, compared with 0.50 for the overall community. The ridit for the disintegrated communities was 0.66.

Stirling County investigators also found that the probability of "caseness" was higher for low socioeconomic groups (similar to the findings of Hollingshead and Redlich)[14] (p. 316).[5] In contrast to recent surveys, such as the ECA study,[25] they found a higher probability of psychiatric disorder in the older age groups. Women were more likely to experience psychiatric disorders than men (p. 255).[5] As might be expected from their hypotheses, the investigators found that degree of religiosity was associated with a lower probability of disorder (though this finding was true only for men) (p. 306).[5] These findings held for individuals, independent of the level of social integration of the community in which the person lived.

In a follow-up study 10 years after the original survey, the investigators found that one of the disintegrated areas had undergone remarkable changes and could be reclassified as integrated.[8, 26] Its economic opportunities had increased, communications had improved (secondary in part to television), and some people within the community began to exert much more leadership than they had previously. Accompanying this change was a significant decline in psychiatric illness at follow-up compared with the initial survey. The investigators concluded that a change in the social ecology of a community was accompanied by a change in the mental health status of its residents.

The Midtown Manhattan Study

Investigators at Cornell University fielded the largest of the studies in the United States in the 1960s, in midtown Manhattan. The founder of the study, Thomas Rennie, like Alexander Leighton, worked with Adolf Meyer in Baltimore. Rennie emphasized that social psychiatry is etiological in its aim, but that its point of attack is the whole framework of contemporary living.[8, 27] Originally planned as a cross-sectional study (in 1953), the Midtown Manhattan investigators followed up the sample 20 years after the original survey.[6, 7, 28]

The investigators proposed a stress-strain model of mental disorder onset,[6, 8] based on Hans Selye's *General Theory of Adaptation*.[29] Noxious environmental factors were labeled *stress*, and the reaction to stress was labeled *strain*. This labeling was analogous to engineering definitions in which stress is applied to a physical structure, such as a bar. The reaction of the bar to the stress was called strain. According to Langner and Michael, coinvestigators with the project,

> We know that personality, the sum of a person's relatively reliable ways of acting and reacting, can become deformed because of stress. That deformation, that strain, we may call mental disorder. ... In other words, strain is a reaction to the external environment. (pp. 6, 7)[6]

The investigators focused on the 20- to 59-year age group in midtown and attempted to assess the frequency of impaired mental health functioning (they also tried to classify some diagnostic types, such as psychotic, neurotic, psychosomatic, personality trait, and probable organic trait). A distribution of mental health impairment from the Midtown Manhattan study is presented in Table 6.2.

"Depression" was found by the rating psychiatrist in 23.6% of the respondents and was considered for most participants to be a tendency to assume a pessimistic viewpoint toward life situations, health problems, and interpersonal relationships. According to Langner and Michael, people in the low socioeconomic status (SES) category exhibited a unique variety of depression:

Table 6.2 Distribution of Midtown Manhattan Respondents According to Severity of Symptoms and Associated Impairment

Category	Percentage Rating
Well	18.5
Mild symptoms	36.3
Moderate symptoms	21.8
Impaired	23.4
Marked symptoms	13.2
Severe symptoms	7.5
Incapacitated	2.7

> *The depressive quality of the lower SES outlook is typified by the item, "I am in low, or very low, spirits most of the time." Along with depression, the Lows exhibit pervasive feelings of futility. … Their alienation from others and political apathy are reflected in their strong agreement with such statements as, "These days a person doesn't really know whom he can count on." And, "Most public officials are not really interested in the problems of the average man." … Thus the complex of depression and futility, political apathy and lack of trust in others and oneself is more typical of the lower class. (p. 462)[6]*

The investigators developed a method for evaluating overall stress that included parents' poor physical health, parents' poor mental health, childhood economic deprivation, childhood poor physical health, childhood broken homes, parents' character negatively perceived, parents' quarrels, disagreements with parents, poor physical health, work worries, SES worries, poor interpersonal affiliations, marital worries, and parental worries. They found that the accumulation of stress factors predicted poor mental health functioning.[6] No individual stress factor, however, was associated with increased impairment. Risk for poor mental health functioning secondary to stress varied significantly across SES even though the average stress scores did not vary by SES. In other words, the risk of mental health impairment increased with increased stress much more markedly among the lower SES groups than the higher SES group. In other words, life stress led to a greater risk for mental health impairment among people who were more vulnerable because of lower SES.

An association between lower SES and higher rates of mental health impairment has been noted in many studies. Dohrenwend and Dohrenwend,[8, 15] in a review of studies before 1970, stated that in psychiatric epidemiology "the most consistent result is an inverse relationship between social class and reported rates of psychological disorder" (p. 165).[15] Even so, the explanation for this association has not been fully explained. Possible reasons for this association include the following: poverty leads to mental illness; social drift, that is, persons with mental illness drift down the SES ladder; poverty leads to social disintegration; and genetic factors (people with mental illness marry others with mental illness) (p. 172).[8]

Social stress was individually assessed, yet setting the study in midtown Manhattan was thought to ensure the inclusion of people in the sample who experienced many of the negatives of urbanization. Srole and Fischer described the initial framework of the study as follows:

> *Among the enduring thematic strands that weave through the long fabric of Western thought is the conviction that contemporary man is in a condition fallen from an earlier height of simplicity, virtue, and well-being. ... One key tenet in this ideology is the pervasive conviction ... that mental health in the population at large has long been deteriorating, and at an accelerating tempo during the modern era. ... We will refer to this trend in the psychiatric literature as the "Mental Paradise Lost" doctrine. ... Exponents of the Paradise Lost doctrine hold urbanization, and the big city in particular, to be the prime villain behind the presumed trends of deteriorating mental health in recent centuries. (pp. 77–79).[30]*

Srole and Fischer, in retrospect, argued against this tenet. In the 20-year follow-up of the initial study (a follow-up that presents many methodological challenges to interpreting the data), they found that midtown respondents exhibited no significant net change in mental health, there was no appreciable difference in changes by gender, and people did not become more impaired as they aged.[28]

Categorical Versus Dimensional Assessment in Psychiatric Epidemiology

The evolution of psychiatric nomenclature toward specific psychiatric disorders, solidified with the advent of the *DSM–III*,[31] as I discuss in chapter 2. It was even more marked in the transition in case ascertainment from the social epidemiologic studies of the 1960s to the psychiatric epidemiology of the 1980s and 1990s.

Psychiatric epidemiologists of the 1950s and 1960s were strongly influenced by the work of the U.S. Army Research Branch on screening during World War II.[32, 33] They began to use small batteries of symptom questions with fixed alternative response formats. The batteries included questions about a variety of physical and psychological symptoms thought to be related to psychiatric disorders, including probes for psychological (e.g., anxiety and depression) and physical (e.g., cold sweats) problems. The scales were never found to be valid for identifying "case-ness" but continued to be used because they were economical to administer and intuitively attractive. Many investigators used the instruments for screening and complemented their use with more detailed clinical judgments (as I describe for the Stirling County study).

Sociologists have tended to come down on the side of such a dimensional assessment; that is, each person receives a score on a continuous scale of general-ized psychological impairment, with no clear point to designate a threshold between those with and without a presumed illness.[34] Two reasons have been given for preferring a dimensional approach: (a) the relationships between predictors and syndromes of psychological distress are more accurately captured in statistical mod-els that specify dimensional representations of distress, and (b) there is a lack of evidence for the existence of true discrete mental illnesses that account for the patterns observed among symptoms.[35]

Prototypical examples of dimensional scales include the 22-item Langner scale used in the Midtown Manhattan study[36] and the 20-item *Health Opinion Survey* used in the Stirling County study.[21] Yet these scales were originally developed to screen for the presence or absence of mental illness, not to provide a dimensional perspective of the burden of mental health. Even the dimensional scales called for a threshold beyond which a "case" could be identified. Kessler suggested that the cut-point debate (regarding where one draws the line for identifying a case using a dimensional scale) focused initially on a narrow question, "What is the correct cut-point to define clinical significance of psychiatric symptoms?"[34] Yet the challenge of labeling theorists broadened the question (those who proposed that mental illness was a social construction operationalized by labeling persons as either mentally ill or well).[37, 38]

Link and Dohrenwend demonstrated that these unidimensional screening scales typically include questions about a wide range of symptoms that cross many different psychiatric disorders.[33, 34] Despite the heterogeneity of symptoms, these screening scales were highly correlated with measures of self-esteem, helplessness-hopelessness, sadness, and anxiety.[33] The cluster of these symptoms was associated with what Jerome Frank labeled "demoralization."[39] Link and Dohrenwend therefore postulated and demonstrated that demoralization was a condition that is likely to be experienced in association with a variety of problems including physical illnesses and specific psychiatric disorders, as well as stressful life events. They further estimated the frequency of demoralization to be as high as 25% in the general population; approximately one half of the demoralized population was also suffering from significant clinical impairment. (The finding of symptoms spread across multiple domains is reflected in the high frequency of comorbidity of specific psychiatric disorders, as I describe next in the discussion of the NCS.)

The loading on this one factor does not mean that more discrete clusters of symptoms are not present, or if they are present, are unimportant.[34] For example, clusters of antisocial personality and schizophrenic symptoms are fairly clear, yet no clear clusters distinguish depression and anxiety.[34]

The ECA study, which I describe, departed drastically from the dimensional approach, dispensing with a screening instrument altogether and assessing the symptoms of specific psychiatric disorders, such as major depression. The ECA method of ascertaining cases of the *DSM–III* psychiatric disorders would not have been possible without the specific operational criteria for those disorders presented in the *DSM–II*[31] and the subsequent development of a highly structured instrument to determine the presence or absence of the criteria symptoms, the *Diagnostic Interview Schedule* (DIS),[40] which could be administered by nonclinical interviewers. Even so, clinicians continue to use screening instruments to evaluate those who might experience a specific disorder. The *Center for Epidemiological Studies Depression* scale[41, 42] and the *Beck Depression Inventory*[43] are examples of the scales used to screen for depression.

Neither the dimensional approach nor the categorical approach adequately describes the actual presentation of psychiatric morbidity in community surveys. Perhaps future studies will use the two approaches in tandem. Even if symptoms of depression do not cluster clearly, clinicians still think categorically about the presence or absence of major depression and other psychiatric disorders. Frequently, treatment decisions (and reimbursement) are based on if people are considered "cases." Therefore health services planning might require the use of categorical diagnoses to estimate the number of "untreated" people on the basis of accepted clinical operational diagnoses.[44] These utilitarian needs drove in large part the move from the dimensional approach to the categorical approach of psychiatric diagnosis in the second wave of community-based epidemiologic studies of psychiatric disorders, such as the ECA and NCS.

The New Psychiatric Epidemiology

The Epidemiologic Catchment Area Study

The ECA program broke the mold of the psychiatric epidemiologic studies of the 1960s. The broad aims of the program were to estimate the incidence and prevalence of specific psychiatric disorders, search for etiologic clues, and aid in planning health services use.[9] The ECA program derived from some of the many and diverse recommendations of the President's Commission on Mental Health, which was commissioned by Jimmy Carter and chaired by Rosalyn Carter.[45]

Significant new methods were introduced into the program. First, the program focused on estimating the prevalence and 1-year incidence of specific psychiatric disorders as defined in the *DSM–III*.[31] The previous focus on global mental health ratings ran counter to the new and emerging nomenclature (major depression was a specific example, as I described earlier in this book). To this end, a standardized interview, the DIS, was developed. It permitted lay interviewers to assess the presence and severity of specific criteria symptoms, on which the operational criteria of the *DSM–III* were based.[40] The same survey instrument was administered to participants twice, 1 year apart. This strategy permitted the assessment of incidence—that is, the onset of new cases—and prevalence—that is, the frequency of existing cases. In addition, the diagnostic instrument permitted the assessment of current (designated as 1-month, 6-month, and 1-year) prevalence estimates and lifetime prevalence estimates. Collection of data on their use of psychiatric, general health, and other human services coincided with collection of the data to estimate whether a participant was a case.

A second aspect of the methods implemented by the ECA was the integration of data from community samples and people in treatment. The sampling method permitted investigators to follow people who normally resided in the community but who might currently be in a treatment facility. Participants could be interviewed within the facility. In addition, people residing in prisons and long-term care facilities were included in the survey. Thus ECA investigators estimated the overall burden of psychiatric disorder for the entire population, including participants in treatment and participants who met diagnostic criteria but who were not in treatment. The focus of the populations studied was the individual Community Mental Health Center catchment areas, geographic areas with populations of 75,000 to 250,000.

Five sites were selected, and approximately 3,000 persons were sampled and interviewed at each site: New Haven, Connecticut; urban St. Louis, Missouri and surrounding rural areas; east Baltimore, Maryland; urban and rural areas in the

Piedmont of North Carolina; and two areas in Los Angeles, California, one of which included a high frequency of Latinos. Older persons were oversampled in New Haven, Baltimore, and North Carolina. The Baltimore, St. Louis, and North Carolina sites included a significant proportion of African Americans. Special studies were included in New Haven and Baltimore to follow the chronically mentally ill. Studies of sexual abuse and psychiatric problems secondary to a drought were added in North Carolina (yet these were not central to the goals of the ECA).

The combined 1-year prevalence estimate for any DIS psychiatric disorder for people 18 years of age and older was 28.1%.[46] The 1-year prevalence for any mood disorder was 9.5%; of these, 5.4% met criteria for dysthymia, 1.2% met criteria for bipolar disorder, and 5.0% met criteria for unipolar major depression (some dual diagnoses were permitted). The lifetime estimate for major depression was 7.5%. The 1-year incidence for major depression (the number of new cases divided by the number of participants not experiencing major depression at the first interview) was 0.3%.[47] The prevalence estimates appeared high to some investigators, and therefore they later corrected these estimates to ensure that the participants who met symptom criteria also reported impairment secondary to the symptoms.[48] Using the corrected estimates, they found that the overall 1-year prevalence for all DIS disorders among persons 18 years of age and older was 18% in the ECA. The adjusted 1-year prevalence for major depression was 4.0%. The overall estimates of the burden of mental health impairment were similar for the ECA project, the Stirling County study, and the Midtown Manhattan study, though the approach to identifying cases was quite different. Even so, many criticized the ECA study for underestimation of the mood disorders, especially major depression.

For this reason, investigators explored the frequency of subthreshold disorders, and the one studied most was minor depression. (Diagnostic criteria for minor depression can be found in the appendix of the *DSM–IV–TR*, though in the published epidemiologic studies many different criteria were used.)[49] For example, Eugene Broadhead, in a reanalysis of the ECA data from North Carolina, estimated the frequency of minor depression with mood disturbance to be 5% and minor depression without mood disturbance to be 23%.[50] Lew Judd, in a reanalysis of ECA data from all five sites (but using somewhat different criteria), estimated the current prevalence of what he and his colleagues labeled *subsyndromal depression* to be 14.6%.[51] In both of these studies, the investigators demonstrated that people who met criteria for the subthreshold conditions also experienced impairment in function (but the impairment was not as severe as in people with major depression).

Judd and colleagues took a further step in interpreting the findings from the ECA data coupled with experience from the Collaborative Study of Depression:[52]

We were surprised to find that the course of major depression is expressed by fluctuating symptoms that represent stages in the disorder rather than discrete depressive disorders. Thus, depressive symptoms at the major, mild, dysthymic and subthreshold levels are all part of the long term clinical structure of major depression. ... Residual subthreshold symptoms were significant enough to affect the quality and completeness of recovery. ... Patients who retained these symptoms when they recovered were more likely to experience a chronic course of illness and relapse than patients whose recovery was symptom free. ... Patients were symptomatic 60% of the follow-up period. ... The degree of psychosocial impairment was directly related to the severity of depressive symptoms. ... Patients functioned poorly when their sympoms were severe and functioned well when they were asymptomatic. ... Clinicians [should] treat all levels of symptoms in major depression, including residual. (p. 5)[53]

In other words, most of the community burden of depression was actually major depression writ large.

The extension of the umbrella of depression as a reified disease, whether labeled major or minor depression, has been challenged in the lay press. Stanley Jacobson wrote the following, in response to a consensus statement regarding minor depression in older persons:

The authors ... want to apply their medical interpretations and their pharmacological treatment across the board, beyond the so-called clinically depressed ... to those who are unhappy without apparent reason, the theory being that these conditions [i.e., minor depressions] negatively affect quality of life and are associated with increased risk of comorbid medical illness and clinical depression. ...[On the other hand], a depressive reaction to life experience is one thing, and vulnerability to a diagnosable disease called depression is another. ... [Consider] depression as a personality trait, a tendency to experience feelings which varies in strength from person to person. The disposition is not pathological but normally distributed, stable personality trait that neither increases nor declines with age. (pp. 46–51)[54]

Horwitz reflected on the revolution in diagnosis that underlay the ECA (p. 1ff).[35] At the beginning of the 20th century, Freud freed psychiatry from asylum psychiatry, focused on a small number of psychotic conditions, and broadened the profession to a specialty that treats a wide range of neurotic conditions. The *DSM–III* marked the second revolution by overthrowing the broad, continuous, and vague concepts of dynamic psychiatry and reclaiming the categorical illnesses, what Horwitz called "diagnostic psychiatry." Some have claimed that diagnostic psychiatry returns psychiatry to its theoretical roots at the beginning of the 20th century.[55] In contrast to asylum psychiatry, however, diagnostic psychiatry casts its net very wide (the *DSM–IV* classifies nearly 400 distinct disorders).

Despite the move to discrete disorders, many people in the community meet criteria for at least one disorder. Many of them are seeking help for their emotional suffering. Each year about 15% of the adult population of the United States seeks some type of professional treatment for mental health or addiction problems (though most do not seek that help from psychiatrists).[46] Between 1985 and 1994, the number of prescriptions for psychotropic medications soared from 33 million to about 46 million.[56] "A huge cultural transformation in the construction of mental illness has occurred in a relatively short time," said Horwitz (p. 3).[35] This transformation is unique in psychiatric history. Even so, the public health cry is that people with major depression are not seeking care, and the ECA documented that vast numbers of persons who met criteria for a psychiatric diagnosis in the community were not treated.[57] The percentage seeking some type of professional help, however, has increased in recent years (to more than 50%).[3]

The National Comorbidity Survey

The NCS followed the ECA by 10 years.[11] The survey was mandated by the U.S. Congress to study the co-occurrence (comorbidity) of substance-abuse disorders and other psychiatric disorders. In many ways the goal of the survey was similar to that of the ECA, but the methods were modified. The NCS was designed to take the next methodological steps beyond the ECA. First, the NCS was based on *DSM–III–R*[58] rather than *DSM–III* disorders.[31] Second, the questions permitted cross-classification with the *International Classification of Disease*.[59] Third, the NCS was carried out in a national sample as opposed to multiple local samples.

In contrast to surveying five catchment areas, the NCS sampled nationally by means of a multistage, area-probability sample of people 15 to 54 years of age in the coterminous 48 states. Fieldwork was carried out between September 1990 and February 1992. The survey was administered in two parts. More than 8,000 persons received part 1, which included core diagnostic questions. From those initially screened, 5,877 respondents (which included those with any lifetime psychiatric diagnosis, all participants between the ages of 15 and 24 years, and a random sample of other respondents) received a more detailed questionnaire, which included a review of potential risk factors and questions about service use.

Diagnoses were generated by a modified version of the *Composite International Diagnostic Interview*.[60] Nearly 50% of respondents reported at least one lifetime disorder, and nearly 30% reported at least one disorder during the 12 months preceding the interview.[11] The most common disorders were major depressive episode, social phobia, and simple phobia. Comorbidity (more than one diagnosis in one's lifetime) was frequent. Fewer than 40% of those with a lifetime disorder had ever received professional treatment, and fewer than 20% of those with a recent disorder had been in treatment during the 12 months preceding the survey. Women were more likely to experience mood and anxiety disorders, and men had higher frequencies of substance abuse and antisocial personality disorder. Most disorders were less frequent at older ages and with higher SES.

The 1-month prevalence of major depression was 4.9% overall. The frequency was relatively higher in females, young adults, and people with less than a college education.[61] The prevalence estimate for lifetime major depression was 17.1%, with a similar demographic distribution to the 1-month prevalence. People with major depression were more likely to use general medical services and specialty mental health services than those without.[62] The study was replicated 10 years after the original. (I describe the results at the beginning of this chapter.)[3]

The comorbidity between alcohol or substance abuse and other psychiatric disorders was high.[63] Whereas the frequency of any mood disorder without use of alcohol was 11% in men, the frequency increased to 16.7% with any alcohol problems and 23.6% with alcohol dependence. This pattern persisted for women, though the frequencies were higher (50% if the woman was dependent on alcohol). Comorbidity overall was high, with 92% of people with major depression having at least one lifetime comorbid disorder.[64] If a participant experienced any disorder found on the *Composite International Diagnostic Interview*, he or she had a 60% chance of experiencing at least one other disorder. Lifetime comorbidity was the norm in this study.

The NCS brings to the forefront the entire concept of comorbidity. Horwitz suggested that the symptoms of most psychological dysfunctions are not direct indicators of discrete underlying disease entities but instead stem from general underlying vulnerabilities that might assume many different overt forms, depending on the cultural context in which they arise (pp. 109–111).[35] Though more severe disorders, such as schizophrenia, appear discrete, nonpsychotic disorders, especially depression and anxiety, often occur together (hence the interest in comorbidity if one is wedded to discrete disorders). The pattern persisted in clinical settings. In one study of depression in outpatients, 65% of 373 patients with major depression had a comorbid anxiety disorder—23% with panic, 36% with social phobia, 24% with post-traumatic stress disorder, and 15% with generalized anxiety disorder.[65] In another study, 41% with major depression were also diagnosed with comorbid anxiety disorders such as post-traumatic stress disorder and simple phobia.[66]

Is there evidence that these comorbid disorders might actually result from the same pathophysiological origin? In a study of female twins, investigators concluded that major depression and generalized anxiety disorder derive from the same genetic factors. In contrast, environmental risk factors that predispose to "pure" generalized anxiety disorder episodes might be relatively distinct from those that increase risk for major depression.[67] There is also considerable crossover through time from one diagnosis to another, especially within the diagnosis of depression and between depression and anxiety.[51,68] Treatments such as cognitive behavioral therapy and pharmacologic treatment with the selective serotonin reuptake inhibitors seem to work for multiple disorders.[69] Perhaps a better explanation is that some people have a general vulnerability to psychological dysfunctions that expresses itself in different ways, depending on the social circumstances.

Individuals recruited for clinical trials are dissimilar to individuals treated for major depression in typical outpatient clinics.[70] Eighty-six percent of the clinic patients in one study would have been excluded because of a comorbid anxiety disorder or substance-use disorder, insufficient severity of depression, or current suicidal ideation. Fifty-four percent would not have been entered because of insufficient symptoms. Rather than comorbidity, perhaps a better explanation is that the symptoms are nonspecific indicators of a common, broad, underlying vulnerability (the magnitude of comorbidity is in part an artifact of the syndromal approach to diagnosis). There is virtually no specific etiological cause for any particular nonpsychotic disorder.

As I described previously,[48] the higher-than-acceptable frequency of disorder found in the community-based studies led investigators to reclassify current psychiatric disorder on the basis of dysfunction and presence or absence of symptoms. By combining the ECA and NCS for persons ages 18 to 54 years, they estimated that the 12-month prevalence was 18.5%. The percentage remains a hard sell (though perhaps not as hard as in the past). Many policy makers cannot accept that fully one fifth (or nearly one third if the unadjusted estimates from the NCS are used) of Americans experienced a psychiatric disorder that required professional intervention during any given year. Yet the sell has been easier for the specific diagnosis of major depression. Perhaps it is easier to accept the estimate because of the perceived effectiveness of medications coupled with the propensity to focus general emotional distress on specific diseases (as I discuss in more detail in chapter 7).

Is the Frequency of Depression Higher Today than in the Past?

One question that repeatedly arises is whether the frequency of depression is increasing in the United States. In other words, are we in fact entering an age of melancholy?[71] Clinical and community-based epidemiologic studies appear to provide the data from which this question can be answered. In a large clinical study, major depression exhibited a strong secular trend toward increased lifetime risk. Depression had emerged at an earlier age in the younger people surveyed than the older ones.[72] Results from the major community-based epidemiological studies confirm the view that depression is more frequent among younger people (and therefore that the overall frequency of depression is increasing).[61,73] The data documented a sharp increase in the frequency of major depression among men and women in the birth cohort born during the years 1935 to 1945.[74]

Three effects must be accounted for to answer this question: age, period, and cohort. If the frequency of depression onset decreases as age increases (as appears to be the case),[75] then as the population ages, the overall frequency of depression would decrease if other effects are held constant. Period effects are societal factors that affect the entire age range (or a portion of that range). Analysis of the clinical sample of depressed individuals and their relatives mentioned previously suggested that a powerful period effect can be responsible for the secular trend toward increased rates of major depression.[72] Investigators found that the rates of onset of depression in siblings of the probands (the patients being studied) between ages 15 and 50 years doubled between the 1960s and 1970s. These period effects also were found in the community survey from 1960 to 1980.[74] Cohort effects are the effects experienced by the birth cohort into which a person is born. Younger birth cohorts appear to be carrying a higher burden of depression.[73,76–78] In addition, the higher frequency of depression among younger birth cohorts can accompany a higher frequency of other disorders, such as drug and alcohol abuse. Yet comorbid drug and alcohol abuse does not totally explain the increased frequency of depression.[79]

Studies that consider age, period, and cohort effects simultaneously are difficult to carry out without considerable bias, and these studies have been challenged. Poor recall among older adults can decrease the reported lifetime frequency of depressive episodes.[80] Older respondents might also be less likely to label major depression as "depression"; that is, as a psychological or emotional problem.[81] Recent studies of children have not found a higher frequency of depression among younger birth cohorts.[82] A group that reanalyzed the result from the clinical study reported previously[76,83] found significantly larger cohort sizes for the younger birth cohorts and therefore concluded that method effects probably explain a larger portion of the secular trends reported. There is no clear necessity to include changing environmental effects into quantitative genetic modeling. Suffice it to say that current evidence is mixed regarding a secular trend toward increased frequency of depression.

Among the psychiatric disorders, depression is the most frequent cause of suicide.[84,85] Suicide rates were tracked carefully during the 20th century,[84,86] and so suicide rates during the past few decades could help us determine if depression is increasing in frequency. The overall frequency of suicide has not changed in the United States during the past several decades and has remained in the range of 11 to 12 per 100,000 per year. Even so, suicide is the third-leading cause of death in youths 15 to 24 years old. Some recent trends are of interest. Despite the significant increase in use of antidepressant medications (more than 10% of the general population),[56,87] rates of suicide have not declined appreciably in the United States, and this discrepancy has targeted an important area for further study.[88] In a study of England and Wales, from 1950 to 1999 suicide rates doubled in men ages 15 to 44 years. It appears that men in successive birth cohorts born after 1940 carry increasingly higher risk for suicide.[89] In contrast, suicide rates have decreased in Sweden, and the decrease has been attributed to the introduction of the selective serotonin reuptake inhibitors.[90]

Other studies of suicide suggest important temporal trends. In a study from Great Britain, an increase in suicide rates from 1981 to 1991 was found to be associated with an increase in social fragmentation, though not with poverty as such.[91] From 1970 to 1997, suicide rates among adolescents in the United States have tripled, even as rates for other age groups declined (overall rates remaining about the same).[92] When economic status is held constant, reduction in parent's time available to adolescents (such as monitoring their behavior) is hypothesized to be an important contributor to the increased frequency. In a provocative finding, suicide rates are increasingly higher in rural areas than in urban areas (thus substantiating Srole's critique of the Mental Paradise Lost hypothesis).[93] One explanation is that rural residents, especially women, are at increased risk for social isolation. Again the evidence is mixed, and more study of the trends is called for.

Who Benefits from the New Psychiatric Epidemiology and Major Depression Writ Large?

Wakefield suggested that a valid psychiatric disorder exists when some internal psychological system is unable to function as it is designed to function and when this dysfunction is defined as inappropriate in a particular social context.[94] The symptoms of many of the most common psychiatric disorders vary from time to time and from place to place in ways that are socially structured to fit predominant cultural models. Shorter argued that this effect can be seen in the changing diagnosis of vague physical symptoms, specifically the transition from hysterical paralysis to chronic fatigue syndrome.[95]

7

A Lesson from War
Syndromes

> No doubt they'll soon get well; the shock and strain
> Have caused their stammering, disconnected talk,
> Of course they're "longing to go out again,"...
> They'll soon forget their haunted nights; their cowed
> Subjection to the ghosts of friends who died
>
> —Siegfried Sassoon, *Survivors*, 1917 (foreword)[1]

The first Gulf War was a success story, at least initially. We won the war decisively, remarkably few soldiers were killed or wounded given the large deployment to the Gulf, and most of our soldiers returned soon after the final battles. Years after the war was over many Gulf War veterans surfaced complaining of headache, joint pain, abdominal pain, sleep problems, and other symptoms. This surprised the military and the health care profession. Their symptoms were coalesced into a new diagnosis—Gulf War syndrome. A presidential commission was established, and the National Research Council was called on to shed light on the emergence of these symptoms and to explain their cause. Many medical scientists redirected their research to this new syndrome. The Gulf War appeared to give birth to a new disease. Or did it?

Changing concepts of "war syndromes" during this past century mirror the retreat of social psychiatry and the rise of highly medicalized diagnoses, such as major depression. In fact, the progression of psychiatry through the past 60 years, especially its diminishing focus on social factors as the origin of emotional suffering, comes into sharp relief as we look at war syndromes. Military psychiatry usually falls outside the interest of the public and general psychiatry. Nevertheless, the recent and unexpected physical and psychiatric sequelae of the Persian Gulf War (often labeled Gulf War syndrome or illness) has brought war syndromes to the center stage of health care providers and the public at large.

Each of the major conflicts in which the United States has participated during the past 150 years has produced physical and emotional problems for the participants that have not been easily categorized or explained by physical causes. During each conflict, however, a particular characterization of these problems has emerged. The names given them include "shell shock" during World War I, "combat exhaustion or fatigue" during World War II, "post-traumatic stress disorder" following the Vietnam War, and "Gulf War syndrome" following the Persian Gulf War (as noted previously). Of course, soldiers were exposed to physical toxins from the environment, such as mustard gas during World War I and Agent Orange during the Vietnam War, yet these syndromes were not found to be associated with these toxins.

These afflictions are not merely the same problem presenting in different ways. Some, such as combat exhaustion, are by definition limited to the period of combat. Others, such as Gulf War syndrome, came to public attention years after the conflict was over. In addition, the combat conditions vary for soldiers from one war to the next. The debilitating trench warfare of World War I in no way compared with the plight of the soldiers waiting for conflict in relative safety for weeks on end during the Persian Gulf War. Old stressors have disappeared and new agents of destruction have emerged. Fear of mustard gas during World War I gave way to fear of nerve gases such as sarin during the Persian Gulf War. Yet an interesting pattern emerges when we review these nonspecific (though at times severe) syndromes and the accepted explanations for the cause and potential cures of the syndromes.

A CASE IN POINT

John sought medical consultation at a Veterans Administration outpatient clinic in 1994. He was a member of a support unit during the Persian Gulf War of 1990 to 1991, stationed in Saudi Arabia for nearly 2 months before the ground invasion began in early 1991. He followed the ground troops into Iraq and spent nearly a month in Iraq before being relieved. After returning to his home base in the United States, he completed his prescribed 4 years of military service in 1993. Following discharge he entered college to complete a bachelor's degree and pursue his career goal of teaching and coaching in a high school. John had joined the military initially because he was not certain what to do with his life at the age of 19. In addition, he wanted to take advantage of the financial support for education that a tour of duty would provide.

Once he began school, he realized that he just was not the same as before. His sleep was fitful, and he seemed to experience aches and pains all over his body. Before entering the military, John had been an excellent athlete, starring on his high school football team. Only a knee injury prevented him from continuing his athletic career in college. Therefore, he thought the frequent though not disabling pains seemed "unlike" him. He also had trouble concentrating at school and was concerned that he might fail two of his courses that semester. Though not a strong student, he nevertheless believed that he was more disciplined in his studies following military service and was confident that he could complete the requirements for a college degree. Instead, he found himself sitting for hours at a time over his books, his mind wandering continually.

Overall, John had enjoyed his time in the military. Though he originally thought he would be a "fighting soldier," he soon realized that he was better adjusted to support work, especially as a driver and mechanic. The first 2 months in Saudi Arabia had been frustrating but not threatening. "I knew they were shooting those Scuds, but I never really worried about them. The alarms went off every day but we never saw or heard an explosion." When he followed the ground troops into Iraq, "the fighting was over by the time that we arrived on the scene. I never felt in danger." Even so, the month in Iraq had not been easy for John. He could never forget the sight and smell of the dead bodies of the slain Iraqi soldiers. "I had never been around dead people before. At the time, we all had a job to do, so I did pretty well during the day but I started having trouble sleeping at night thinking about those dead bodies. You can't believe how thankful I was to return to the States. And you better believe that after that month I never considered re-enlisting."

The doctor treating John told him, "I can't find anything really all that wrong, but I know that you have been through a lot and that war is tough." John decided just to do the best he could, for he did not know what else he could do. His concentration did improve, and he managed to pass his courses. He did a little better each semester while in college. Two years after the initial appointment, in 1996, John returned to the clinic. He asked the doctor, "Do you think I have this Gulf War syndrome that everyone is talking about? I still have difficulty sleeping and I have more aches and pains than I should at my age. Even though I work out regularly, they just don't go away."

The Civil War: A Prelude

As early as the Civil War, treatment of mentally ill soldiers was recognized as important to their welfare.[2] The Union Army identified 2,410 cases of "insanity" and 5,213 cases of "nostalgia." In addition, 200,000 soldiers deserted whom some classified as mentally ill (though this classification can certainly be challenged). Given the limitations of medical care, much less psychiatric care, during the most devastating American conflict ever, we can safely assume that many Civil War soldiers experienced nonspecific physical and psychological problems that could have accompanied them the remainder of their lives.

Da Costa[3] evaluated 300 soldiers referred to him during the Civil War.[4] He thought he recognized a pattern of symptoms: shortness of breath, palpitations, sharp or burning chest pain particularly on exertion, fatigability, headache, diarrhea, dizziness, and disturbed sleep. He found no consistent sign of physiologic disease among these soldiers, and most appeared to be in fair overall health. Of the men he evaluated, 38% recovered.

Calhoun recognized another syndrome, which he labeled *nostalgia*.[5] This term was introduced to describe initially highly enthusiastic soldiers who expected an early end to the conflict but became disenchanted as the war dragged on. Characteristics of nostalgia cases included constricted affect, social estrangement, disciplinary problems, substance abuse, mistrust of command, and alienation. Many of nostalgia's characteristics apply to what we now label as post-traumatic stress disorder (chronic and delayed). For nostalgia, however, no specific traumatic event was necessary to make the diagnosis.

The legacy of the Civil War contributed to our overall understanding of ill-defined expressions of illnesses, according to Edward Shorter.[6] Following the war, two general categories of war-related illnesses were recognized. The first category was a poorly understood group thought to be associated with physiologic disease and organic pathology. This syndrome was characterized by the similarity of reported symptoms and the high frequency of diarrhea and other infectious diseases preceding the onset of the syndrome. The second group, characterized by a mixture of physical and psychological symptoms, was attributed to wartime stress. Symptoms associated with wartime stress were not specific enough to establish a diagnosis, yet the loosely used term *neurasthenia* was incorporated. Neurasthenia was considered to be "functional"; that is, it was hypothetically organic but exhibited no tangible tissue change. That such a term was used reflected the climate of medical uncertainty and the uncertainty of patients about what was madness (psychologic) and what was nerves (physical). Patients and doctors sought a bridge—an organic-*sounding* disease term to explain psychiatric-*looking* illness behavior (p. 229).[6] In 1869, Beard suggested that a large number of nervous symptoms in neurasthenia were actually the result of physical exhaustion of the nerves.[7] The range of symptoms he included as resulting from nervous exhaustion included dyspepsia, headaches, paralysis, insomnia, anesthesia, neuralgia, and rheumatic gout. A rest cure was the usual therapy prescribed.

World War I

During World War I, the neuropsychiatic disorder of most interest was shell shock.[2] Officers initially sought a traumatic etiology for shell shock, suggesting that the condition emerged after the explosion of shells, producing a concussive effect to the brain of the victim. That explanation failed, for many soldiers who developed shell shock were nowhere near the explosion of any shells. Medical personnel therefore theorized that the behavior was either preconditioned as constitutional and neurotic or class specific and derived from some personal failure, such as lack of character or being a weakling. Naturally, this explanation was not acceptable to the soldiers, who firmly believed that they were ill. In part because of the protest of the soldiers, all medical personnel were instructed to label these disorders as "not yet diagnosed (nervous)" as the war neared its end.

In addition, medical personnel learned that if the condition was not treated early, it became refractory. Soldiers who were evacuated from the front, specifically to England, experienced symptoms particularly resistant to treatment. From these discoveries, the three-pronged approach to treatment of immediacy (treat the soldier as close to the front as possible), simplicity (use basic treatments such as rest and encouragement), and centrality (develop a central point to coordinate the treatment of all psychiatric casualties) emerged.[2]

A syndrome similar to Da Costa's syndrome emerged in World War I. It was called "effort syndrome," "soldier's heart," or "neurocirculatory asthenia."[4] Soldiers with this condition reported shortness of breath, palpitations, chest pain, fatigue, headache, dizziness, confusion, concentration problems, forgetfulness, and nightmares.[8] A consensus emerged that effort syndrome was not caused exclusively by unique wartime exposure, because many soldiers reported having similar symptoms before the war. Medications did not improve their symptoms. A structured rehabilitation program, with a graduated exercise regime and encouragement from a supervising medical staff, was effective. Franklin Jones noted that the military learned that time away from the unit weakened bonds and permitted the rationalization of symptoms.[2] "If I am not sick, I am a coward. I cannot accept being a coward, therefore I am sick." If the physician attributed the symptoms to a heart condition, recovery was hindered (so physicians were advised not to tell soldiers that they had a heart condition).

Novelists, biographers, and poets wrote of the emotional dysfunction that can result from trench warfare and the advent of modern weaponry. World War I was unlike any war previously fought (even though the casualties resulting from the U.S. Civil War were staggering). Robert Graves, in *Good-bye to All That: An Auto-biography*, documented the loss of innocence that occurred as a result of the war.[9] When he was deployed to the front, he believed he was leaving England for the last time. He bid farewell to his birthplace and life as he knew it. England and the modern world would never be the same. He vividly described life in the trenches, the loss of dear friends, and the absurdity of government bureaucracy. In *The Great War and Modern Memory*, literary critic Paul Fussell located the 20th century's literary and martial birth in the British trenches of World War I.[10] He traced events from pre-1914, a time without radio, TV, or any movies to speak of, when the populace had implicit faith in their press, their king, and progress, to the postwar era's fear of technology and despair. He proposed that its pessimistic influence shaped much of the British literature during the next century.

World War II

World War II ushered in, at least on the surface, a significant increase in psychiatric services. These services began with the psychiatric screening of every inductee (an effort that greatly exceeded the capabilities of medical personnel, leading to many 2-minute psychiatric consultations).[2] The screening, supposedly done to avoid exposing men with psychological vulnerabilities to the stress of war, failed on two counts. First, many potentially excellent soldiers were screened out serendipitously. Second, the screening in no way prevented psychiatric casualties. William Menninger, in a review of World War I and World War II statistics, found that the initial rejection rate and the rate of psychiatric breakdowns were much higher during World War II.[11]

A deeper analysis of the screening program led to the conclusion that "social and situational determinants of behavior were more important than the assets and liabilities of individuals involved in coping with wartime stress and strain" (p. 1024).[12] The theory of ultimate vulnerability was promulgated and usually expressed as "everyone has his breaking point."[13] Gilbert Beebe and John Appel found that if only psychiatric casualties occurred at the battlefront, there would be a 95% depletion by company combat by day 260 (though this never happened because of transfer, death, and other factors).[14] Therefore, periodic rest was essential. Even so, the "short timer's syndrome" emerged—an anxious, tense state that emerged as the tour of combat neared its end, even though substantial rest and relaxation were available.

Craig Hyams found that the effort syndrome continued to be important during World War II among the British.[4] It was generally considered to be a psychoneurosis and not a medical disease. Acute combat stress reaction (battle fatigue, combat exhaustion, or operational fatigue) also became better understood—frequently manifested as fatigue, palpitations, diarrhea, headache, impaired concentration, forgetfulness, or disturbed sleep. The syndrome appeared best treated with the triad of immediacy, simplicity, and centrality, as I described previously. Medical personnel tried to avoid diagnoses such as "war neurosis." In fact, the terms *war neurosis* and *traumatic neurosis* presented a paradox. Traumatic suggested some stress from without. Neurosis suggested individual vulnerability. An external stress might trigger internal vulnerabilities but could not cause them.

Rather, the term *exhaustion* was initially used in World War II, then *combat exhaustion*, then *combat or battle fatigue*.[2] The military wanted to avoid a definitive diagnosis that emphasized the liabilities of individuals and ignored the setting in which a failure of adjustment had occurred. The military also relearned the importance of "forward treatment" (brief therapy and rest near the battlefront).

World War II shaped the thinking of psychiatry for many years afterward. For example, the concept of combat exhaustion helped set the stage for the social psychiatry of the 1950s and 1960s. Combat exhaustion was defined by the *DSM–I* as follows:[15] "Combat reaction is often transient in character. When promptly and adequately treated, the condition may either clear rapidly or it may progress into one of the established neurotic reactions. The term is to be regarded, therefore, as a temporary diagnosis [and] applies to more or less 'normal persons.' The stress in such cases is intolerable."[16] In the *DSM–I* the category of "gross stress reaction" was included, the direct descendent of combat reaction. Ironically, in the *DSM–II* (published in 1968, the year of the Tet Offensive of the Vietnam War) the category was dropped.[17]

This view of a gross stress reaction, in turn, shaped the approach to services. Grob described the prevailing view at the end of the war:

> If the rigors of military life and the stress of combat—not the structure of personality—fostered mental breakdowns, then it followed that careful and intelligent planning could reduce the number of

psychological casualties. All individuals, after all, were at risk.
(p. 194)[18]

Could this view of treating psychological casualties in war be transferred to civilian life? Appel and Beebe, even after conceding that environmental stressors were more diverse and less amenable to centralized control in civilian life than the military, expressed the belief that institutions of government, industry, education, religion, and communication possessed sufficient means to undertake efforts to remove or ameliorate some of the situational stresses that adversely affect mental health.[19] (These views helped fuel the social psychiatry and Community Mental Health Center movement and derived from successes of World War II.)

The belief that soldiers in World War II recovered without further problems, however, was not accurate. George Vaillant and colleagues followed 152 ex-soldiers, initially interviewed in 1946, for nearly 50 years.[1, 20] More than 10% of this group reported symptoms of war neurosis. In 1995, the surviving veterans were reassessed. Most of the men who reported combat-related symptoms in 1946 reported that the symptoms persisted during the nearly 50-year interval, neither improving nor worsening. Memories of wartime combat do not appear to fade easily.

The screening instruments developed during World War II, though they were not proved effective in screening out vulnerable soldiers and not effective in predicting who would experience problems in battle, became the foundation for the screening instruments used in the community-based social psychiatric surveys of the 1950s (see chapter 6).[21]

The Korean War

The Korean conflict followed closely on the heels of World War II. Similar approaches to care were applied, and overall psychiatric casualties accounted for only about 5% of the medical out-of-country evacuations during the war.[2] Acute combat stress continued as an important problem during the Korean conflict, though the Korean War was somewhat different because more combat soldiers than support personnel were deployed—a prelude to future conflicts. Marren reflected on the stress experienced by support personnel following the armistice:[2]

Troops removed from the rigors and stresses of actual combat by the
Korean armistice ... continued to have psychiatric difficulties
... stresses relegated to the background or ignored in combat

are reinforced ... time for meditation, rumination, and fantasy
increases ... absence of gratifications, boredom, segregation from
the opposite sex, monotony ... fears of renewal of combat, and con-
cern about one's chances in and fitness for combat are psychologic
stresses that tend to recrudesce and to receive inappropriate empha-
sis in an Army in a position of stalemate. (pp. 719–720)[22]

A dynamic view of the soldier interacting with the social environment emerged from the Korean conflict. Rather than focusing on biological vulnerabilities or childhood traumas, this view considered the stability of the soldier's social ecology.[2] For example, the soldier must balance seeking relief from the press of war, such as a discharge home, and committing to his fellow soldiers who recognized that he was not alone in the difficult situation. The success in achieving this balance played itself out eventually in the soldier's overall adaptation. This view of the individual in the context of society has many similarities with Leighton's views of social integration and striving sentiments (see chapter 6).[23]

The Vietnam War

The basic principles of military psychiatry had been immediacy (treatment should be begun as quickly as possible), proximity (treatment of the disorder as near the front as possible), and positive expectancy (early intervention would correct the problem). The paradigm changed dramatically following the Vietnam War.[24] During the initial buildup in Vietnam, psychiatric services were fully in place.[2] Combat stress casualties, however, were rare during the buildup and during the heaviest months of fighting. Fewer than 5% of cases were labeled combat exhaustion, far lower than in previous conflicts. Some speculated that the type of combat—brief skirmishes followed by rests in a secure base camp—did not permit fatigue and anxiety to buildup.[25] During the war, however, a number of hidden casualties emerged, such as reckless sexual behavior leading to a high frequency of sexually transmitted diseases, disciplinary infractions, and drug abuse. And Vietnam would forever be linked with another problem of significant consequence —post-traumatic stress disorder.

Though the intuitive view of post-traumatic stress disorder is that the condition results from an overwhelming stress, some believe that the condition is aggravated by the discontents of soldiers in low-intensity, ambivalent wars.[2] In retrospect, post-traumatic stress disorder appears to have been a serious problem for prisoners of war exposed to harsh treatment during World War II and for German veterans of

World War I. Yet the disorder reached the center stage of military psychiatry only following Vietnam.

In Vietnam, the psychologically wounded soldier gave way to the psychologically wounded veteran. Once again, the military experience helped shape our overall psychiatric nomenclature. A new diagnosis emerged (though the problem was far from new). The inclusion of post-traumatic stress disorder in the *DSM–III* documented that American psychiatrists and soldiers had accepted that severe traumatic events could lead to behavioral disorders, which could become manifest after a delay of months or even years.[26] Post-traumatic stress disorder, unlike other disorders that are reactions (e.g., adjustment reactions), results from very special circumstances outside the usual experiences of everyday life, such as rape.

The Persian Gulf War

During late 1990, nearly 700,000 soldiers were deployed to the Persian Gulf in anticipation of a war to remove Iraq's troops from Kuwait following an invasion of Kuwait by Iraq earlier that year. After weeks of bombing, the actual invasion of Kuwait and Iraq resulted in just a few days of battle. Many American troops remained in the Gulf, however, following the invasion. According to Martin, the United States fielded a psychologically healthy army.[27] In addition, few soldiers actually participated in frontline combat.

The number of soldiers evacuated from the Southwest Asia theater between August 1, 1990, and August 1, 1991, because of psychiatric impairment, was small compared with the numbers from many previous wars. Despite the low frequency of frontline combat, soldiers were still exposed to stresses of war (inflicting or observing death, inflicting or receiving friendly fire, observing the horror of human remains, and encountering the victims of war—the men, women, and children killed, wounded, or made homeless). In many ways, the Gulf War was the perfect U.S. Army war because it fit the American doctrine regarding the reasons for a just war (in contrast to Vietnam), our training for war, and our ground arsenal (the United States fielded the best-trained and best-equipped army in its history).

Soon after returning home from the Gulf War, some veterans reported symptoms including myalgia, fatigue, neurocognitive difficulty, and problems with mood.[28] Early on, this constellation of symptoms was suspected to represent a mysterious illness of undiscovered etiology. The constellation of symptoms has been referred to as Gulf War syndrome. The frequency of complaints has been high. A population-based survey from Iowa, fielded during 1995 to 1996, included veterans deployed to the Gulf and Gulf War–era control individuals (soldiers deployed to noncombat locations).[28] Fifty percent of the deployed veterans and 14% of the controls reported health problems that they attributed to military service during 1990 to 1991. A factor-analytic study of the reported symptoms revealed three factors that could be loosely labeled: somatic distress, psychological distress, and panic. The authors concluded that the frequency and distribution of symptoms did not support the existence of a unique Gulf War syndrome but did reflect a range of symptoms attributed to multiple causes secondary to deployment in the Gulf. The Presidential Advisory Committee on Gulf War Veteran's Illnesses reached a similar conclusion:

> *Although some veterans clearly have service-connected illnesses, current scientific evidence does not support a causal link between the symptoms and illnesses reported today by Gulf War veterans and exposures while in the Gulf region to the following environmental risk factors assessed by the Committee: pesticides, chemical warfare agents, biological warfare agents, vaccines, pyridostigmine bromide, infectious diseases, depleted uranium, oil-well fires and smoke, and petroleum products. Some of these risk factors explain specific, diagnosed illness in a few Gulf War veterans. ... Prudence requires further investigation of some areas of uncertainty. ... Stress is known to affect the brain, immune system, cardiovascular system, and various hormonal responses. Stress manifests in diverse ways, and is likely to be an important contributing factor to the broad range of physiological and psychological illnesses currently being reported by Gulf War veterans. (summary, chapter 4)[29]*

This report and its findings appear quite reasonable. Studies have substantiated the role of stress in physical and psychiatric illness, as I discuss in far more detail in chapter 10. In one such study, U.S. Army reservists in graves registration (body recovery and identification) duty experienced a high frequency of psychological symptoms, including anxiety, anger, depression, and multiple somatic complaints. Almost one half met criteria for post-traumatic stress disorder.[30] The authors left room for further explorations of multiple etiologic factors yet recognized the central role of the stress of combat and war. Exponents of the stress hypothesis to explain physical and emotional suffering following the Gulf War came under dramatic attack. Veterans (and their supporters) wanted a specific case definition of Gulf War syndrome and a specific cause. (A recent report from the Veterans

Administration supports a solely physical cause of Gulf War syndrome, yet I, and many of my colleagues, believe the role of stress to be central.) They did not want stress to be emphasized among the causes that might lead to the delayed physical and mental health consequences of service in the Gulf.

One of the more vocal spokesmen against stress as an etiological factor in Gulf War syndrome has been Robert Haley (an epidemiologist in Dallas). First, he and his colleagues devised a case definition of Gulf War syndrome that focused on cognitive and neurological deficits.[31] Second, they attempted to identify specific objective neurological dysfunction associated with this case definition.[32] In other words, they proposed a specific disease category, with specific symptoms and physical signs—a tightly bound operational diagnosis. They made the case that there is a core Gulf War syndrome, not a collection of multiple-symptom presentations that overlap one another. They criticized previous studies associating psychiatric symptoms with Gulf War syndrome, suggesting that the psychiatric symptoms are no more prevalent in Gulf War syndrome than in the general population.[33] (Overall this is true. Remember, however, that soldiers are more healthy physically and psychologically than the general public. In addition, soldiers deployed to the Gulf reported more psychiatric symptoms than soldiers deployed elsewhere during the Gulf War era.) Finally, they dismissed stress as a minimal contributor.[34]

A recent study has been cited to support Haley's view, though it is far from clear that it does so. Ismail and colleagues compared Gulf veterans with physical disability to Gulf-era veterans from the United Kingdom not deployed to the Gulf.[35] Only 24% of the disabled Gulf veterans had a formal psychiatric disorder (with very few suffering from post-traumatic stress disorder), whereas the prevalence of psychiatric disorders in nondisabled veterans was 12%. This finding makes sense, for psychiatric disorder is more likely among persons with physical disability.[36] Their conclusions, however, were that psychiatric disorders do not fully explain self-reported ill health in Gulf veterans. Formal diagnoses (such as major depression or post-traumatic stress disorder) do not always capture the general reaction to the stress of being in a combat area. The symptom constellations found more frequently among Gulf War veterans do not usually meet criteria for a specific psychiatric diagnosis.[28, 37] The lower frequency of post-traumatic stress disorder is not surprising, given that the percentage of soldiers who experienced a specific traumatic event in the Gulf was probably much lower than in Vietnam.

The pressure from advocacy groups to explore a specific biological cause for a specific disease (Gulf War syndrome) has been difficult for the federal government to avoid, even when the weight of the scientific data falls on the stress of war as the major contributor to the psychiatric symptoms (of which depression is among the most frequent). In an Associated Press report from November 2, 2002, we read,

> *The Department of Veterans Affairs' plan to sharply increase funding for research into Gulf War illnesses marks a turning point in how the government perceives the problem, the leader of a veterans group said Friday. "We've had to fight tooth and nail to convince people that Gulf War illness was more than stress," said Steve Robinson of the National Gulf War Resource Center, an umbrella group of 60 veterans organizations. The department announced this week it would make up to $20 million available for research in 2004.*

The belief that Gulf War syndrome is not due predominantly to stress and that a specific cause can be identified has triggered the change in the approach taken by the Veterans Administration. Veteran lobbying for increased funding to find "the cause" in large part has led to this approach.

Let me hasten to add that the veterans are not to be criticized in their quest for a specific disease with a specific cause. Causative agents from the physical environment of these soldiers might yet be found to have contributed to some of the morbidity they experienced (though the probability that physical causes will explain a sizable percentage of the morbidity is quite small). Studies should be pursued. The government should not be criticized for searching thoroughly into toxins from the physical environment that might contribute to morbidity and mortality. But the social milieu of military life, the admission of stress of separation from family, and the harsh conditions of the desert are just not accepted as equally (or perhaps more) important. Responsibility falls to the individual to overcome the stressors. Failure to meet that duty is counter to the soldier's view of self. Unfortunately, previous experience that suggests all soldiers might be pushed to the breaking point under certain conditions seems to have been lost on our society currently.

Lessons from War Syndromes

In my view, the response to the physical and psychiatric morbidity that has been a residual problem among Gulf War veterans represents a vivid example of trends in our society as a whole. People want their problems named and they want them solved. The vagueness of social stressors as an explanation (not to mention the implication that an inability to adapt to stress reveals a personal deficit) coupled with general nihilism regarding the ability to change society fuels the search for specific causes and cures.

In addition, people today might not be as willing to tolerate symptoms as they might have been in the past. Agnes Miles, some years ago, recognized this tendency. She argued,

> The threshold at which the problems and discomforts of daily life become unacceptable is, as it were, being progressively lowered. In modern industrial societies people's expectations regarding standards of living have been and are rising. The argument is not so much of a life genuinely free of problems but rather of a general expectation that problems are capable of solution. ... In addition, a proliferation of professional helpers has developed (health workers). One result is that people turn to their doctors with a range of minor physical and psychological symptoms which previously seemed to be acceptable parts of daily life. It is also the knowledge that remedies are available for sleep, to relieve tension, to lift depression, etc. (p. 192)[38]

Shorter expanded this argument in his study of unexplained medical symptoms, especially pain and fatigue:

> The ... symptoms of pain and fatigue are not very different from those of the 1920s. There are two significant differences. Sufferers today are more sensitive generally to the signals their bodies give off and they are more ready to assign these symptoms to a given "attribution," a fixed diagnosis, a particular disease. This increase in illness attribution stems in part from the loss of medical authority and from the corresponding increase in the power of the media to suggest individuals into various fixed beliefs. These new patterns come from a distinctively "postmodern" disaffiliation from family life. (p. 295)[6]

Our culture witnesses a kind of collective hypervigilance about the body. Much more of this illness is now channeled to the doctor's office, as people redefine themselves as patients. At the same time, mistrust of physicians has increased.

Shorter continued his argument by suggesting that what is different today is that the influence of the mass media takes precedence over what was once called "medical authority." The mass media are interested in specific diseases that can be named (such as Gulf War syndrome) and in specific biological causes. The psychosocial paradigm excites little interest among the press, for it is not particularly exciting. The rejection of psychiatric diagnoses by persons with a mixture of psychiatric symptoms that cannot be easily categorized and the embrace of specific diagnoses tend to be viewed as much more emphatic than the normal reactions of medical patients to psychiatric consultation. Riding this wave of specificity and attribution is major depression.

Changes in family structure and the sociocultural milieu in particular, what some have labeled *postmodernity* (I return to this theme in chapter 8), have increased people's vulnerability to fixed ideas about illness. People are more isolated as they desire individual self-actualization over commitment to the family as an institution, according to Shorter.[6] The fragility of social networks then removes "feedback loops"; that is, the hour-by-hour give-and-take found among people who live together. The resultant social isolation intensifies the tendency of individuals to give themselves fixed self-diagnoses (they cannot work through the nuances of their suffering). The advantage of living closely together with others is that one can test one's ideas. The isolated individuals are therefore more prone to diagnosing themselves with diseases widely publicized in the media.

Veterans of the Gulf War truly suffer from the effects of that war, and their pleas for help should not go unheeded. Rather, investigators and the public must acknowledge and investigate the stress of war and the strain that stress places on the soldier during and following the conflict. Investigating the overall stress associated with war in no way dampens the investigation of specific noxious agents, such as nerve gasses or fumes from oil-well fires. Both investigations must proceed in parallel.

The Attribution of Symptoms

If we consider the symptoms of Da Costa's syndrome of the Civil War, the effort syndrome of World War I, battle fatigue during World War II, and Gulf War syndrome, we find they have many symptoms in common, and many meet the symptom criteria of minor depression in the *DSM–IV*: anxiety (agitation), sleep disturbance, medically unexplained physical symptoms, problems with concentration, and fatigue.[4, 39] Yet the attribution of these symptoms has varied remarkably during past years. We must not hasten to assume that these symptoms express a single disorder that has been labeled differently over the years, for that assumption does not capture the dynamic nature of these symptoms. We must also not assume that the symptoms represent psychosomatic illness with no physical etiology to be explored. At the same time, however, each of these syndromes arose in the midst of great psychosocial stress. To some extent their history reflects the attitude at the time to the stressors of war of soldiers in particular and society in general. In other words, the symptoms are framed to reflect current societal attitudes. The same is true for how society has framed the emotional response to social stress over time, as I describe in chapter 3.

Gulf War syndrome, when perceived as one specific disease with clear yet undiscovered causes in the physical environment, can be an example of societal framing of nonspecific symptoms into an understandable entity. We might see the name of a behavior change over time as the social context in which the name is used changes.[27] For example, excessive complaints of physical symptoms due to trauma in civilian life in times past might have been termed "malingering." The same complaints might be labeled "cowardice" in the military. These labels, however, did not fit the actual experience of conflict. World War II led to exhaustion or fatigue—both tied to battle or combat, with the behavior defined as an environmental challenge that could affect everyone. Therefore, a combat stress reaction, a behavior caused by a particular environment in a special place and time, was so named today because it satisfied the "framing of illness."[40]

At the time of World War II, commanders accepted that fear was normal and that they could and should so inform their soldiers, do preventive therapy, and demand posttraumatic intervention.

Shorter believed that the medical framing of such symptoms did not occur until the 18th century, with the advent of new theories about "nervous disease."[6] Since that time, the framing has changed given the context. For example, the hysterical paralysis of the late 18th and 19th centuries gave way to chronic fatigue in the late 20th century. This labeling is unfair to the people who suffer the profound disabling fatigue that lasts for months and is accompanied by numerous symptoms.[41] Actual chronic fatigue syndrome occurs in less than 3% of the general population, though the frequency of fatigue as a symptom might be as high as 50%. But today there is a propensity for people who experience fatigue to frame their symptoms as chronic fatigue syndrome. This framing results as much from the media as from any other source of information. Much of the fatigue in our society is the body's response to stress or unhappiness, orchestrated by our culture.[6] Legitimate symptoms are ascribed to a specific underlying organic disease (rather than a stress response) for which the patient could not possibly be blamed.

Yet the origin of these symptoms is masked by cultural framing. Arthur Kleinman suggested that symptoms of depression and anxiety resulting from social causes are best understood, not as discrete diseases but rather as nonspecific bodily (psychobiological) forms of human distress (p. 59).[42] Social scientists ask, "Why must we distinguish these problems as specific disorders, such as major (or minor) depression and generalized anxiety, simply because at times they exhibit distinctive forms of symptom presentation, when they share the same social origins?"[43-45]

Demoralization and despair due to severe family, work, or economic problems trigger syndromes of distress that have biological and psychological correlates. The clusters of these symptoms are often labeled "psychiatric disorder," but they have been reconceived by social scientists as the psychobiological sequelae of social pathology and human misery generally. Would they not more parsimoniously be considered simply as social distress?

The social scientific critique can be heard in psychiatry, yet the approach to psychiatric nomenclature is not likely to change. In fact, the current psychiatric diagnoses do "work," as I describe in previous chapters. Nevertheless, whatever treatment the patient receives, the fact that the doctor gave a diagnosis and started a treatment has social implications. The sufferer becomes a patient, his or her hitherto unorganized feelings of worry and so on having been accounted for and explained by the diagnosis. Medical legitimization for being ill has been given. This is true whether the diagnosis is combat exhaustion, Gulf War syndrome, hysterical paralysis, chronic fatigue syndrome, or major depression. The person can therefore take comfort in the relative security of knowing the origin of the problem, whether its true origin is known. To name a condition is to feel some control over it.[46]

Joyce Carol Oates,[47] in her New York Times review of Andrew Solomon's The Noonday Demon[48] (a book in which Solomon described his personal journey with depression), suggested our current infatuation with depression might be akin to hysterical epidemics of the past. She referred to Elaine Showalter's Hystories: Hysterical Epidemics and Modern Culture,[49] in which Showalter suggested that hysterical epidemics require at least three ingredients: physician-enthusiasts and theorists; unhappy, vulnerable, and suggestible patients; and supportive cultural environments promulgated through the mass media. When these three ingredients are present, a unified theory of a vague syndrome emerges. Oates probably went too far, yet her critique is food for thought.

8

Things Fall Apart: Society and Depression in the 21st Century

Things fall apart; the centre cannot hold; Mere anarchy is loosed upon the world.

—W.B. Yeats, *Selected Poetry* (p. 99)[1]

In this chapter and the next I make recommendations for a rebirth of social psychiatry, albeit in a different form from the social psychiatry of the 1960s. I devote chapter 9 to suggestions for a revival of empirical research in social psychiatry, and I devote this chapter to what C. Wright Mills identified as the "sociological imagination," a perspective that can be of great value to psychiatrists as they treat their patients today.[2] Mills described the need as follows:

> *What they need ... is a quality of mind that will help them to use information and to develop reason in order to achieve lucid summations of what is going on in the world and of what may be happening within themselves. ... The sociological imagination enables its possessor to understand the larger historical scene in terms of its meaning for the inner life. ... It enables him to take into account how individuals, in the welter of their daily experience, often become falsely conscious of their social positions. Within the welter, the framework of modern society is sought, and within that framework the psychologies of a variety of men and women are formulated. By such means the personal uneasiness of individuals is focused upon explicit troubles [experienced by the individual] and ... indifference [experienced by society]. (p. 5)[2]*

Psychiatrists need a sociological imagination, and they need to help their patients to broaden their sociological imaginations.

Social theorists propose that modern Western civilization is undergoing a significant transformation.[3-6] Jane Flax described it as follows:

> Western culture is in the middle of a fundamental transformation; a "shape of life" growing old. The demise of the old is being hastened by the end of colonialization, the uprising of women, the revolt of other cultures against white Western hegemony, shifts in the balance of economic and political power with the world economy, and a growing awareness of the costs as well as the benefits of scientific and technological progress. (p. 5)[7]

I believe that underneath the superficial return to "traditional values" and trends toward a revival of American imperialization, the observations of Flax remain cogent, despite apparent trends to the contrary. The transformation has shaken the foundations of the way we think, feel, and behave. The old "sacred canopy"[8] of modern progress has blown away and the biting chill of anomie now settles on city and state (p. 25).[6] This has led to what Clifford Geertz called "the gravest sort of anxiety" (p. 99).[9] Such anxiety results from a sense that we have lost our foundations, and chaos reigns. Chaos and its resultant anxiety cannot be tolerated for long.[10] Depression, a signal to withdraw, is perhaps a natural adaptation to this grave anxiety.[11] For example, Todd Gitlin, in *Media Unlimited*, suggested the barrage of images that dominate our chaotic culture precipitates depressive withdrawal.[12] Western society is now characterized by instability,[6] supersaturation,[5] and isolation.[13] People dwelling in such a society will naturally react to that society.

A Case in Point

Tom, a law student at a local university, felt the bottom had dropped out of his life 3 months prior to consulting a psychiatrist. He could not sleep, he had difficulty eating, and his energy was "just gone." Everything seemed meaningless. Going on seemed useless. Despite these problems he continued to perform well in school and suspected that most of his friends had no idea that he was suffering. His symptoms diagnosed as major depression by his family doctor, Tom took an antidepressant medication for about 6 weeks. The antidepressant helped him sleep better and maintain his weight. He lacked energy but wondered if he was actually tired or just bored with what he was doing. "Bored," however, did not describe how he felt.

Tom attended a few sessions with a psychologist to whom he was referred for cognitive behavioral psychotherapy. He liked the psychologist, but he could not connect the therapy with his feeling that the bottom had dropped out of his life. When asked in therapy what situations led him to experience depressive symptoms, he answered that he felt anxious, lonely, and dislocated when he thought about his life. When asked, "What about your life led to these feelings?" he answered, "Everything yet nothing in particular." When asked to give an example, Tom could not identify a specific time during the past week when he became depressed. When pressed about his depressive thoughts, Tom challenged the psychologist to give him good reason why his thoughts should not be depressed. "Just look around. If you think about it, why not be depressed?" Therapy was going nowhere, so Tom decided to stop. He then sought a psychiatrist to help him sort through his continued discomfort. When asked by the psychiatrist, "Can you tell me why you have come to see me?" Tom answered, "I can't really explain. I seemed to be doing OK, but then everything just seemed meaningless."

Tom continued, "When I say the bottom dropped out, that is about as clear as I can get. I feel better taking the medication, but I still can't find my footing. A couple of nights ago I was watching TV, just to relax. I became more anxious. The TV was making me anxious. That's not quite true. There was nothing all that special about the program, just another sitcom. But all these images kept hitting me—buy this, learn that, go here, stay away from there. I went to check my e-mail. Thirteen messages. Contacts everywhere, but who could I really count on as friends? I checked the *Times* on the Internet. Information at my fingertips. But what information can I trust? I seem to be swimming in images, facts, experiences, relationships. You name it. But I don't know if I am swimming with the current or against it. I can't even find the current in this river."

"I hang out with my friends, but their conversation is frankly inane. 'Did you see that ballgame last night? Arizona really looks strong this year.' So what. Teams win, teams lose, and nothing changes. This same conversation will be going on next year—just substitute Kentucky for Arizona. My girlfriend wants some distance because she wants to find herself. Fine. Maybe we are both lost. I go to class. Thought law was pretty straightforward. Turns out you can argue virtually any situation from any side you wish. What am I to believe? Who am I to believe? Does anyone care what anybody believes? Maybe I'm kidding myself. I'm not swimming. I'm treading water. I thought the bottom dropped out. Maybe there never was a bottom."

Tom met all the criteria for major depression. The family physician prescribed a drug, and Tom partially responded. To Tom, however, something loomed in the background from which he could not escape but that he had kept somehow hidden. Recently, the "floodgate opened," and that gate let in "a river of thoughts, feelings, images and I have been swimming in them ever since." He could no longer find himself.

The psychiatrist faced a dilemma. Did distorted thinking that could be corrected by psychotherapy actually describe Tom's thinking? Would a better medication restore his sense of self? How could Tom find meaning? Could Tom's depression have clarified rather than clouded his thinking? Did more insight into the society in which he lived lead to the bottom's falling out? Tom appeared to suffer from what some have labeled an "existential crisis," the inevitable crisis that occurs when the defenses used to repress existential anxiety are breached, thus permitting one to become truly aware of his basic situation (p. 207)[14] (p. 167).[15]

Should Tom's existential crisis and resultant depression be of concern to his psychiatrist? Yes. Throughout most of the 19th and 20th centuries psychiatrists have accepted the responsibility to understand the fit of their patients in the world and the bodies and brains of their patients. To understand the world of their patients, psychiatrists cannot simply rely on scientific sociological and anthropological study; rather such understanding is largely intuitive yet informed by the study of the social context from which emotional suffering arises.

Psychiatrists, Patients, and Society

Patients cannot be divorced from place. The Hippocratic physicians recognized the importance of context millennia ago. They advised,

> Who ever wishes to investigate medicine properly should proceed thus: in the first place to consider the seasons of the year, and what effect each then produces. Then the winds ... in the same manner, when one comes into a city to which he is a stranger, he should consider his situation, how it lies as to the wind and the rising of the sun ... one should consider most attentively the water ... and the mode in which the inhabitants live, and what are their

pursuits, whether they are fond of drinking to excess, and given to indolence or are fond of exercising and labor. (p. 19)[16]

Philippe Pinel (1745–1826), the 19th-century theoretician and reformer, examined the treatment of persons with mental illness in France. He found the insane chained! To understand the treatment of the mentally ill, one must see the chains.[17] The horrid conditions of the mental asylums of his day could be changed, a change he labeled "moral treatment." Such treatment required that society view not only the insane but also the society as sick, deserving, and requiring medical treatment. Pinel could not separate the behavior of the insane or their treatment from the conditions under which the insane lived day after day in the asylums.

Freud took a more pessimistic but equally contextual view of his patients in *Civilization and Its Discontents*.[18] He proposed that people must restrict their natural hostile and aggressive tendencies to become members of an organized social system. These restrictions are a necessary price to pay for living together. Even so, living in a restrictive society does not relieve guilt feelings, a guilt that leads to a universal discontent that necessarily accompanies social life. Despite his early focus on the innate drives and impulses of the individual, Freud became more and more fascinated by the social context of his practice as he aged.[17] He wrote,

> My interest, after making a lifelong detour through the natural sciences, medicine and psychotherapy, returned to the cultural problems which had fascinated me long before, when I was a youth scarcely old enough for thinking. (p. 72)[19]

Adolf Meyer, in his discussion of the treatment of children and their parents, encouraged the broader view:

> [We need] a body of concrete facts, generally applicable concerning such matters as the balance of work and play, and rest, the management of discontent, of disappointment, the acceptance of one's grades and the proper reaction thereto, the reaction to criticism, the family problems, the choice of time and conditions of pregnancies, the economics and practice in the care of the mother and infant. (p. 472)[20]

More recently, Irvin Yalom, in his book *Existential Psychotherapy*, called those involved with modern psychiatry back to treating their patients in context.[14] Exis-

tential psychotherapy addresses the ultimate concerns of people. The dislocation of
people from their social environment is such a concern:

> *There are moments when the curtain of reality momentarily flutters*
> *open, and we catch a glimpse of the machinery backstage. In these*
> *moments, which I believe every self-reflective individual experi-*
> *ences, an instantaneous defamiliarization occurs when meanings*
> *are wrenched from objects, symbols disintegrate, and one is torn*
> *from one's moorings of "at-homeness." ... In these moments of deep*
> *existential anguish one's relationship to the world is profoundly*
> *shaken. (p. 358)*[14]

Situating patients in the context of society is no small task at the turn of the
21st century. Societal transformation increases the likelihood of being torn from
one's moorings of at-homeness. As one writer described our current society, "Truth
is stranger than it used to be."[6] Many patients have been shaken loose from their
roots. They feel, as did Tom, that they are treading water in a river with no shore in
sight. How can therapists understand this strange new world in which they and
their patients live? Social theorists have suggested that the rapid transformation
described previously by Flax is the historical passage from modernity to postmodernity in Western society.[4, 7, 21, 22] How are we to understand this passage? In what way
does this passage provide a fertile ground (if at all) for the emergence of depression? I propose that the transition from modernity to postmodernity is key to understanding the social origins of depression.

The Birth and Growth of the Modern

Modernity was based in the Enlightenment, a designation of an era generally
agreed to have emerged in 18th century in England, France, and Germany. Medieval society emphasized ecclesiastical authority, the supernatural, the unseen, and
revelation. In contrast, the Enlightenment displaced authority with reason. For
example, unconditional belief was replaced by Rene Descartes's radical skepti-
cism.[23] Supernatural and unseen forces were displaced by the discovery of natural
laws that govern the visible universe (such as the discovery of gravity by Isaac
Newton). Revelation retreated as a source of knowledge. Every aspect of culture
was illuminated by reason.

According to John Locke's philosophy, humankind had the power to discern
and distinguish, to combine simple into complex ideas, to discover relations

between ideas, and to engage in abstraction (p. 307).[24] The goal of such reasoning was the search for certainty and the focus of that search was humans studying humans. Alexander Pope captured the spirit of the Enlightenment by his phrase "the proper study of mankind is man." The concept of God evolved to that of a mathematical scientist who knew everything simply because he had a perfect insight into the laws of reason (p. 44).[25]

The seeds of modernity, however, took two centuries to fully flower. Only during the early and mid-20th century did the characteristics of modernity dominate Western society. What are these characteristics? Modernity is characterized by a dominant spirit (p. 14).[6] John Dewey was among the most representative proponents of the spirit of modernity in North America.[6, 26] He described the changes from the premodern to the modern world as a growing belief in the power of the individual mind and therefore a belief in progress. Dewey's modern man was self-assured and in control of his own destiny. If he follows his own reason, he is autonomous—a law unto himself. He could hold dominion over nature and himself.

Modernity is also characterized by a belief in linear progress.[21] Modernity breaks with any and all preceding historical conditions. Never-ending, internal ruptures and fragmentations constantly reform humankind. This break with the past lays the foundation for successive achievements in the future (p. 10).[21] Continuous movement leads to continuous improvement. Progress promises power, growth, and transformation of the world and us. Such optimism initiated a utopian view of the future.[3] Progress progresses toward truth. Truth, however, is not absolute truth but utilitarian truth. Modern truth is judged by the question "what works?" Truth therefore also evolves by successive approximations. Despite its utilitarian foundations, the search for truth proceeds toward an essence—a fundamental *thing-in-itself* (pp. 32–33).[5] Any discipline claiming to use the scientific method can also claim to search for an essence. Form follows function, and function derives from the scientific method.

The foundation of modernity therefore is science and its application through technology. The efficient machine is the metaphor and myth that embody human aspirations of modernity.[27] If machinery lies at the center of the modern conceptions of the person, then autonomous reliability should be the hallmark of the mature person. The well-designed machine resists deterioration and functions reliably (p. 44).[5] A well-designed society should lead to social harmony, freedom from disease, and prosperity for all.[21] If we unlock the secrets of nature, then we unleash much benefit for humankind. The grand narrative of modernity is humanly engineered progress (p. 30).[5]

Modernity, however, is not without its problems. The engine of modernity disrupts the sense of place and time for people. Anthony Giddens characterized the modern social institution by (a) an increased pace of change, (b) an increased scope of change (transglobal), and (c) new types of institutions (p. 16).[3] The dynamism that drives this change depends on the separation of time and space and their recombination as well as the breaking down of social systems followed by a reflexive ordering and reordering of social relations. Time in the past was linked with place. The clock dislocated time from place. Modernity and its accompanying technology (such as the telephone) also tears space away from place by fostering relations between "absent" others.

Modernity also promotes what has been called the "modern self," a self that is not without its problems.[5, 13, 28] The modern self is self-secure, self-formed, self-conscious, and therefore autonomous. Moderns seek a unique identity. Autonomy is the hallmark of moderns (p. 44).[5] Modern people are inner-directed people.[13] It is as if such people are directed by a psychological gyroscope that sets them on an inescapably destined goal. Given this self-sufficiency and autonomy, moderns no longer find or perceive that they need to find their identity in the local community. When moderns are grouped together in crowded places, such as a city, they are a lonely crowd.[13]

Science teaches that the world is composed of fixed and knowable entities. Despite the autonomy of moderns, they should be no less mysterious than the objects around them. The modern self is therefore a firm and recognizable character (p. 39).[5] That character is open to observation through techniques such as psychoanalysis and psychological testing. The quest for identity and the sense that one can grow to know one's identity pervaded modern psychology, as explicated by Erik Erikson's description of the adolescent's search for identity.[29] This quest in turn heightens the sense of drama created by the progressive revelation of the true character of the protagonist in a novel, such as the fisherman in Hemingway's *Old Man and the Sea*.[30] Erikson wrote, "In the social jungle of human existence there is no feeling of being alive without a sense of identity" (p. 36).[28]

A Thoroughly Modern Psychiatry

Psychiatry at the beginning of the 21st century is modern psychiatry to the core, and herein rests a problem. For one, psychiatry has virtually eliminated the mysterious. Freud explored the mysterious unconscious, and Jung extended that exploration to the even more mysterious collective unconscious.[31, 32] Explorations of the unconscious took on an almost religious significance, and many accused these psychoanalysts of actually founding an alternate religion.[33] Today, psychiatry has rejoined mainstream medicine and holds empirical science sacred. Psychiatry focuses on the observable, and at least implicitly debunks the mysterious. Therefore psychiatry has lost depth even as it has gained precision. Is the trade-off necessary?

Additional evidence of a movement from the mysterious to the thoroughly modern can be found in the disappearance of "giants" in the field of psychiatry. Undoubtedly this is true for other fields as well. As late as the 1960s, psychiatry venerated its leaders, many of whom were not only charismatic, almost mythical, but also extremely influential in shaping the field. These leaders included Freud, Jung, Harry Stack Sullivan, Adolf Meyer, and others from early in the century. Contemporaries who were known by virtually all U.S. psychiatrists during the 1960s included Karl Menninger, Roy Grinker, and Francis Braceland.

Early in the 21st century, I suspect that the major advances in psychiatry are not coupled with the investigators who have produced these advances. Most advances are joint efforts by teams of investigators throughout the world. Psychiatrists, even those who are members of the American Psychiatric Association, often cannot name the current president of the association. Many factors contribute to the loss of giants in any field, including the maturity of the field, specialization, and growth. Yet a thoroughly modern psychiatry is not an individually authoritarian psychiatry. Giants no longer dominate modern psychiatry. Instead, faceless teams and committees shape psychiatry (such as the committees that constructed the *Diagnostic and Statistical Manual of Mental Disorders*).[34] The mystery and charisma of past leaders has been replaced by a well-run, yet impersonal, machine.

Modern psychiatry strives to solidify the modern self, especially through the new generation of psychotherapies.[35] People can be transformed. The depressed can be freed of depression, freed to be their autonomous selves.[36] Once freed, their approach to society will be one of adapting, happy with the status quo. Pharmacotherapy and cognitive behavioral therapy assume that perfecting the self biologically and psychologically is the road to mental health. The elements of importance in understanding and changing human behavior are fixed and knowable entities. Given the focus on understanding the mechanisms of the brain as the basis for understanding behavior, the metaphor of the brain as machine unfortunately rings true.[37]

Psychiatrists view the progress of the field as linear (we know more now than we ever did, we are on the right track). We have standardized the methods of knowledge acquisition (the scientific method rules as never before). The number of therapeutic tools, especially medications, is growing at an ever-increasing rate. New technologies, especially methods for scanning the brain (including magnetic resonance imaging or MRI, spectroscopy, and positron-emission tomography or PET) are being perfected at a rapid rate.

The reliance of modern psychiatry on clinical trials implies that the truth about theory, and therapy, is established by whether it works. We have entered an age of practice guidelines, an age in which we are provided an algorithm for using the tools available to us.[38] These practice guidelines are based on empirical evidence of therapeutic efficacy. Modern psychiatry does work (see chapter 2), and psychiatrists are optimistic about its future. Given the competitive market place, psychiatry is very much in a productive mode, seeing more patients in a shorter period of time. In fact, the machine metaphor for modern man can be expanded to a machine metaphor for modern psychiatry.

Psychiatry today is thoroughly modern. Psychiatry today works. But is this thoroughly modern utilitarian psychiatry missing something?

The Challenge to Modernity

Modernity brought its discontents.[4] These discontents sprang directly from the main thrusts of modernity. Autonomy led to isolation.[39] Increased urbanization led to the breakup of the local community, and the routines of everyday life were disrupted. People could no longer rely on face-to-face relationships to communicate and to orient themselves. These trends furthered the sense of isolation. Civic loyalty and personal responsibility were deposed by the cry for personal entitlements.[4] Belief in unremitting progress was thwarted by events such as World War I, the Great Depression, World War II, and the war in Vietnam. A counterculture arose in protest to modern themes during the 1960s. Even the scientific method and the progress of science have been challenged.[40–42] Cultural progress at times appeared to revert to cultural regress, such as the increased influence of fundamentalist religions and anti-intellectualism.[43, 44]

One window into the discontents with modernity was the rise of modernism during the late 19th and early 20th centuries. Modernism, in contrast to modernity, was the radical aesthetic transformation that accompanied late modernity. This international movement arose in the poetry, fiction, drama, music, painting, architecture, and other arts of the West, subsequently affecting the character of most 20th-century art.[45] A modernist work is associated with unfamiliarity and difference. It shakes the solid foundations on which modernity is built.[46] It probes deep into the unconscious layers of modernity and confronts modernity with its own hidden anxieties. Within fiction, the modernistic novel confronted modernity with primitivism and the uncurtailed expression of the unconscious as found in James Joyce's *Ulysses* and Joseph Conrad's *Heart of Darkness*.[47, 48]

The solidity and optimism of modernity therefore has given way to a more nuanced, skeptical, and at times cynical view of humankind. Blind acceptance of science and technology evaporated, just as blind acceptance of ecclesiastical authority evaporated with the Enlightenment.[42] The modern self has given way to the "other directed" self,[13] the "de-centered" self,[6] and the "saturated" self.[5]

The Challenge to Modern Psychiatry

Modern psychiatry is relatively free of nuance, yet modern society and the persons who dwell therein are not. Within a nuanced and complex society, psychiatry has perhaps fallen victim to the same tendency as some conservative religions (and perhaps other movements); namely, a fundamentalist retreat. Could such a retreat in psychiatry have any similarity to the rise of global religious fundamentalism? Religious fundamentalism represents one of the most puzzling phenomena of the world as we know it today.[43, 49] The information age and the unpredictable flow of power and influence (such as the global sensitivity of the economy to single uncontrolled events) leads to an inability of society to provide stable and predictable meanings to the individual.

Therefore personal and communal identities become centrally important, such as feminism, environmentalism, God, and family. For example, developing an identity becomes a central preoccupation among many religious movements, especially more fundamentalist and evangelical groups. These personal quests are grounded communal identity. Zigmunt Bauman believed that the infinite possibilities of consumerism could lead to a dizzying experience of infinite possibilities.[50] As a reaction, fundamentalism can offer a respite from the infinite choices available.

The ascent of images in modernity is at once revealingly modern and confusingly modernistic. Imaging in psychiatry provides a poignant example. On one hand, the use of MRI enables us to view the brain in ways impossible with plain x-rays that barely revealed brain structure at all. (The electroencephalogram provided additional information yet was very crude.) Not only can we view tumors and brain atrophy, we can view the brain at work through functional MRI and PET scanning. For example, we can compare brain metabolism in the depressed and nondepressed.[51] We can give a person a task and then view functional scans to determine how the brain of that person varies with different clinical states, such as Alzheimer's disease, compared with normals.[52]

Yet what are we viewing? At one level we are viewing reconstructed images. The MRI, for example, does not actually photograph the brain but rather reconstructs an image from the brain based on the radio frequency signal generated by atoms in the brain exposed to a strong external magnetic field. The scans look real, yet the skill of the radiologist is needed to interpret the light and dark shadows that emerge and perhaps are artifacts. In other words, we can observe findings on the MRI that we cannot observe with the visible eye (or the microscope), and likewise we can observe changes in the naked brain that we cannot observe with MRI. Seeing an MRI, therefore, is believing "almost."

At another level, however, what is the meaning of what we see?[53] A neuroradiologist commented, "Suppose a patient's brain scan reveals an unexpected degree of atrophy; we may never speak to that patient in quite the same way again. The light behind the patient's eyes may be forever dimmed in our own" (p. 13)[54, 53] In other words, what is real—the person with whom we interact or the image we obtain through our modern imaging techniques?

Kay Redfield Jamison, a mental health professional who wrote about her own battle with bipolar disorder, observed,

> There is a beauty and an intuitive appeal to the brain-scanning methods, especially the high-resolution MRI pictures and the gorgeous multicolored scans from PET scan studies. With PET, for example, a depressed brain will show up in cold, brain-inactive deep blues, dark purples, and hunger greens; the same brain when hypomanic, however, is lit up like a Christmas tree, with vivid patches of bright reds and yellows and oranges. Never has the color and structure of science so completely captured the cold inward deadness of depression or the vibrant, active engagement of mania. (p. 194)[55, 53]

For Jamison, it appears the image became almost more real than the experience of the disorder.

Psychiatry during the past few decades has sought to replace spiritual, moral, and political understandings of madness with the technological framework of psychopathology and neuroscience, culminating in the "decade of the brain."[56] As I described previously, the new nomenclature has dramatically shaped how we think about emotional suffering and society's response to suffering.[57] If psychiatry is the product of a culture preoccupied with rationality and the individual self, what sort of mental health care is appropriate in a world in which such preoccupations are waning? How appropriate is Western psychiatry for cultural groups who value a spiritual ordering of the world and an ethical emphasis on the importance of family and community?

Psychiatry today might be helping millions of people through medications and psychotherapy, yet how will psychiatry cope with a shift from cultural optimism and vitality toward cultural cynicism and demoralization?[58, 59] The once unchallenged ethic of personal responsibility has been superceded widely by frustrated entitlement.[60, 61] Cultural preferences have shifted away from great art, literature, and the humanities toward seeking a quick fix through drugs, rock music, television, unrestrained sex, and shallow advertising, according to some.[62] Such trends have been referred to as *cultural regression*. Could psychiatry unintentionally contribute to this regressive trend? Is psychiatry buying into the culture of the quick fix? Is psychiatry unwittingly contributing to a cultural regression? Robert Fancher, for example, wrote,

> *The culture of cognitive therapy devalues those attributes of mind most likely both to create culture and to take us beyond the status quo—imagination, passion, and the courageous, painful process of bringing new ways of thinking and living to birth. It amounts to an endorsement of the middlebrow life under the authority of "good mental health." (p. 248)*[35]

The current emphasis on difference highlights the ambiguities inherent in understanding the mood of another. The typical psychiatric stance is to view depression as different ("If I am depressed, I am different from you and something must be wrong with me."). Therefore the goal of treatment is to reduce the difference.[63] The state of the psychiatrist who is not depressed is assumed to be the natural state. The goal of therapy is to reduce the difference; that is, to naturalize the depressed into the nondepressed. Deconstructionists today, in contrast, seek to "de-naturalize some of the dominant features of our way of life; to point out that those entities that we unthinkingly experience as 'natural' are in fact 'cultural'; made by us, not given to us."[6, 64] This type of critique is well recognized by psychiatrists in the writings of R.D. Laing.[65] Laing proposed that the schizophrenic state was in fact the natural state. Only the schizophrenic understands the world as it really is.

A thoroughly modern psychiatry therefore faces a world that no longer unambiguously embraces modernity, a world that experiences the fragile and fragmented edges of the modern thrust. The response of society to modernity has been described as the emergence of the postmodern critique.[4, 21, 50] Others have suggested that modernity has entered its full maturity. The descriptions of the discontents remain similar regardless of the interpretation.[3]

The Emergence of the Postmodern Critique

The postmodern critique is to most persons a trendy concept relegated for the most part to academic debates on ivory tower campuses. Postmodern themes, however, shape the lives of virtually all people in the United States. The postmodern critique, as applied to later 20th-century Western culture, is the affirmation of the void and loss of hope left by the failure of the scientific and the rational. The postmodern critique also leaves us with a feeling that we cannot fill that void. Postmodern themes are therefore society's gut response to our decline in confidence.[66] Lyotard argued, "The word postmodern ... designates the state of our culture following the transformations which, since the end of the 19th century, have altered the game rules for science, literature, and the arts" (p. xxii).[22]

By its nature, the postmodern critique defies definition yet defines an era. A reaction to the solidity of modernity, the era of the postmodern critique is characterized by a "playful acceptance of surfaces and superficial style, self-conscious quotation and parody" (p. 294).[67] We have moved to a light and liquid era.[68] The era of the postmodern critique is usually considered a reaction to a naive yet earnest confidence in progress and a reaction against objective or scientific truth. At its core, the postmodern critique is a denial of any fixed meaning, any correspondence between language and the world, any fixed reality (pp. 294, 295).[67]

Postmodern themes, however, are not abstract concepts confined to the academic with little relevance to the warp and woof of everyday life. Rather, they challenge and critique the complex, interlocking network of symbols, practices, and beliefs at the heart of our society's structure. We consciously and unconsciously react to this challenge and critique. For example, despite the diversity of race and ethnicity, religion, and regional subcultures in our society, Roger Lundin argued that there are cultural patterns deeply imbedded in our past and our character. Those patterns can be witnessed in sports, the media, and advertising. They reflect the covert meaning we impress on our experiences (p. 3).[66] When those patterns are challenged, we react.

Postmodern themes emerge in many areas of our lives. Whereas modernity emphasized production, our current era emphasizes consumption.[68] Disney has become a byword for postmodern consumptive culture, according to David Lyon:

"Disneyfication" is the act of assuming, through the process of assimilation, the traits and characteristics more familiarly associated with a theme park ... than with real life ... parks encourage the consumer to relate to America as a spectacle rather than as an object of citizenship ... make social conflict temporary and abnormal, emphasize individual rather than collective action ... it fails to make sense of the present or to provide a plausible vision of the future, sacrificing "knowledge" for staged spectacles organized around soundbites of history and culture ... deep questions of good and evil are rendered shallow through this process ... a process that diminishes human life through trivializing it ... amusing ourselves to death. (pp. 3, 4)[49]

The postmodern critique, the extreme expression of the era, attacks the foundation of all our understanding. Nothing remains sacred or certain. In other words, the critique reminds us that there is always another perspective to any perspective we employ when trying to understand the world around us, always another meaning for any meaning we ascribe to what we hear and say, always another person or group whose reality is different from our own.

The postmodern critique at times presents an outrageous assault on the apparent core values of the mainstream. For this reason, many can dismiss it as marginal rather than central to our everyday lives. We can attribute the postmodern critique to a radical political movement that cuts against rationality and decency in our society. For example, curiosity alone might encourage some to read Stanley Fish's book titled *There's No Such Thing as Free Speech.*[69] Few, however, take him seriously. We know that free speech is our constitutional right.

Denish D'Souza, however, took the postmodern critique quite seriously on university campuses in his book *Illiberal Education.* He framed his argument against the critique, however, as "we versus they."[70] The "they" are a marginal group of 1960s-bred professors who have achieved tenure status and student activists who challenge traditional values through the veil of critiquing the racist, sexist, homophobic, and class-biased structure of college campuses (a microcosm of society). To confront this radical political and social agenda, according to D'Souza, mainstream society must rally to defend unity and traditional values. Efforts such as the battle to abolish affirmative action are based on the belief that our society does not discriminate against diverse races or ethnicities, religions, or other minorities and that the postmodern critique is unjustified. Efforts that encourage values training imply that larger society has common values or at least a basis for discourse about values.

Do these common values exist in our society? The pattern any one of us perceives to be dominant competes with multiple other patterns in full view by most of us. The plethora of channels available on cable television ranges from an old-time gospel hour to the Playboy Channel. Though I feel in my element watching *Murder, She Wrote*, most persons with whom I work and around whom I live do not. Though I construct a worldview, I am well aware that multiple competing views exist even in the small societal niche I inhabit. I know that my view does not dominate. I am therefore less confident with my view than in times past. The postmodern critique has shaken the security for many. The society we inhabit favors no dominant pattern of culture, and we delude ourselves if we believe larger society shares our beliefs and values.

The Postmodern Critique and Depression

How are persons responding to postmodern themes? One means by which they adapt (or maladapt) to these societal themes is depression (though other responses include anxiety or wonderment). Much of the natural emotional response to the postmodern experience is a negative experience. Depression captures the essence of this experience. Depression also captures the paradox of an emotion that at once appears foreign to human nature (even foreign to self) and in part expresses the core of the postmodern self. The experience of a severe depression often includes not only a sense of not being one's self ("This isn't like me and I don't understand what is happening to me.") but also the loss of orientation, meaning, and hope ("I feel alone with no meaning to my life and have no hope.").

Some writers on postmodern themes take a very different view of the mood set by these themes.[4] They exude a sense of celebration as they escape modern assumptions and expectations. They relax in the "playground of irony and irrelevant pastiche, where pluralism and difference contrast with the older 'terrorism of totalizing discourses". ... Ecstasy, enthusiasm and even emancipation are promised in the postmodern" (p. 75).[4] As foundational thought is dissolved, each person defines his or her own historical tradition. Michel Foucault, for example, advised, "Prefer what is positive and multiple, difference over uniformity, flows over unities, mobile arrangements over systems" (p. 76).[71] Yet this is not the prevailing mood.

What is the value to psychiatrists in examining postmodern themes? I propose two areas of inquiry. First, postmodern themes have helped shape the mood of Western society and should therefore be considered in the investigation of the causes of depression. In other words, we have witnessed a transformation in the social origins of depression during the past 30 years, the era most theorists attribute to the postmodern critique. Second, the very nature of depression has been transformed in part by postmodern themes. Psychiatry should therefore consider postmodern themes as a risk for and architect of depression. Episodes of depression emerge from a social context. That context or background is characterized by themes that render a person more vulnerable to individual stressors.

A wide range of terms have been employed to describe the immediate experience of depression—feeling down, blue, or unhappy; or being dispirited, discouraged, disappointed, dejected, despondent, sad, or despairing. Yet other descriptions place the experience in a larger context, a context that often couples depression with postmodern themes—meaninglessness, hopelessness, self-denigration, nihilism, fragmentation, alienation, disorientation, suspiciousness, and loneliness. These terms are intermixed in descriptions of the depressive experience, by persons afflicted and persons who minister to those afflicted. In other words, the description of the experience by the depressed at once attempts to express their feelings and behavior as well as their perception of their role in the sociocultural environment. Such dual expression is difficult. Therefore, one of the most distinctive aspects of depression is the inability to describe the experience: "I don't know what is wrong with me. I don't know what to tell you." The example of Tom describing his feelings to the psychiatrist exemplifies this inability.

A pervasive theme of the postmodern critique is *loss of hope*, which can be thought of as a summary of more specific themes.[72, 73] Christopher Lasch, in *The Culture of Narcissism*, noted that, with the ending of the 20th century, other things were perceived by society to be ending as well.[72] Hints of catastrophe haunt our times. People busy themselves with survival strategies. People have withdrawn from societal concerns to personal preoccupations. We therefore live for the moment as we lose confidence in the future. Andrew Delbanco, in *The Real American Dream*, suggested that something died during the later 1960s, with the reform impulse degenerating into solipsism.[73] Instant gratification became the hallmark of postmodern life with a parallel repudiation of the state and other institutions as a source of hope.

Loss of hope is also a core symptom of depression.[74] Delbanco wrote,

> *Human beings need to organize the inchoate sensations amid which we pass our days—pain, desire, pleasure, fear—into a story. When that story leads somewhere and thereby helps us navigate through life to its inevitable terminus in death, it gives us hope. ... We must imagine some end if we are to keep at bay the ... suspicion that one may be adrift in an absurd world. The name for that*

*suspicion—for the absence or diminution of hope—is melancholy
... the dark twin of hope. (pp. 1, 2)*[73]

The swelling prevalence of depression in Western society perhaps reflects an increasingly dominant hopelessness within society. Next, I explore eight specific themes associated with loss of hope and the ascent of depression, the ways in which psychiatry has traditionally countered these themes, and the risks that modern psychiatry will overlook the themes.

The first theme is *loss of story*. Owen Flanagan proposed that one view of the self is as a "center of narrative gravity"; that is, as a biography or autobiography (p. 209).[75] Whether the narrative is realistic (and he suggested that the answer lies somewhere between), it performs a key function as "an organizing principle" with causal efficacy. In other words, the cause of our thoughts and behavior in part derives from the story of our lives that we tell to ourselves. For example, the answer to the question, "Why did you change jobs?" typically takes the form of telling a story: "I have been working for years in order to gain experience in sales, so when this opportunity to devote more time to sales presented itself, I could not turn it down."

The postmodern spirit undermines an individual's story. Barnaby Barratt, in a review of the postmodern critique and psychoanalysis, noted,

> *The unification of individuality as a continuous, constant, and cohesive story line from birth to death and the identification of the mundane world with the universe of possibilities begin to crumble. There is no longer an authentic identicality or unity to be anticipated from the events of personal life. ... There ... never was ... an ultimate authenticity of personal life waiting to be articulated.* (p. 102)[76]

To some extent the nature of the more psychoanalytic therapies is to critique and undermine the stories we tell of our lives, ostensibly to find the true story. Yet the process of analysis, and self-analysis, which is so typical of postmodern humankind, can leave that center of narrative gravity dismantled at the end rather than reconstructed.

Our stories, however, are not isolated. Narrative has a twofold usage. On one hand, the narrative is the unique story of an individual. On the other hand, narrative is embodied in the community and specifically in the stories that shape the community; that is, metanarratives. These embodied narratives ground the worldview of a given community. Alastair McIntyre wrote, "There is no way to give us an understanding of any society, including our own, except through the stock of stories which constitute its own dramatic resources. Mythology, in its original sense, is at the heart of things" (p. 216).[77] Our individual life stories reside within a larger purposive narrative that allows room for agency, responsibility, and hope (p. ix).[78] Yet the postmodern critique challenges the larger story, the metanarratives of our lives. According to Lyotard, "Simplifying in the extreme, I define postmodern as incredulity toward metanarratives [the stories carried by a society, such as stories of great leaders in the past]" (p. xxiv).[22]

Spiegal reflected on the role of stories in therapy,

> *What was once regarded as "insight" or "truth" about early development through memory recall and episodes interpreted via dreams and free association is now proposed to be a form of storytelling. Humans ... are fascinated by stories with a beginning, a middle and an end (hence the reaction against the postmodern which undermines narrative). ... In part, it is "man's search for meaning." ... The philosophical shift from "ultimate" truth to a "narrative" truth implied that actual causation was elusive but clinical causation was composed by the story makers—the patient and the doctor. (pp. 66, 67)[79]*

A traditional role for psychiatry was assisting people to uncover, formulate, and come to grips with their story. With the advent of a thoroughly modern psychiatry during an era when narrative and metanarrative are seriously challenged, psychiatry is missing a grand opportunity to minister to the needs of its patients in the context of the fluid society in which they reside. Structured interviews controlled by the psychiatrist to elicit symptoms of specific psychiatric disorders, such as major depression, mute the stories of our patients' experiencing depression. Structured interviews ignore the larger context, the metanarratives, within which our patients reside.

A second theme is the *loss of language*. Perhaps the arena in which the postmodern spirit has been most visible is the arena of literature and literary critique.[66] The canon, that is, the societal consensus of literary classics, has been based, in large part, on a judgment of the author's ability to appropriate unique yet effective language to express a feeling or tell a story. The postmodern critique has attacked the Western canon, and rightfully so. The accepted canon of the first half of this century was dominated by Western white men. Feminine and African American literature, as well as previously unknown works from alternative cultures, such as the culture of Native Americans, have now been recognized as not only stylistically sophisticated but also more effective than Dickens or Melville in expressing the feelings of late-20th-century Western society. For example, writings by African Americans were largely ignored by the keepers of the canon until recent years.

Yet the postmodern critique undermines the concept of the "telling my story." The meaning of the text is the meaning ascribed by the reader, not the writer. The text no longer belongs to the writer. Words strung together by a writer (or speaker for that matter) no longer provide a window into the mind of the writer. For example, the suffering described by the author of a novel, such as the suffering and existential despair felt by Antoine Roquentin in Jean-Paul Sartre's *Nausea*, is no longer about the author but about the reader. In other words, language cannot be trusted to communicate thoughts and feelings, only stimulate thoughts and feelings in the hearer or reader. Depression, though marked by feelings too deep for words, cries to be heard. The depressed seek to be understood, yet modern psychiatry reinterprets the emotional suffering of the depressed into its own symptomatic language, a language that must fit the procrustean bed of the *DSM–IV*. The psychiatrist hears what he or she wants to hear.

Psychiatrists are in an excellent position to hear their patients at the very time when these patients cry that they are not heard. Yet modern psychiatrists all too often ascribe meaning to select symptoms expressed by patients rather than assisting patients in their search for the meaning beneath the language, as illustrated by Tom in the example. By imposing operational criteria onto our diagnostic assessments, we selectively listen for some symptoms and look for some signs while selectively ignoring others. In the case example, Tom was not heard by the psychologist in part because the psychologist was "listening for" a specific trigger for the depressed mood and Tom could not identify a specific trigger.

A third theme is the *loss of self*; that is, loss of a core sense of identity. During the modern era, views of the self became optimistic and objective rather than reflective.[78] With the influx of the postmodern critique, however, the self has become decentered. Robert Solomon described the postmodern era as the era of the end of self.[80] The reflective self of philosophers such as Descartes (1596–1650) (who authored the phrase "I think, therefore I am") evolved over time into the intentional self of the modern era. Brentano (1838–1917) insisted that every act of the self must have an object other than itself, that it is always directed toward an object (p. 101).[80] The self is about objects; that is, an objective self.

The objective self of the modern era, in turn, has been rejected by the postmodern critique as not recognizing the pretensions of a self-centered self. A first-person description of self is deemed suspect. "We're not first of all consciousness but rather social creatures, products of genetics, language, and culture-bound education" (p. 196).[80] Any single theory of human nature is doomed to destruction and therefore any continuity perceived in the self is deceptive.

Psychiatry has traditionally worked to strengthen the identity and sense of self.[28, 81] Yet modern psychiatry might unwittingly contribute to the fracturing of the self. Descriptions of depression as a chemical imbalance, emphasis on depression as a disease (apart from the real you), and focus on treating the depression without attention to the person treated (such as the 15-minute medication check) separate depression from the self who is experiencing the depression.

A fourth theme derives from the celebration of diversity—*loss of unity*. The postmodern critique celebrates the potential for expression by many communities previously silent in our society. Even as we embrace diversity, 21st-century Western society is far from a unified acceptance and value of the diverse perceptions, beliefs, values, and behaviors within our society. Though the rights of expression by previously silent communities are emphasized, all communities are not respected equally. This partially derives from a characteristic of postmodern society. Even as postmodern critics thrust onto the public scene a plethora of beliefs and behaviors, they devalue the beliefs and behaviors of the dominant culture.

Traditional psychiatry had considerable interest in unifying diversity. Freud, for example, focused on unifying themes across cultures that could explain cultural variation.[18] Jane Murphy, in a groundbreaking article, described the almost uniform frequency of schizophrenia across different cultures if the investigator appreciates the diversity in presentation given the context of the culture.[82] Cultural sensitivity has been a theme expounded by psychiatric anthropologists such as Arthur Kleinman throughout their careers.[83, 84] Modern psychiatry, in contrast, is much less attuned to cultural diversity and to cultural issues. The medicalization of emotional suffering has rendered attention to cultural factors of less importance. For example, the use of antidepressant medications is far more frequent among Whites than among African Americans in our society.[85] Yet little attention has been directed toward understanding this difference in use beyond an expressed concern about disparities in the delivery of mental health services (undoubtedly a contributor but probably not the only contributor).

A fifth theme is *loss of trust*. According to this theme, the deception and oppression that pervade our society can be addressed only by what Ricoeur labeled the "hermeneutic of suspicion" (pp. 32–36),[86] (p. 16).[66] Reality is not what it used to be.[6, 87] Customs that we have taken for granted through much of our lives are but local conventions, and we accept them primarily by sheer force of habit. Reality, therefore, is nothing more than the shared worldview of small communities. In a diverse society, how can your worldview be evaluated compared with mine? I should be more accepting of your worldview and more suspicious of mine. Yet as I seek to ground my own beliefs, I am likely to become even more attached to my worldview and more suspicious and rejecting of yours. This leaves people with a sense of being at the margin of society as a whole. It leaves them feeling, if there is no overall worldview, isolated and alienated. To counter this isolation, people often develop strong attachments to subcultures, mistrusting other cultures within society, or a perception of independence from all groups, therefore mistrusting all who strongly adhere to one view versus another.

Modern psychiatry finds itself competing, as a subculture of sorts, with a plethora of other subcultures (nontraditional therapies) in part because people at the margins of society, for example, those with fundamentalist beliefs, seek counselors from their own culture.[88] Modern psychiatrists are embedded in the empirical sciences, yet find themselves trying to communicate with patients embedded in a religious orientation that does not trust science. When, for example, psychiatrists and fundamentalist religious patients attempt to communicate, they might feel they are being pulled away from their own communities into a vacuum, and they therefore retreat from this vacuum to a worldview where they feel more comfortable. Perhaps the psychiatrist and the patient wish to communicate, yet the gap appears too wide to bridge. If psychiatry is to be effective within this social context, it must attempt to understand the subcultures from which its patients emerge.

A sixth theme is *loss of orientation*. The liberation of self that results from the postmodern critique of constraining social customs and beliefs is frequently accompanied by confusion and disorientation (p. 36).[6] We discover that our perceptions are flawed, our foundations shattered, and we live in a society characterized by few or no attachments. Our response is a loss of any secure sense of order and predictability in the world.[6, 39] More than one author has considered the movie *Blade Runner* prototypical of the postmodern condition.[4, 21, 89] David Harvey described the postmodern Los Angeles of *Blade Runner* as follows:

> The sense of the city at street level is chaotic in every respect. Architectural designs are a post-modern mish-mash—the Tyrell Corporation is housed in something that looks like a replica of an Egyptian pyramid, Greek and Roman columns mix in the streets with references to Mayan, Chinese, Oriental, Victorian and contemporary shopping mall architecture. ... The aesthetic of Blade Runner ... is the result of "recycling, fusion of levels, discontinuous signifiers, explosion of boundaries, and erosion." (p. 311)[21]

Psychiatry, through most of the 20th century, has sought to bring orientation to its frequently disoriented clientele. At the most basic level, orientation to reality is a mainstay in the treatment of persons with memory impairment secondary to dementia. Psychotherapists who work with schizophrenic patients also focus on reality orientation. Psychotherapy, especially the cognitive behavioral therapies, attempts to reorient the faulty logic of the depressed to a more accurate understanding of their relations to the world around them.[36, 90] Unfortunately, the fragmentation of mental health care in recent years undermines and perhaps contributes to the loss of orientation that postmodern society exacerbates. Even as psychiatry appears oriented around an empirical and rational approach to the care of the mentally ill, the delivery of mental health care services is far from appearing to consumers as a meaningful, coordinated response to emotional suffering.

A seventh theme is *loss of meaning* (p. 11).[66] A central theme of the postmodern critique is the abolishment of authority. One meaningful explanation for existence is not exchanged for another. Rather, all explanations are equally brought under suspicion. The postmodern impulse is to overthrow all entrenched beliefs and attitudes, whatever those beliefs and attitudes might be. Nothing remains sacred. Stephen Carter, in *The Culture of Disbelief*, suggested that beliefs are not so much attacked as restricted and trivialized.[88, 91] For example, an orthodox Jew who enlisted in the army wished to wear his skullcap under his army cap. He was not permitted to do so in the name of religious freedom and the separation of church and state. Religious beliefs are accepted as long as they are not expressed in words or actions toward others of a different persuasion. What does it mean to be an orthodox Jew if one cannot practice one's beliefs? As described by David Lyon, "Like ice-floes on the river during spring break-up, the world of meaning fractures and fragments, making it hard even to speak of meaning as traditionally conceived" (p. 11).[4]

Psychiatrists have through most of the 20th century recognized the importance of meaning to individuals' mental health.[14, 92] Victor Frankl, in *Man's Search for Meaning*, described a therapeutic approach to psychotherapy that actually underlies many forms of psychotherapy today — logo (or meaning) therapy.[92, 93] He claimed that all humans strive to find meaning and purpose, which are essential for human fulfillment and happiness. He ascribed this search to a latent spirituality within all people. This latent spirituality can become manifest in many different forms, and the task of the therapist is to nurture rather than suppress these expressions. The therapist's task is to comprehend some coherent pattern, some meaningful gestalt, in what the patient presents as random and tragic events of life.[14]

When depression is medicalized, the psychiatrist all too quickly answers the question, "Why did I become depressed?" with "You have a chemical imbalance." That answer does not consider the heart and soul of the question (p. 136).[88] Thomas Moore, in *Care of the Soul*, wrote,

> *The great malady of the twentieth century, implicated in all of our troubles and affecting us individually and socially, is "loss of soul." ... It is impossible to define precisely what the soul is ... [yet] we say certain music has soul or a remarkable person is soulful. ... Soul is revealed in attachment, love and community, as well as in retreat. (pp. xi–xii)[94]*

Many doctors now recognize the need to take a spiritual history from their patients during the overall evaluation.[95] A spiritual history assesses the role of comfort and support of spiritual beliefs, the influence of beliefs on medical decisions, potential conflicts between beliefs and medical care, membership in a spiritual community, and spiritual needs that should be addressed. Such a history expands the horizons of the clinician, yet is segregated from the remainder of the evaluation. Spirituality remains marginal to the meaning of the malady. Somehow the medical model for depression misses the soul of the experience, an experience that cuts to the core of meaning for persons.

A final theme is *nihilism*, a term that has incorrectly been applied to persons who do not believe in a particular set of absolute values. Nihilism is more pervasive, suggesting a state of believing in nothing, having no allegiances and no purposes (p. 263).[67] Though the concept of nihilism was first widely used during the later 19th century in Russia, it might be more relevant today than a century ago. One description of nihilism begins, "Here is the ultimatum of our camp: what can be smashed should be smashed; what will stand the blow is good; what will fly into smithereens is rubbish; at any rate, hit out right and left—there will and can be no harm from it" (Vol. V, p. 515).[96] In other words, nihilism completes the postmodern attack by leaving nothing in its wake. That nothingness perhaps defines the existential experience of depression.

David Karp, describing his own depression and the experience of depression in a postmodern world, wrote,

> *In an emerging postmodern world the construction and maintenance of a integrated self becomes deeply problematic because the social structures necessary to anchor the self have themselves become unstable and ephemeral. ... There is always an element of*

doubt in our relations with others. ... As a person with depression,
I am sometimes inclined to embrace such an unrelievedly negative
view of America's present and future. ... The postmodern condition
unquestionably contributes to a collective identity crisis since a
culturally fragmented society produces fractured and dis-eased
selves ... [yet] I have tremendous faith in the capacity of human
beings ultimately to refashion them-selves and thereby also the
world now denying them the conditions for good mental health.
(pp. 186–187)[97]

Psychiatrists must be aware of the social and cultural forces that impinge on, shape, and in many ways define the mental health of their patients. Yet psychiatrists must not throw up their hands in despair but must rather be aware.

The Revival of
Social Psychiatry

9

A Call for Basic Social Science
Research in Psychiatry

Research in social ... sciences has established a reasonably consistent set of findings relevant to the community context of health: there is a considerable inequality between neighborhoods and local communities; a number of health problems tend to cluster at the neighborhood and larger community level; [and] community-level predictors common to many health-related outcomes include concentrated poverty and/or affluence, racial segregation, family disruptions, residential instability, and poor-quality housing.

—*New Horizons in Health*, a report published by the Committee on
Future Directions for Behavioral and Social Sciences Research at the
National Institutes of Health (p. 93)[1]

If social psychiatry is to be reborn, it must be reborn, in my view, from a foundation of empirical research; that is, research based on observation and research that bases conclusions on the evidence available. Though empirical research alone does not ensure that a more inclusive and integrated approach to patient care is implemented, empirical research is the clear bridge to the biological sciences. For example, the randomized clinical trial to determine the efficacy of a medication is the standard empirical approach in clinical medicine to identify those medications that are beneficial in the treatment or prevention of disease. Such research also ensures a necessary caution that was absent during the 1960s, an era when social psychiatry encompassed theories that ran far ahead of the evidence for those theories.

During the past 30 years, social research has been relatively stagnant among psychiatrists but has matured significantly in other disciplines. Now is the time for psychiatry to take full advantage of the maturity of the social sciences and to create and develop a new wave of basic social psychiatric research. Now is the time for psychiatry to train a new generation of psychiatrists grounded in the basic social sciences who can participate in interdisciplinary research to explore the impact of social forces on the frequency and distribution of psychiatric morbidity, especially depression.

Social science research has a long, though not central, history in the National Institutes of Health, especially in the National Heart, Lung and Blood Institute and the National Cancer Institute.[1] Such research is fundamental to a comprehensive understanding of disease etiology and to the promotion of health and well-being. For example, the National Cancer Institute has insisted on a major role for behavioral research. All Comprehensive Cancer Centers must include a program in primary and secondary prevention apart from chemotherapeutic, surgical, and radiation interventions. Not all institutes have developed their social scientific initiatives as persistently.

The Committee on Assuring the Health of the Public in the 21st Century, convened by the Institute of Medicine of the National Academies, recommended in 2002 that action be taken to adopt a population health approach that considers the multiple determinants of health (p. 3).[2] Specifically, they recommended that the National Institutes of Health increase the portion of its budget allocated to population and community-based research that addresses population-level health problems, involves a definable population and operates the level of the whole person, and focuses on behavioral and environmental (social, economic, cultural, physical) factors associated with primary and secondary prevention of disease and disability in populations (p. 16).

The National Institute of Mental Health, following an auspicious beginning I documented in previous chapters, has all but abandoned social scientific research. Some vestigial projects persist but are barely visible. A basic social science of psychiatric disorders is almost oxymoronic to neuroscientists. On one hand, even the most emphatic biological psychiatrists would not argue that the social environment does not shape and drive psychiatric disorders such as major depression. On the other hand, few biological psychiatrists can conceive of, much less produce, a research plan to explore the social causes of depression. Clinical psychiatrists daily attend to the social forces affecting their patients if they are to practice effectively, as I describe in chapter 8.

Nevertheless, the social sciences have, throughout the latter half of the 20th century, held a tenuous relationship with psychiatry that remains marginal today.[3] Could there be a bias against the social sciences within psychiatry? Certainly the failure of the social psychiatry movement of the 1960s has soured the view of many psychiatrists toward the social sciences. Society perhaps is biased against the social sciences in general, some believing that social science is not true science, others equating social science with socialism, and still others viewing social forces as an unnecessary "add on" to the biological base of medicine. Reductionism flourishes in psychiatry as in all of medicine despite its discredit by many philosophers of neuroscience.[4, 5]

Investigators attempt to find the most basic biological cause of maladies such as depression, and once those basic causes are even partially identified, the investigation is closed to social causation. Notwithstanding the bias against the social sciences in psychiatry, investigators in primary care, social medicine, and public health are progressively introducing materials from social sciences into their disciplines.

Yet another factor can stifle basic social research by psychiatrists. Emotional suffering has been medicalized. The consequences of life in the 21st century are being increasingly defined and treated through illness constructions grounded in the biological features of individuals.[6] For example, the abdominal pain felt by a patient on a surgical ward is often viewed by the surgeon as "the gallbladder in room 166" rather than as "Mrs. Smith is suffering a lot of pain from what is probably a blockage by gallstones." As biological mechanisms are clarified, social context becomes further ignored.

Margot Lyon described the close associated process of "functional autonomy."[6] Functional autonomy in medicine refers to the way in which illness categories, such as major depression, are treated as if they are autonomous from the contexts in which they exist. For example, major depression caused by stress in the workplace can be treated with a medication without attention paid to the workplace. Peter Kramer, in *Listening to Prozac*, quoted Donald Klein's concept of functional autonomy: "A cause engenders an adaptive response (function) that persists after the termination of the cause (autonomy)" (p. 75).[7] Symptoms become uncoupled from their origins. Consequently, there is no longer a reason to suspect that the origin of a symptom will contribute to healing that symptom.

The concept of functional autonomy of symptoms folds neatly into a psychiatry that focuses on pharmaceutical interventions and psychotherapeutic interventions that emphasize adaptation. This concept gained considerable strength during the era when psychiatrists and the general public were becoming more critical of years spent probing into one's past to improve present emotional well-being with psychoanalysis. The social origin of depression also became less attractive as a subject for study as pharmaceutical interventions became the norm. By almost any measure, at least on the surface, a pharmacological solution is less expensive than a social intervention. It is no wonder that Michael Norden, in *Beyond Prozac*, wrote that we live in "serotonin depleting times."[8] A neurochemical explanation of the origins of our emotional angst is sufficient.

Emotion, however, especially the emotion of depression, cannot be abstracted from the context of our society. Depression, of course, cannot be understood if we do not understand the psychobiology of depression. In addition, depression must be understood as caused and shaped by the social and historical context from which it emerges.[6] Depression is at once social and individual. On one hand, it is precipitated and formed by society. On the other hand, emoting depression shapes the social contacts of depressed people. Emotion is foundational to the very fabric of social life.

In this chapter I propose that we launch a new wave of basic social science research in the service of the mentally ill. This new wave must avoid the social activism that doomed the first wave. It must take full advantage of the advances in the social sciences during the past 25 years, advances of which most psychiatrists are unaware. Young psychiatrists who are considering a career in research should be encouraged to consider the basic social sciences, such as anthropology, sociology, social psychology, and social epidemiology, and the basic physical sciences, such as molecular biology and neuropsychopharmacology. I review two areas to illustrate how the basic social sciences can be applied to understanding the causes of depression—depression in the workplace and the social ecology of depression. In other words, risk factors for depression should be considered that are not strictly tied to the individual. The application of basic social science to the study of depression is a step away from methodological individualism (see chapter 1).

A CASE IN POINT

What prevents violence? An investigative team in Chicago proposed that, in addition to personal characteristics, social and organizational characteristics of neighborhoods explain variations in crime rates.[9] They theorized that, just as individuals vary in their capacity for effective action, so too do neighborhoods. Many factors can decrease neighborhood effectiveness, such as a high rate of residential mobility (people moving into and out of the neighborhood), race and class segregation that can fuel concentrations of poverty, and a sense of powerlessness to effect change within the community.

The investigators studied more than 300 neighborhood clusters and classified them in a number of ways. Residents were asked about collective social control, specifically about the likelihood that their neighbors could be counted on to get involved if they (a) saw children skipping school, (b) saw children spray-painting graffiti on a local building, or (c) learned that the local fire station was threatened with major budget cuts. They also were asked about social cohesion and trust, specifically how strongly they believed their neighbors were willing to help one another, if they viewed their neighborhood as close knit, and if people in the neighborhood got along with one another. Survey participants also were asked how often they had noticed violent acts in the neighborhood during the 6 months prior to the survey. Police records were also reviewed for reports of violent crimes.

The investigators concluded that they could reliably assess perceived collective efficacy; that is, the perception by the neighborhood members that they could, as a group, get things done. In the past, measures of perceived efficacy have been primarily limited to individual (or self-) efficacy. Collective efficacy was found to be an important factor in rates of violence. The investigators also found that a concentration of poverty and frequent movement of residents in and out of the neighborhood (i.e., decreased residential stability) were important predictors of objective (from police records) and perceived violence in the neighborhood. In addition, neighborhoods that scored higher in informal social control, cohesion, and trust experienced lower rates of violence. Therefore, impoverishment and social mobility (indicators of social disintegration) as well as the lack of communal efficacy were important predictors of violence above and beyond individual risks for violence.

What prevents violence? Neighborhoods that work in part prevent violence.

Social Epidemiology

The scientific study of the social causes of disease has increasingly come under the umbrella of social epidemiology.[10] Social epidemiology in the United States grew in part (perhaps in large part) from the psychiatric epidemiology of the 1950s and 1960s.[11-14] Achieving a coherent and complete theory of disease causation, according to social epidemiologists, requires obtaining social and biological data that are consistent with each other with regard to a specific disease.[15] For example, we must understand the chain of events that leads from how membership in a social group relates to behavior patterns that can expose people to methods for transmitting noxious agents, through how these agents cause tissue changes, and finally to how these tissue changes cause disease. The great contribution of early social epidemiology was the ability to incorporate this multilevel thinking into a comprehensive picture of disease causation. Unfortunately, the methods were crude and the results were frequently challenged.

John Cassel, during the waning days of psychiatric social epidemiology of the 1970s, asked the critical question for social epidemiology:[10, 16] Are there categories or classes of environmental factors that are capable of changing human resistance in important ways and making subsets of people more or less susceptible to ubiquitous agents in our environment? He argued that environmental conditions capable of producing profound effects on host susceptibility involve the presence of other members of the same species or, more generally, certain aspects of the social environment. Cassel posited that at least one of the properties of stressful situations might be that the actor is not receiving adequate evidence that his or her actions are leading to anticipated consequences. The evidence for this adverse consequence includes the powerlessness brought on by social disorganization, migration, discrimination, poverty, and low support at work. He also proposed a series of protective factors that might buffer the individual from the deleterious consequences of stressful situations, specifically social support.

I also explore the ecological approach to the study of depression in society. When we investigate the social origins of depression, we typically consider those social factors that are attributed to the individual being studied, such as stressful life events and the absence of individual social support. A basic social science of psychiatry must also consider those social and organizational characteristics of larger units that are not solely attributable to the collective characteristics of individuals in these larger units. People today occupy many social spaces, such as neighborhoods, work environments, and religious organizations. Each of these environments can independently contribute to the emotional well-being of persons residing in them. Sophisticated methods are being developed in the social sciences that permit psychiatric investigators to study these environments as environments and to determine their independent contribution to the emotional well-being or the emotional suffering of the people who inhabit these environments.

Depression in the Workplace

Americans are working longer hours today than at any time during the past 50 years. In 1933, the U.S. Senate passed a bill that would have made the standard workweek 30 hours (anything more would be overtime).[17] The workforce, however, has opted for more goods and less time. During an era when American productivity is several times what it was in 1930, we now work on average nearly 2,000 hours a year (much more than 40 hours a week when holidays and vacation time are considered), 350 hours (9 weeks) more than Western Europeans.

The number of hours worked (one marker of workplace stress) and adverse mental health are consistently associated in scientific studies.[18] Stress in the workplace is a powerful social stressor. According to *USA Today* (October 29, 2002), 7 out of 10 employees say they feel "moderate" to "great" stress on the job. The four top causes of their stress are demands on the job (54%), coworkers (20%), the boss (10%), and layoff fears (8%).

Workplace stress is especially troublesome in a developed country such as the United States, for work is so central to the identity of our citizens. Four important reasons have been proposed for the centrality of work and occupation in advanced industrialized societies.[19] First, having a job is a principal prerequisite for continuous income opportunities. (This can appear self-evident to Americans, yet income in many countries is not directly associated to continuous employment.) Second, training for a job and achievement of occupational status are the most important goals of primary and secondary socialization. Through job and education, personal growth and development are realized. Third, occupation defines a most important criterion of social rank in advanced societies. That is, we naturally form our opinions of others based in large part on their occupation. Furthermore, the type and quality of occupation, and especially the degree of self-direction at work, strongly influence personal attitudes and behavioral patterns in areas that are not directly related to work, such as leisure, family life, education, and political activity.[20] Finally, occupational settings produce the most pervasive and continuous demands during one's lifetime, and they absorb the largest amount of active time during most of our adulthood.

Despite the centrality of work to our emotional well-being, a MedLine review of the two most widely read psychiatric journals in the United States, the *American Journal of Psychiatry* and the *Archives of General Psychiatry*, from January 1993 to December 2002 revealed only one article that investigated work-related stress as a predictor of psychiatric symptoms or disorder. In 1997, Redford Williams and colleagues published in the *Archives* results from a study of female workers in which they found that high job demands and low decision latitude were associated with a pattern of psychological factors consisting of increased negative emotions such as anger, depression, and hostility.[21] The virtual absence of studies of work-related stress as a risk for psychiatric disorder in these journals is due not so much to the editorial policies of the journals but rather to the dearth of interest in such studies by psychiatrists. The public often follows the lead of psychiatry. In the *Women's*

Health Weekly report on depression in women, no mention is made of work-related stress as a contributor to depression.[22]

In contrast, the impact of depression on workplace performance has been featured in these same journals. For example, in one study of more than 15,000 employees of a major U.S. corporation that filed health claims in 1995, workers with depression incurred an average of $1,341 in mental health care costs and $3,032 in nonmental health care, more total than workers with diabetes, heart disease, and hypertension.[23] When sick days (average of 9.86 for depressive disorders) were included, the annual cost was $5,415 ($7,906 for comorbid depression and a physical illness) adjusted for age, gender, race, and so on. One fifth of the costs of depressive illness were related to disability pay. That translated into $2.2 million total expenses to the corporation secondary to depression. The authors of this study featured the benefit of treating the depression on performance at work, not changing the work environment to prevent depression. Another recent study estimates that the cost of depression to employers each year in the United States exceeds $31 billion.[24] The reasoning by of these teams of investigators is that better treatment of depression will reduce loss of productive work. Work-related stress receives virtually no attention.

Results from studies of the association of work-related stress and depression have been published in other journals, such as the *Lancet*, the *British Medical Journal*, the *British Journal of Psychiatry*, the *American Journal of Public Health*, and *Psychological Medicine*. Christopher Tennant recently reviewed the topic in the *Journal of Psychosomatic Research*.[25] He found consistent evidence that work-related stress predicted depression in longitudinal studies. In one study of blue-collar workers in Japan, "lack of control over work," "unsuitable jobs," and "poor workplace relations" were significant predictors.[26] In another study, noise was a particular stressor at work among blue-collar workers.[27]

Studies of white-collar workers expose other specific risks for depression.[25] A classic study of white-collar workers (male and female civil servants) was fielded in the United Kingdom (the Whitehall II Study).[28] Psychological morbidity was predicted by poor work social supports and high job demands. Much of the social class difference in depression was explained by the psychosocial work environment.[29] Among managers, in another study, workload and role ambiguity predicted depressive symptoms.[30] In yet another study, specific work tasks, such as supervising teaching, driving, skilled machine operation, and people contact, contributed to nervous strain and depression.[31]

Health care workers, especially direct care staff and women, have been identified as experiencing more psychological morbidity than the general population.

For nurses, ambiguity about authority and perceived lack of social support at work contributed to burnout-related absenteeism in one study.[32] (The symptoms of burnout are very similar to those of depression.) Among workers in long-term care facilities, workload and related stress predicted both depression and increased physical symptoms.[33] Among child protection workers, work environment and work hassles predicted burnout.[34] In general, among direct service providers, social environmental variables, especially conflict in relationships and poor social support at work, predict depression and burnout.[25]

The perception that a job is a good job or a bad job also predicts work-related stress and depression.[35] As I note next, jobs with a high degree of control and low demand are optimal.[36] Joseph Grzywacz and David Dooley, using data from two large cross-sectional surveys, classified jobs into five categories, from "optimal" to "inadequate."[35] They found that a substantial number of adults are working in inadequate or barely adequate jobs. Of those employed, 20% in one study and 33% in another study worked in inadequate or barely adequate jobs. Though the highest prevalence of depression (31% and 23%, respectively) was found among the unemployed, inadequate jobs were consistently associated with higher depression scores as well (17% and 18.6%, respectively).

Specific characterizations of work-related stress have been examined by a number of investigators. The most widely used method to measure work-related stress is the Job Demand-Control model (JDC model) initially proposed by Karasek.[36] This model predicts that job strain and subsequent physical or psychological illness, or both, results from the interaction of job demands and job control.[37] Two hypotheses drive this model: (a) the combination of heavy job demands along with low control over one's own tasks and conduct during the working day precipitates "high strain"; and (b) learning, personal development, and active participation in workplace social life for those with "active jobs" (characterized by high demands and high control) lead to better adaptation to the workplace. Job demands basically refer to psychological demands such as mental workload, organizational constraints on task completion, and conflicting demands. Job control is the decision latitude of the worker, such as the freedom to determine how to best meet job demands or perform job-related tasks. The opportunity to use skills and make decisions reduces possible adverse effects of heavy psychological demands.[36]

A group of investigators analyzed data from the Whitehall II study I described previously to explore the influence of low control at work (and home) on depression while taking into consideration the effects of gender and social class.[38] Women and men with low control either at work or at home experienced an increased risk of developing depression and anxiety. Women in the lowest or middle employment grades who also reported low control at work or home were at most risk for depression and anxiety. Men in the middle grade with low work control were at risk for depression whereas those in the lowest grade were at risk for anxiety. Men in the middle and highest grades were at greatest risk for depression and anxiety if they reported low control at home. Obviously home life and life at work interact as risks for depression.

One of the most stressful aspects of work is the loss of employment or chronic unemployment.[35,39,40] Depression is a common outcome of job loss and unemployment.[40–42] Financial strain is perhaps the most significant factor in the pathway from job loss to depression. Richard Price and colleagues followed for more than 2 years nearly 800 people who had lost their jobs.[39] They found that financial strain is the most significant mediator of the relationship between job loss and depression. Ron Kessler and colleagues found that financial strain accounted for 90% of the explainable variance between job loss and mental health problems.[43] In England and Wales, investigators found a clear association between unemployment rates and suicide rates among men and women from 1921 to 1995.[44]

Can depression be an adaptation to work-related stressors?[45] Unlike some other psychiatric disorders, depression is very prevalent and therefore can serve some protective role. The social navigation hypothesis suggests that depression plays two complementary roles in dealing with particularly important and troublesome social problems: focusing limited cognitive resources on planning ways out of complex social problems (ruminative and more associated with less severe depression), and motivating close social partners to provide problem-solving help (motivational and more associated with more severe [major] depression).

Still another hypothesis is that depression is a cry for help.[46] Perhaps the days missed from work, days often labeled unofficially as "mental health days," are a cry that the demands of work are overwhelming. A second hypothesis is the social yielding hypothesis. According to this hypothesis, depression is an adaptation that forces the loser of a conflict to cease competing with the winner, accept that he or she has lost, and signal submission to stop oppressive behavior by the winner.[47] Depression can lead to workers' accepting for extended periods of time work situations characterized by high demand and low latitude because they cannot extricate themselves from the subordinate position at work. In contrast to the social navigation hypothesis, the depressive response is not adaptive for the individual in the long run (and perhaps not adaptive in the short run as well).

Depression can be strongly associated with social problems in the workplace. Social problems in the workplace are characterized (a) by social dependency, where the fitness of one social interaction is dependent on the behavior of another, and (b) by interpersonal conflicts of interest. Depressives exhibit many characteristics of enhanced social dependency, including an enhanced desire for social approval.[48] Depressives perceive themselves to be in an unenviable social situation and desire to gain more social approval and success. Their dependent behavior can create further problems.

Depressives also pay closer attention to social information, including social comparison information, and process it more extensively.[49] Depressives are less likely to attribute their success to ability and their failures to chance, perhaps a more accurate appraisal than assuming that all failures result from bad luck. This attributional pattern of depressives is called the depressive attributional style.[50] Depressives also evaluate themselves and others more evenhandedly for personality traits.[51] This increased accuracy applies particularly to social domains and can be beneficial in some work situations. Depressives outperform nondepressives on difficult tasks that tap social problem-solving skills.[52] Specifically, depressives are less likely to make an error in judgment when a person's mental state and behavior are assumed to correspond to a degree that is logically unwarranted by the situation.

Many research questions arise if psychiatrists take work-related stress seriously as a risk for depression:

- Is the number of hours worked per week associated with depressive symptoms such as sleep disturbance, loss of appetite, anhedonia, loss of interest in sex, and agitation when factors such as socioeconomic status, job security, and marital or family conflict are controlled?
- If people with major depression respond to a combination of pharmacotherapy and psychotherapy, does high demand coupled with low control on the job increase the likelihood of relapse into another episode of major depression?
- Do depressed persons holding jobs where working conditions are poor become more active in negotiating for better working conditions if they respond to treatment for the depression?
- Do persons who move from "bad jobs" (such as jobs with high demand and low decision latitude) to "good jobs," other factors being controlled, improve in mood apart from intervention with medication and psychotherapy?
- Is work-related stress more likely to lead to major depression in women than men, in underrepresented minorities than in Whites, and in younger people than older people?
- If a depressed worker responds to antidepressant therapy, yet finds himself or herself in a difficult work situation, is the worker more likely or less

likely to work toward correcting the work environment once he or she recovers from the episode of depression?

In summary, work-related stress is an ideal focus for a revival of the basic social scientific study of psychiatric disorders.

Social Ecology and Depression

Within epidemiology there has been something of a backlash against the apparent individualism of chronic disease epidemiology and a call for a return to more traditional focus on the health of populations and on cultural, social structural, group-level, and environmental influences on health.[10,53,54] The historical origins of public health were essentially ecological, relating environmental and community characteristics to health and diseases.[54,55] Only with the advent of the "germ theory" of disease were individual environmental stressors associated with disease onset in specific persons.

Ana Diez-Roux proposed that multilevel analysis of risk holds potential for reemphasizing the role of macrolevel variables in shaping health and disease in populations.[54] The individualization of risk has perpetuated the idea that risk is individually determined rather than socially determined. In contrast, the study of the effects of collective group characteristics on individual-level outcomes has been termed *contextual analysis*.[56] Individual and contextual variables might cause disease. For example, lifestyle and behaviors are for the most part considered matters of free choice. Yet free choice might not be so free after all. For example, exercise is influenced not only by personal taste, cognitions, and beliefs but also by the local social context and by larger social factors. These factors include the importance of exercise in the society, the need to walk to essential services (e.g., the extent to which a person is dependent on automotive transport), and even the climate (extremes of hot and cold weather can decrease the likelihood of exercise).

James Koopman and John Lynch carried this proposal conceptually further.[57] The sum of an exposure (e.g., an infectious disease) affects the distribution of that disease in a population. In addition, the pattern of the exposure affects the distribution. For example, exposure to an infectious agent in one setting can lead to widespread disease, whereas exposure in another leads to the emergence of sporadic cases. The social context and the geographic setting can help to explain the relative frequency of one disease compared with another, not just individual exposure or genetic susceptibility to the disease.

Medical geographers have called for medicine to return to an earlier emphasis on "place," a renewed focus on place as actually experienced by people and as a context for their lives, rather than on statistical analysis of spatial relationships between individuals, places, and institutions.[58] One reason for the neglect of studies of localities and health within sociology has been the dominance of an individualistically oriented epidemiological paradigm within the sociological study of inequalities in health. Investigators must also consider features of local areas that might influence health, such as physical features of the environment shared by all residents (e.g., quality of air); availability of health environment at home, work, and play (e.g., secure and decent places); services provided to support people in their daily lives (e.g., transportation); sociocultural features of a neighborhood; and the reputation of an area.

An overreliance on individual-level data and measurements can blind investigators to those factors that take the community into account. Community levels of social cohesion, for example, can influence mortality.[59] "Social capital" provides a way to think about connections among individuals.[60] Social capital, the capital that we accumulate through positive interaction within the community, refers to the following:

> Those tangible substances [that] count for most in the daily lives of people; namely good will, fellowship, sympathy, and social intercourse among individuals and families who make up a social unit. ... The individual is helpless socially, if left to himself ... the community as a whole will benefit by the cooperation of all its parts, while the individual will find in his association the advantages of the help, the sympathy, and the fellowship of his neighbors. (p. 130)[61,60]

Social capital is an inherently ecological concept and focuses attention on properties of communities and the processes by which social capital is maintained or diminished in these communities.

Social support, a variable frequently considered at the individual level as a determinant of depression, therefore acts at the individual and societal level.[62,63] Social integration of the community, the degree to which the community fits together, can have a positive effect on the availability of individual social support.[29] Social cohesion, the existence of mutual trust and respect between different sections of society, contributes to the way in which people and their health are valued. Social cohesion means cohesive community relationships with high levels of participation in communal groups. Such cohesion has been associated with better health.[64] For example, cities with stronger civic communities have lower infant mortality rates. Mortality increases during social upheaval. There is some evidence for a differential distribution of social support by social class, but, in general, it does not seem to be a major influence in explaining employment-grade differences in depression.[29] The physical environment can also determine opportunities for social support, for inclement weather can reduce the likelihood of some communal activities.

Mervyn Susser called on epidemiology to broaden its base and move beyond its focus on individual-level risk factors and "black box epidemiology" to a new "multilevel ecoepidemiology."[53,65–69] Epidemiology shares the study of populations, in a general way, with other population sciences such as sociology and population genetics. According to Susser, states of health do not exist in a vacuum apart from people. People form societies, and any study of the attributes of people is also a study of the manifestations of the form, structure, and processes of social forces.

Epidemiology is essentially ecological because the biology of organisms is determined in a multilevel, interactive environment. Identifying risk at the individual level, even multiple risks, does not sufficiently explain interactions and pathways at that level or incorporate the social forces that influence risks to individuals.

Geoffrey Rose provided through his population perspective the critical insight that an individual's risk of illness cannot be considered in isolation from the risk for the population to which he or she belongs.[70] For example, Japanese immigrants to the United States take on the coronary risk profiles of their adopted country and experience more heart disease than native Japanese. (This concept was anticipated by Emil Durkheim, who found that the rate of suicide in a society is linked to collective social forces [see chapter 4].[71] Individual risks come and go, but the social rate of suicide remains predictable.)

Rose asked, "Why does this *population* have this particular distribution of risk?" Identifying population risk can lead to the greater benefit. For example, those clinical trials that attempt to modify individual behavioral risk factors are most successful if they incorporate elements of social organizational change (behaviors are not randomly distributed in the population). Reducing smoking in individuals is most effective when more "no smoking" zones are designated and smoking is prohibited in progressively more social spaces.

Leonard Syme pointed to two limitations of the individual risk-factor approach.[72] First, individual risk factors explain only a part of variations in the occurrence of disease. Second, individual risk factors are difficult to modify by trying to persuade individuals to change their behaviors (such as quitting smoking). There has been limited benefit among persons at especially high risk (e.g., people experiencing very high blood pressure), but these efforts have made limited contributions to reducing disease rates in the whole population. In contrast, when the frequency of smoking drops for an entire population, individual smoking is more likely to cease.

The ecologist analyzes the effects of the social and physical environment on the health of individuals or populations. Ecological studies have been attacked frequently in epidemiology.[53] The "ecological fallacy" is the mistake of making causal inferences from group data to individual behaviors. For example, if color televisions are associated with coronary heart disease, one must not make the mistake of attributing coronary heart disease to watching color television. Other factors common to both can be causative, such as lack of exercise and the diet found in affluent societies. Nevertheless, social epidemiologists argue for the importance of an ecological perspective that takes into account humans' habits, modes of life, and relationships to their surroundings. Emphasis on the ecological fallacy encourages three equally fallacious notions: that individual-level theories of the cause of disease are better than community-level models, that community-level associations between potential causes of disease and the frequency of disease are simply substitutes for individual-level correlations, and that community-level variables do not cause disease.[73] For example, the atomistic[74] or individualistic[75] fallacy incorrectly infers information about the environment from data on individuals. Individual analysis can assume that married women have more friends than widows, but this might not be true in retirement communities. Individual characteristics depend on the community setting.

Social ecology can be especially relevant to depression. Preliminary evidence suggests that the structural characteristics of neighborhoods are related to major depression and suicide. In a study of neighborhoods in Illinois, investigators found that depressive symptoms were higher in the more socioeconomically disadvantaged neighborhoods when the effects of individual socioeconomic and demographic characteristics were taken into account.[76] The investigators also found that, under conditions of low poverty, residents of neighborhoods with little residential turnover had lower levels of depression and anxiety than residents of more residentially mobile neighborhoods. Under conditions of high poverty, however, residents of neighborhoods with little residential turnover had higher levels of depression and anxiety than residents of more residentially mobile neighborhoods.

Eric Silver and colleagues reexamined data from the Epidemiologic Catchment Area study.[77] After controlling for individual characteristics, they found that neighborhood disadvantage was associated with higher rates of major depression and substance abuse, and that neighborhood residential mobility was associated with higher rates of schizophrenia, major depression, and substance abuse. On the basis of the work from the Chicago neighborhood project in part (as I described previously),[9] these investigators defined neighborhood disadvantage as neighborhoods with a lower socioeconomic status, racial or ethnic heterogeneity, and residential mobility. They theorized that these characteristics undermine the ability of community residents to join together to realize their common values and to solve experienced problems. The odds for major depression, taking into account age, individual race, education, income, and living arrangements, were 1.14 for the neighborhood disadvantage index and 1.21 for the neighborhood mobility index.

In a study of more than 600 parliamentary constituencies in Great Britain, mortality rates from suicide from 1981 to 1992 were higher in constituencies that also were rated higher in social fragmentation and poverty.[78] The investigators estimated poverty from census data on unemployment, car ownership, overcrowded housing, and housing tenure. They estimated social fragmentation from census data, using private renting of housing, single-person households among those older than 65 years, the percentage of persons unmarried, and mobility in the previous year. They also used abstention from participation in elections to assess social fragmentation. Constituencies with absolute increases in suicide and poverty during the 10 years of the study tended to have greater increase in suicide over the same period. Social fragmentation predicted suicide more strongly than poverty.

Some can argue that in such studies, the individual characteristics basically mediate the neighborhood context, and if enough individual characteristics are controlled, then the neighborhood characteristics will cease to be associated with depression and other psychiatric disorders. Another explanation, however, gives more weight to the neighborhood characteristics. W.J. Wilson, in *When Work Disappears: The World of the New Urban Poor*,[79] proposed that the long-term socioeconomic and marital prospects of residents of socially and economically disadvantaged neighborhoods become compromised because of high rates of joblessness, poor systems of education, and limited marriage markets.[77]

In other words, individual social and economic disadvantages are reinforced by the disadvantaged neighborhoods in which these people live. Given the strong association between individually experienced stressful life events, impaired social support, and depression,[62,80,81] neighborhood social disorganization can increase the likelihood of stressful events and limit the amount of social support available to individuals.[77] New statistical methods, specifically hierarchical linear regression, are tailor-made for such analyses.[82] Using these models, the contribution of an individual's risk can be separated from the contribution of the neighborhood's risk.

Many research questions arise from this ecological perspective:

- Do urban-rural differences in the frequency of depression persist today as they have in the past? If so, when individual factors are controlled, can ecologic factors (derived from census data) help refine these differences in prevalence by geographic locale?
- Do regional differences in the frequency of depression persist after controlling for individual risk factors? If so, can ecologic factors relevant to these regions be identified that are associated with depression? Examples of regional differences might include the long-term economic problems of the rust belt in the midwestern United States or the significant recent economic downturn in Silicon Valley.
- Do regional differences in the frequency of depression hold equally for all racial and ethnic groups? If not, what factors might explain the differences?

A new generation of psychiatric investigators, grounded in the basic social sciences, would be well equipped to explore the importance of social ecology on the origins of depression in the community. Yet this new generation must be trained. The National Institute of Mental Health is most anxious to attract more psychiatrists to psychiatric research, and they are to be applauded for this effort. The institute recognizes that fewer women and men entering psychiatry are training for research academic careers. Yet the emphasis in training for research has been almost exclusively an emphasis on basic biological research and the design of clinical intervention trials. Basic social science research should be added to the research training agenda of the institute if psychiatrists are to effectively expand their understanding of the origins of depression.

10

Emotion: A Link between Body and Society

We do not weep because we are sad, but rather we are sad because we weep.

—William James, *Psychology: The Briefer Course* (p. 375)[1]

I ... treat specific emotions ... as culturally constructed judgments, that is, as aspects of cultural meaning systems people use in attempting to understand the situations in which they find themselves. ... They are socially negotiated.

—Catherine Lutz, *Culture and Depression* (p. 65)[2]

A debate has been waged far too long regarding nature and nurture, genes and environment, biological and social. E.O. Wilson, in describing the "webwork of causal explanation," lamented,

The explanatory network now touches the edge of culture itself. It has reached the boundary that separates the natural sciences on the one side from the humanities and humanistic social sciences on the other. ... From Apollonian law to Dionysian spirit, prose to poetry, left cortical hemisphere to right, the line between the two domains can be easily crossed, ... but no one knows how to translate the tongue of one into that of the other. ... Few can deny that the division between the two cultures is a perennial source of misunderstanding and conflict. (p. 125)[3]

If a new and meaningful basic social science of psychiatry is to emerge, science must recognize and incorporate body, brain, mind, and society. Yet this science should not demand that we propose a grand theory that suggests that depression accounts for every contributing factor. Grand theories have been proposed to integrate the physical, psychological, and social origins of depression, and these theories are overwhelming conceptually and virtually impossible to investigate scientifically.

For example, Hagop Akiskal and William McKinney proposed a "unified hypothesis" with "the depressive syndrome ... conceived as a psychobiologic final common pathway" (p. 286).[4] They identified five broad processes or domains: a genetic predisposition, developmental factors such as early parental loss, psychosocial events or stressors, physiological stressors, and personality traits. Varying admixtures of these processes "conceivably converge in those areas of the diencephalon that modulate arousal, mood, motivation, and psychomotor function" (p. 290). They postulated that a "diencephalic final common pathway" interlocks "processes at chemical, experiential, and behavioral levels that, in language of neurophysiology, translate into a functional impairment of the diencephalic centers of reinforcement" (p. 300). The "diencephalic final common pathway accounts for the shared clinical features seen in the heterogeneous group of depressive disorders" (p. 300).

At the least, this unified hypothesis is extremely complex and difficult to grasp for the public and most practicing psychiatrists. Such hypotheses also become caught on the horns of various dilemmas. For example, can a grand theory accommodate the fact that enough social stress leads to clinically significant depression in almost everyone? Can such a theory accommodate the opposing views that a severe depressed mood is an extreme point on a dimension instead of a qualitatively unique disease?

In place of a grand theory, I propose that future study of body and brain within the context of society be linked through constructs familiar to both, specifically emotion.[5] Depression is, if nothing else, an emotion. An informed study of emotion is a key link between body and society, given its rich history in biology, psychology, sociology, and anthropology.[6] Emotions, according to some, have evolved as ways of matching physiological responses with environmental demands and signaling the organism's state.[6, 7] The empirical study of emotions should buffer the tendency of the biological sciences toward reductionism and the social sciences toward social construction.

The extreme biologic model of emotion is manifestly reductionistic.[8] According to this model, emotions are clear reflections of disordered somatic processes. The critical clinical task of the physician is to decode patients' discourse by relating emotions to their biological referents to diagnose a disease entity. Descriptions of symptoms are meaningful only if they accurately reflect biological reality. For example, David Rowe proposed that emotional states are "surprisingly immune to 'objective' social circumstances."[9] He proposed that people inherit genes, and genes form the recipes for their nervous systems. People with different nervous systems respond to the world differently. Yet he went further. People expose themselves to different social environments in large part based on their social circumstances. In other words, people make their environments based on their genes.

The extreme position in the social construction of emotion has argued that all emotions are social products and that natural (biological) phenomena have little relevance to emotion.[10] Emotions, such as depression, are to be interpreted in terms of the meaning society gives and to the roles designated for persons with symptoms, such as "mentally ill." Some societies might appear to be almost totally free of the emotion of depression, for the absence of the social construct leads to the absence of the emotion.

The symptomatic expression of an emotion, as I attempt to demonstrate next, derives from the body and brain and the societal context in which it is expressed. The understanding and interpretation of an emotion must simultaneously take into account the body and brain and the social context, not assume that one is foundational to the other. At least two lines of argument support this view of emotion as a link between the body and brain and society. First, no single gene (or combination of genes) has to date been conclusively linked to depression; that is, a gene that causes depression has not been identified.[11] Therefore, genes must work in combination with the environment to cause the emotion of depression.

A recent study confirms the joint combination of genes and the social environment.[12] In this study, a variation (polymorphism) in a gene that transports serotonin (a chemical messenger in the brain) was associated with the response of individuals to stressful life events. The gene alone does not lead to depression. Nevertheless, people with a common variant of the normal gene and who experienced multiple stressful life events were much more likely to develop depression than people who experienced the same number of events but who had the normal gene. The study is preliminary and must be replicated. Even so, it demonstrated that the combination of body and brain (a gene that predisposes a person to develop depression) and social context (the experience of stressful life events) contributes to a higher risk for the emotion of depression. This study provided evidence of the link between body and brain and social context through emotion, yet it does not help us understand the mechanisms by which the body interacts with society to create an emotion. The approach to the study of the biology of emotion is qualitatively different from the study of emotion embedded within its social context and must proceed for a time in parallel. Yet there are points of contact where the link can be clarified.

In this chapter I review two examples where the link has become more clear—social zeitgebers and allostatic load. Social zeitgebers refer to those personal relationships, social demands, or tasks that serve to entrain biological rhythms,

rhythms that are core to the psychobiology of depression.[13] For example, we can feel hunger around the time dinner is usually served and not before because we have been trained to expect dinner at a particular time each evening. The allostatic load hypothesis links the psychosocial environment to physical disease and psychiatric disorders (such as depression) by means of neuroendocrine pathways.[14] Allostatic systems (*allo* meaning variable) are those bodily systems that help keep the body stable; that is, adapt to changes in the environment by themselves being able to change (such as the change in hormone levels under different circumstances) (p. 6).[15] The price paid by the body and brain to make these changes over time is wear and tear on the organism, such as an increased vulnerability to depression.

A Case in Point

Rebecca was 67 years old when she first sought consultation with a psychiatrist. She was referred from a retirement community to which she had moved 1 year prior to the referral. Rebecca cried frequently during group meetings at the home. These crying episodes were usually brief, but they seemed unusual to the staff, and some of the residents were expressing discomfort when Rebecca was in a group with them because they feared she might lapse into a crying spell. Her husband had died a few years before she moved into the retirement community.

The nurse who referred Rebecca did not believe it was grief for her husband or the move to the retirement community that caused the crying spells. Rebecca had settled into the community with ease and had made many friends from the outset. Nevertheless, her mood was "up and down" and when it was down she would openly cry at public gatherings, usually referring to refugees from the tribal wars in central and southern Africa. Friends would console her, and she would recover from these outbursts after a short time. Nevertheless, she would refer to the refugees frequently during public gatherings. Other residents at the community could not make sense of Rebecca's concerns for the refugees. She seemed to be overreacting. She was too emotional. And the crying spells were becoming more frequent.

After consulting the psychiatrist, Rebecca told of her frustrations in mobilizing the retirement community to support relief work in Africa. "These old people still have plenty of energy and tons of money. What's wrong with them? Are they going to sit around all day, read the newspapers about suffering in the world, only to return untouched to their bridge games? Don't get me wrong. I really like the people where I live and I know that they are no different than most people. Yet there is so much pain and suffering in the world. My heart goes out to the refugees in Africa. The more I read, the more I hear, the more upset I get. How can we ignore them?"

Had Rebecca always felt as she described her feelings to the psychiatrist? Had she, before her husband died, experienced these periods of grief for refugees in Africa? "I do cry more in public than I did in the past. Yet I have always been an openly emotional person. I was raised in a Pentecostal Church and we have always been encouraged to express our love for God and love for others openly. In fact, we went by that old biblical adage, 'Rejoice with those who rejoice and weep with those who weep.' How can we truly understand the suffering among others if we don't feel some of what they feel? How can we feel what they feel if we don't express our feelings? I don't hold anything back.

"The number of people suffering in Rwanda and the atrocities that they are experiencing are so much worse than causes for which I have worked in the past that I just feel worse. There are millions of people for whom there seems to be no hope. In the past there always seemed to be hope. I think I also cry because the situation seems so hopeless to my friends that they choose to close their eyes and ears rather than try to help. It overwhelms them and therefore they don't want to think about it. I probably get a little angry with them when they want to change the subject."

"I believe the thing about Rwanda which makes me feel so bad is that I see these pictures on TV and in the newspapers and they just break my heart. I read of the numbers of people submitted to atrocities and it just overwhelms me. When I think of Rwandans, I think of individuals. Maybe it is a mother whose children have been grabbed away from her and she sees her child butchered. Maybe she has seen the same thing happen to her husband. If this were happening in England our entire country would be mourning but since it is happening in Africa it seems far away to us. My husband and I traveled to Africa many times. We got to know these people. And they are people, real people. They have hopes and fears like the rest of us. I weep for these people."

"I don't go around with a cloud hanging over my head all the time. But I am not happy. I don't see how I can be happy when I think of the Rwandans. Let me ask you a question. When you see a patient who is very sad, say a patient with severe depression, don't you think of that patient after she leaves your office? I have some friends who are counselors. I know that they have to leave their work at the office like everyone else. They see so many people struggling emotionally that if they took it all to heart they would become very depressed themselves. But can you guys just turn it off? I could never turn it off."

After further questioning and examination, the psychiatrist was convinced that Rebecca met criteria for a major depression. He decided to run a test, the dexamethasone suppression test, to determine if her neuroendocrine function was normal. The results confirmed that her regulation of cortisol was abnormal.[16] Dexamethasone is a synthetic steroid; if a tablet is given to the body, the body identifies the dexamethasone as cortisol. Then the body turns off its own production of cortisol. If the body's regulation of cortisol is not working properly, the body continues to produce cortisol. An abnormal dexamethasone suppression test documents that the body continues to make cortisol. It cannot shut off production of cortisol, and this inability can be a marker that the body, when depressed, cannot turn off its stress response.

The psychiatrist further decided to perform an overnight sleep study and discovered that Rebecca experienced one of the typical findings among people who are depressed, namely, that the first episode of dream sleep during the night occurred more quickly than expected; that is, a shortened rapid eye movement latency.[17] When people are depressed, their normal sleep cycle is disrupted. Though neither of these tests is diagnostic for major depression, the psychiatrist wished to gather evidence that Rebecca's depression was biological. He then prescribed a sedating antidepressant, nefazodone. Rebecca returned in 4 weeks and reported that she was sleeping better and did not feel as emotional. The nurses at the retirement community reported that she was better. Yet she emphasized to the psychiatrist that she continued to "feel for the Rwandans. That is never going to change. I hurt for them. I am just an emotional person."

Emotion, a Link between Body and Society

Emotion provides a unique conceptual link between the body and brain and society. As I noted previously, depression is an emotion. To the psychiatrist, *feeling* is a positive or negative reaction to an experience and is usually contrasted with thought (p. 222).[18] Feelings of interest to psychiatrists are usually divided into mood and affect. The term *affect* is used to describe differentiated specific and transient feelings directed toward objects. Sylvan Tompkins defined *affect* as "sets of muscular and glandular responses located in the face and also widely distributed throughout the body, which generate sensory feedback that is either inherently 'acceptable' or 'unacceptable' " (p. 142).[19] *Mood* is a more prolonged and prevailing feeling state or disposition. *Emotion* is often used to describe the physiological and psychosomatic concomitants of mood, yet the common use of *emotion* usually encompasses affect and mood. For example, a person whose affect changes frequently is considered "emotional." The person who is persistently depressed experiences a disorder of emotion. There is an enormous range across what could reasonably be called "normal emotion." Yet abnormal emotions, if witnessed in the extreme, are easily recognized. A severely depressed man is noticeable to all around him.

Some suggest that individual emotions range along a continuum, as points fall within a bipolar space in which one dimension captures pleasure-displeasure and another captures the level of arousal.[20, 21] A second model suggests that emotions are not continuous or seamless but rather discrete events. The usual emotions included in lists of discrete basic emotions are anger, fear, joy, pleasure, frustration, and sadness.[21, 22] Some of these basic emotions, though they can appear quite close in terms of pleasure-displeasure and level of arousal, lead to very different behaviors. For example, anger can lead a person to fight, whereas fear can cause a person to retreat. Psychiatrists generally favor a more discrete view of the emotions. Mood (or emotional) disorders include abnormal expressions of discrete emotions, such as sadness (major depression), fear (panic disorder), and happiness (bipolar disorder).

Emotion is traditionally thought to arise from a diathesis; that is, a constitutional disposition or predisposition. This constitutional disposition forms the tendency to develop an emotion, but psychosocial factors are associated with the type, quality, direction, expression, and interpretation of emotion. Even as emotion arises from a diathesis, however, it is inherently social. Our feelings are very much affected by those around us. They are also observable and understandable to other people—signaling a nonverbal message (such as facial expressions). Not only is emotion observed by others, it is empathically evaluated. Emotion arises from the body and from the sociocultural context.

Charles Darwin proposed an evolutionary theory of emotion. Emotion is adaptive (yet at times can be disruptive) and is universal across cultures.[7, 23, 24] Emotions are expressed (Darwin emphasized facial expressions). The expressions of emotions are natural, precultural facts (even across species).[2] William James expanded the view that emotions arise from the body.[1, 25] He went so far as to suggest that bodily components of emotion can occur without reaching the threshold of consciousness. The emotions that are felt, that is, reach consciousness, are no less derivative from the body. Feelings are a kind of perception of our own bodily state. Feelings might even be considered epiphenomena. In other words, we do not smile because we are happy, we are happy because we smile. Theories of the biological origins of depression fit nicely into James's view.

To fully understand emotion, however, we need to understand feelings from the perspective of their connections with the social and historical context in which they emerge.[26] With this understanding, emotion provides a link that permits one to overcome the profound division between the biological and the social without denying the division. It is through bodies that people feel and act in society. Human society is the ground from which emotions of individuals within that society arise (though we tend to think of emotions as interior to the individual).

Emotion is necessary for human social capacity.[27] Social capacity is essential to the formation of strong relational bonds.[28] Emotion is critical to logical and rational function, as Antonio Damasio has so effectively argued in recent years.[27] Emotion has a role in organizing actions.[27] (In this discussion I purposefully bracket consciousness and thought so I can more clearly describe the link between body and society through emotion. Even so, reference to the mind cannot be totally abolished.)

Emotions move us, but they do so by virtue of the social situations in which we find ourselves. Emotion provides the link between the body and the social world.[26] In addition, to understand the role of emotion in the mediation of social relationships, we must conceptualize that role through the body. In other words, emotion is an aspect of our being in the world, as suggested by Sartre.[29]

Catherine Lutz provided a theory and examples of emotion as aspects of cultural meaning systems people use in attempting to understand the situations in which they find themselves.[2] In other words, emotions are socially negotiated. The social context surrounding the person, a context that gives meaning to feeling and behavior, provides criteria for judging one's own emotions and the emotions of others. She distinguished four ways by which cultural context provides meaning to an emotional distress such as depression. First, we can expect to find knowledge in every society that attempts to explain what constitutes behavioral deviance, and the proper responses to it (i.e., therapies). For example, the appropriate and inappropriate expressions of grief are determined by society.

Second, stances taken by society define what is knowable, how it is known, and what is ultimately real. For example, the extent to which a person feels guilt and can express that guilt in large part is socially determined. Third, natural responses to various kinds of recurrent life events, such as frustration, aloneness, and helplessness, are assumed in all societies. Finally, each society defines in some ways the conscious characteristics and forms of these responses.

The Chinese, for example, view feelings as private and embarrassing events that are best not explored.[2] A Western approach to disturbing feelings typically encourages gaining additional psychological insight through exploration of one's feelings. In contrast, the Chinese often resist such intrapsychic explorations of feelings and their expression, for such intraindividual explorations could lead to more serious problems, such as limited social insights. A lack of understanding of what is acceptable in Chinese society places the individual at a distinct disadvantage. The American's "psychological insight" is the Chinese's "self-absorption." The question, "What is she *really* feeling?" is based on the assumption that ultimate psychosocial reality is internal, an assumption antithetical to the Chinese way of thinking.

The distinction between thought and emotion is central to Western psychological theory,[2] parallel to the distinction between mind and body (though this latter distinction is now being challenged).[27, 30] We make the distinction between emotional (or mood) disorders, such as major depression, and thought disorders, such as schizophrenia. In addition, primacy is given to the physiological basis of emotion. As I note throughout this book, depression is conceived as a body-brain problem. Not only does such a view derive from a medical orientation, it derives from the very basis of Western thought. For example, emotion is seen as something requiring control. Emotions come in "waves" (p. 79).[2] Emotions, such as depression, "happen" to the person. For this reason, emotions contrast with thoughts as irrationality does with rationality.

Lutz contrasted Western views of emotion with those of the Ifaluk, a tightly bound community living on an island in the South Pacific (pp. 86, 87).[2] Though the Ifaluk speak daily about their feelings, they do not portray themselves as battling unruly emotions. Rather they view themselves as basically undivided internally. Thoughts are not separate from emotions. In addition, the expression of emotion is almost invariably related to their connection with other people. Emotions can emerge in response to a loss of a valued object to another person, yet they are subsumed to the legitimate drain on one's personal resources in the service of the community. For example, the emotion *nguch* (sick and tired or bored) can arise when someone is continually pestered by requests for cigarettes, yet the request cannot be denied. Overall, one's state of emotional and physical well-being is dependent on others. Individual Ifaluk respond with individual emotions to social events, yet the Ifaluk culture shapes the response of the expressed emotion. To go further, Ifaluk culture predisposes individuals on the island to prescribed and proscribed emotional reactions given the social situation.

Do the Ifaluk experience depression? Marsella argued that depression is a disorder associated with cultures that tend to "psychologize" experience (p. 350).[31] In these instances, experiential states become labeled and interpreted psychologically, and this adds the components of depressed mood, guilt, self-depreciation, and suicidal ideation. At this level, the experience of depression assumes a meaning that is clearly different from that associated with a purely somatic experience of the problem. The Ifaluk do not psychologize depression. They feel emotional distress, and they socialize that distress.

Ronald de Sousa proposed that, of all the aspects of what we call the "mind," emotions are the most deeply embodied.[24] He suggested a contextualist theory of emotion. His basic thesis is that psychological states are not all in the person. Persons are not all in the skin. For one, only in a social context can feelings be named and talked about. (Hardly anyone would fall in love if they had not read about it.) One piece of evidence in support of a contextualist view is that a shift in frame can dramatically alter the character of an emotion. For example, the emotions elicited by a practical joke dissipate rapidly when we learn that it in fact is a practical joke. Emotions are a kind of perception, their roots in the paradigm scenarios in which they are learned give them an essentially dramatic structure. They can play a crucial role in rational beliefs, desires, and decisions by breaking the deadlocks of pure reason. Emotions control and shape reason, and they must be controlled.[27]

If emotions, specifically the emotion of depression, link the body and brain with the social environment, what are the mechanisms by which this linkage occurs? Investigators have proposed many theories.[4, 13, 14, 32, 33] I review two social phenomena that are known to affect the organism physiologically and that have been associated with depression. Social zeitgebers are of interest because, in theory, these environmental cues combine elements of the physical and social environment.[13] When disrupted, the body reacts physically. Allostatic load is of interest because through allostasis the organism simultaneously adapts to a stressful environment and becomes at risk for physical and psychiatric problems.

Social Zeitgebers

One of the more established theories among the biological theories of mood disorders explains the association between depression and biological rhythms.

Biological rhythms are inherent in nature and span a spectrum of periodicities from the almost instantaneous fluctuations of the electroencephalogram to multiyear cycles in the populations of predators and their prey.[34] These rhythms include the sleep-wake cycle, daily fluctuations in temperature, fluctuations in activity and inactivity through the day, and cycling of hormones such as cortisol and melatonin.[35] Biological rhythms are closely tied to the environment of the organism. For example, the sleep-wake cycle is tied to the 24-hour day. Among hibernating animals, the onset of winter leads to preparation for and eventual entry into hibernation.

Biological rhythms are not simply passive responses to cyclic changes in the external environment but rather are generated by endogenous processes.[34] For example, the intrinsic circadian, that is "about daily," period for humans is slightly longer than 24 hours. The circadian timekeeping system free runs at about 25 hours. In a normal environment, however, the circadian system responds to external stimuli that serve as time cues, or zeitgebers. Biological rhythm researchers have long observed the capacity of these external forces to set biological clocks and thus synchronize body rhythms. Zeitgebers serve to entrain the circadian timekeeping system to the solar 24-hour cycle.[36] Entrainment refers to the coupling between the timing of a biological rhythm and its external zeitgeber; that is, the adjustment of the internal clock to the external environment. Physical, psychological, and social factors can act as zeitgebers.[37]

Biological rhythms are of interest to psychiatry because psychiatrists continually search for those biological vulnerabilities that increase the propensity for depression. Sleep disturbance and diurnal variation are characteristic symptoms of major depression. (Diurnal variation refers to the observation that depressed patients often feel worse in the mornings and gradually feel better as the day progresses, in contrast to most people.) Biological changes, such as sleep abnormalities, can even precede the reporting of symptoms associated with the onset of depression.[13] In addition, those who travel across many time zones, such as to Asia from the United States, experience physical discomforts similar to some of the symptoms of depression, such as disruption of their normal sleep, lethargy, and difficulty concentrating, until adjustment is made to the new light-dark cycle.

Biological rhythms that have been associated with depression include daily, weekly, and seasonal rhythms.[36, 38, 39] Not only is the daily sleep cycle disturbed, depression can increase at certain times of the week, such as midway through the workweek, and emerge during certain times of the year, as with seasonal mood disorders. One possible mechanism in seasonal affective disorder is mood variability, a relatively stable characteristic of individuals.[40, 41] Mood variability is linked to emotional reactivity.[42] People with greater mood variability can be more emotionally responsive to external photic (light-oriented) zeitgebers. Persons with a tendency to seasonality can have more mood variability. Work and recreation can serve to entrain circadian rhythms. The calendar week can as well. Periodicity appears to build into mood through the week (7-day mood cycles).[39] People high in seasonality also appear to be more sensitive to external zeitgebers, and this could be linked to their greater variability in mood. Sensitive people follow a traditional mid-week-low, weekend-high pattern.

In humans, social contacts and environment also exert a substantial influence on the synchronization of circadian rhythms.[13, 43] Social zeitgebers are those personal relationships, social demands, or tasks that serve to entrain biological rhythms. For example, sleeping with a partner for many years will entrain the sleep cycle.[44] In addition, these nonphotic social zeitgebers that derive from family and occupational roles set the temporal framework for daily activity and also help to entrain circadian rhythms to the 24-hour solar day. These events collectively create an individual's social rhythms.

Timothy Monk and colleagues developed the *Social Rhythm Metric* to assess social zeitgebers.[45] Eighteen items, such as "Get out of bed," "Have breakfast," "Physical exercise," "Watch evening TV news program," and "Go to bed" are included. The investigator asks the participant to note the time of day that he or she engages in these activities during the 5-day workweek. For each activity, the participant identifies which people are involved in the activity (such as spouse, children, and friends). Higher scores are accorded to participants who engage in more regular activities that are associated with social contacts.

Major life events can act as specific precipitants by disrupting biological rhythms and increasing emotional distress and thus directly precipitate the biomedical features of major depression and cause psychological pain or stress. Cindy Ehlers suggested that, when a couple lives together, each person tends to synchronize his or her rhythms to the partner's (mealtimes, sleeping times, times of activity and rest).[13] At separation from a partner, important social zeitgebers can be lost that affect biological rhythms. In one study, more than half of a group of women going through divorce proceedings showed shortened rapid eye movement latency during sleep (suggesting a disruption of the normal sleep cycle) and had clinical evidence of depression.[46] Feather and Bond suggested that disintegration of a person's arrangement of time, that is, regularity of schedule, might be a sign that depression is emerging.[47]

Social rhythms can especially be disrupted by negative life events such as bereavement. Widowhood, for example, has been conceptualized as a time disturber or zeitstorer, an event that disrupts the entrainment of circadian timekeeping systems. If widowhood and other events, such as job loss, retirement, or parenthood, are zeitstorers, the preservation of normal social rhythms could serve to buffer, or protect, individuals from the development of depressive symptoms and presage a successful adaptation to changes in life rhythms.[48] Yet the rhythm disturbances might lead only to clinically significant depressive symptoms in people who are vulnerable or who experience the most severe symptoms. In other words, depression can lead to social rhythm disturbances, and rhythm disturbances can lead to depression.

Brown and colleagues[44] found, in a cross-sectional study of older people, that spousal bereavement per se was not associated with a lower social rhythm stability (i.e., maintenance of usual social activities at the usual times of the day and week) or activity level except in the presence of a major depressive episode. The emotional disturbance had to be severe enough to meet criteria for major depression for social rhythms to be disrupted. Severe depression was inversely correlated with social rhythm stability and positively correlated with subjective and objective measures of sleep impairment. Higher social rhythm stability was correlated with better sleep in individuals with high activity levels but not in individuals with lower activity levels. A low activity level can be a precursor to social rhythm instability[49] that in turn leads to depression.[50]

Ehlers suggested the following model.[13] Stressful and disruptive life events lead to changes in the social prompts for the individual (social zeitgebers). The loss of social prompts, in turn, leads to changes in the stability of social rhythms (such as regular sleep and regular social activity). The decreasing stability of social rhythms, in turn, leads to a disruption of biological rhythms. Changes in biological rhythms lead to somatic symptoms that increase the vulnerability of people who are biologically vulnerable to depression, such as people with a hereditary predisposition to depression. The outcome is major depression. The model can be reversed. The symptoms of major depression, such as sleep disturbance, can lead to changes in social rhythms, and these changes in social rhythms can disrupt social relationships. Regardless, in this model, biological and social factors work in concert to lead to depression, and they clearly interact.

Allostatic Load

Homeostasis is an organism's need to maintain a steady internal state.[15] For example, body temperature must be kept within a narrow range. If our body temperature rises to 101 degrees Fahrenheit, we have a good reason to stay in bed. If our body temperature drops to 94 degrees Fahrenheit, we experience a severe problem with hypothermia. Yet we live in a world of change, and our bodies must adapt to those changes. For this reason, many of the body's systems operate over a much broader range than temperature, such as the blood concentration of many hormones.

Bruce McEwen introduced the term *allostasis* to describe those systems of the body that range widely to assist the body in maintaining constancy of function in the face of an ever-changing, stressful environment.[14, 15] In other words, allostatic systems help keep the body stable because they are able to change (e.g., changes in body temperature). He described allostasis as a swift and intricately organized system of communication that links the brain, endocrine system, and immune system for defense against physical and psychosocial stressors. For McEwen, *stressors* and *stress* are synonymous in that they are external to the body (unlike the use of *stress* in physics where the term describes the response of an object to external stressors).

One such defense, for example, is increased production of cortisol. Cortisol is a hormone that assists the body in the fight-or-flight syndrome by increasing the availability of glucose, among other actions, to produce energy. Yet many environmental stimuli that ignite the body's response to stress do not call for either fight or flight. Therefore the system built into us to protect us against stress can cause wear and tear instead. For example, prolonged elevation of cortisol inhibits neurogenesis, therefore volume of the hippocampus in the brain shrinks.[51] In addition, prolonged elevation of cortisol is associated with symptoms of depression.[16]

Frans Holsboer noted that, in response to a stressor, the hypothalamic-pituitary-adrenal system is activated, and during a major depressive episode hypothalamic-pituitary-adrenal regulation is usually impaired.[32] In people with major depression, the ability of elevated circulating cortisol levels to curtail their own overactivity through negative feedback is impaired (perhaps through a disturbed corticosteriod receptor function leading to inappropriate suppression of corticotropin and vasopressin in the hypothalamus).[16] When these neuropeptides are secreted into the blood, the result is excessive corticotropin and subsequently cortisol release. Corticotropin also coordinates several behavioral adaptations, such as decreases in deep sleep (slow-wave sleep), appetite, and sexual drive, and increased anxiety.

Depression can be viewed as an adaptive response that is not as adaptable today as in the past. Depression can therefore be protective, yet in its more severe forms it can be toxic to the organism.[52] That major depression is an adaptation gone awry is an idea with a long history. Charles Darwin proposed that pain or suffering of any kind, if persistent, caused depression and lessened the power of action. Even so, depression is well adapted to assist the organism in withdrawal from unexpected stressors.[53] Randolph Nesse asked the question, "Is depression an adaptation, an adaptation gone awry, or a pathological state unrelated to any function?"[7] Clinicians who believe it to be an adaptation can spend years trying to help a patient understand its significance, whereas other clinicians, convinced that it is maladaptive, actively discourage such inquiry. Investigators of Nesse's question must distinguish severe depression from low mood (or mild depression) because low mood might be adaptive. It is difficult to conceive, however, an adaptive function of a severe depression. Yet a mild depression can be of benefit. For example, Celia Hybels and colleagues found that mild depression was associated with increased longevity among women in a controlled study of older adults.[52]

One argument for depression as an adaptation is that it is so common.[7, 54] For example, given the frequency of fevers, even though we usually treat fevers with aspirin, we assume that the fever is signaling either an internal disequilibrium or, more likely, an external infectious agent. In other words, we become feverish for a reason. Given the frequency of depression, should we not assume that the depression is signaling that the organism is stressed? Simultaneous increased secretion of cortisol and the expression of depressive symptoms might reflect depression as a signal of stress and an initial response to the stress.[51]

In addition, there is no clear point in most studies at which pathologic depression can be differentiated from nonpathologic depression, just as there is no clear point at which an adaptive fever can be distinguished from a maladaptive fever.[55] The depressed move from subthreshold to threshold depression and back again easily through time.[56] Mild depression can initially be adaptive, yet becomes maladaptive if it becomes severe, even though the mechanisms that precipitate the depression can be identical.

In what ways can depression be adaptive? Infants appear to have the capacity to arouse pity in and elicit support from others, but there are few data to support this function among adults. Reactions to adult patients with chronic depression are mainly negative.[57–59] George Engel employed the phrase "conservation-withdrawal" to refer to the presumed utility of the "despair" phase of the behavior pattern exhibited by a lost infant monkey.[60] Yet depression, unlike hibernation, is rarely a state of calm conservation.[61] Among some primates, however, depression can have utility as a yielding signal in hierarchy conflicts. It is a signal to the dominant animal that the subordinate animal is no longer a threat.[62]

Of interest, Archana Singh-Manoux and colleagues found that lower subjective social status was associated with a self-rated symptoms scale of depression.[63] The participants in the study were given a drawing of a ladder and asked to "think of this ladder as representing where people stand in society. At the top of the ladder are people who are best off—those who have the most money, most education and better jobs. ... Where would you put yourself on the ladder?" Even when adjusted for employment grade, education, and income, those who perceived their status to be lower were more likely to be depressed. Such a study contains inherent biases, for the depressed can view themselves of lower status because of a poor self-esteem. Nevertheless, as I describe next, the depressed often view themselves more accurately than the nondepressed do.

Investigators have proposed many animal models and tested them for depression as a response to environmental stress.[64] The chronic mild stress model is generated by applications of different unpredictable stressful conditions, such as mild uncontrollable foot shock, food and water deprivation, and so forth. After exposure to these stressors for 2 to 3 weeks, rats show a number of behavioral changes that are maintained for months and are reminiscent of depressive symptoms.[65] The behavioral deficit seen includes anhedonia. In other words, an initial adaptive response becomes maladaptive. Long-term treatment with various antidepressants in this study led to a return to initial levels of food intake. The rats also exhibited sleep disturbance.

Another model is early life stressors. For example, the hypothalamic-pituitary-adrenal axis in rats handled as newborns is better able to shut off stress-elicited corticosterone excess.[64] Myron Hofer showed that the process of mother-infant attachment involves several independent physiological processes in which the mother serves as a "hidden regulator" for the infant.[66] Models of early separation have shown infant monkeys to respond to maternal separation with agitation, sleep disturbances, and screaming.[67] After 1 or 2 days, they become despaired.

Depression is common in people who are pursuing unreachable goals, and it can serve as a reassessment to abandon those goals or even an escape from the situation. The extreme form of escape is suicide.[7, 68] David Hamburg suggested,

> When the subject estimates the probability of effective action is low ... the depressive responses can be viewed as adaptive. ... Feelings of sadness and discouragement may be useful stimuli to consider ways of changing [the] situation. ... Moreover, [the] state of sadness may elicit heightened interest and sympathetic consideration on the part of significant other people. (p. 240)[69]

Low mood might help people to disengage from pursuing a goal that is perceived to be unattainable. Low mood might also suggest alternative strategies when the distance from the goal does not reduce at a fast enough pace.[70] The extant literature supports this idea. Individuals' pursuit of large goals requires their constructing expensive social enterprises that are difficult to reverse—marriages, friendships, careers, reputation, status, and group membership. Major setbacks in these enterprises precipitate life crises. Depression can therefore be adaptive, to decrease investment in the current unsatisfying life enterprise and also to prevent the premature pursuit of alternatives. Failure to disengage can cause depression, and depression can make it harder to disengage (leading to negative feedback loops). In addition, the costs of low mood can be small compared with those of inappropriate high mood (which might not read a situation accurately).

Life events research has moved steadily from lists of events to examination of the individuals in context of the event.[71, 72] This perspective predicts that social factors should influence rates of depression. Depression should be more common in cultures with rigid hierarchies and in those in which life enterprises tend to be huge, vulnerable, and irreplaceable.[73] Media exposure should increase depression, not just by fostering negative social comparisons but also by motivating the pursuit of unreachable goals. Cross-cultural studies confirm that subjective well-being is higher in societies with greater income equality[74] and also that increased rates of depression occur in developed societies.[75]

Yet another theory of depression suggesting that normal adaptive processes can become maladaptive is the learned helplessness theory. Martin Seligman developed the concept of learned helplessness.[76] He concluded that helplessness was a disaster for organisms capable of learning that they are helpless and that the motivation to respond is sapped, the ability to perceive success is undermined, and emotionality is heightened. Organisms, when exposed to uncontrollable events, learn that responding is futile. The fear of an organism faced with trauma is reduced if it learns that responding controls trauma. Fear persists if the organism remains uncertain about whether the trauma is uncontrollable. If the organism learns that trauma cannot be controlled, fear gives way to depression. What produces self-esteem and a sense of competence, and protects against depression, is not only the absolute quality of an experience but also the perception that one's own actions control the experience. To the degree that uncontrollable events occur, either traumatic or positive, depression will be predisposed.

In summary, investigators have proposed two models that link the social environment to physiological correlates of depression—social zeitgebers and allostatic load. Both of these models enable emotion, specifically the emotion of depression, to link society and biology. Of course, both models also provide evidence for the direct impact of biological disequilibrium on emotion. We might imagine an internal negative feedback system that sustains the depressed mood once the process is precipitated by a stressful social environment.

The linkage, however, does not discredit the separate research of emotion from the biological and sociocultural perspectives. These separate investigations must continue, psychiatrists should be familiar with both, and potential links that arise should be explored.

11

The Problem with Soma

Beneto was notoriously good-natured. People said of him that he could have got through life without ever touching soma. [Beneto says to Bernard], 'you do look glum! What you need is a gramme of soma.'

—Aldous Huxley, *Brave New World* (p. 40)[1]

As we have stepped over the threshold of the 21st century, we ask, What is the problem with psychiatry? Psychiatry confronts many problems, yet most of these problems are not as severe as some of psychiatry's critics imply. Psychiatry is not so paralyzed, conflicted, or impotent to be in imminent danger of disappearing or self-destructing. For example, psychiatry is not inventing diseases to treat with its diagnostic classification system, as suggested by Allan Horwitz in *Creating Mental Illness*.[2] The people psychiatrists see in their clinics, by and large, experience significant and severe emotional suffering or behavioral dysfunction. Despite the expansion of the nomenclature, psychiatrists are not treating the worried well.

Psychiatry is not stranded on the rocks of empiricism, in danger of losing its mind as it discovers the brain.[3] I do believe psychiatry has lost some of its soul, for psychiatrists all too often consider their patients through the narrow lens of operational diagnoses, rating scales, brain images, and pills. I have written on this topic previously in *Freud vs. God: How Psychiatry Lost Its Soul and Christianity Lost Its Mind*, a critique of the strange accommodating relationship between psychiatry and religion, a relationship that, from both sides, somehow misses the essence of human suffering.[4] Yet I am hopeful that the natural human impulses of psychiatrists will prevent us from becoming automatons, functioning like computers in collecting diagnostic information and prescribing therapies. After all, we cannot maintain human contact (even if that contact continues a few minutes rather than the 50-minute hour) and shield ourselves from empathy with our patients. We cannot interact with our patients while at the same time ignoring our own feelings, feelings that connect with the feelings of our depressed patients. At the least, our patients will insist that we be empathic and that we meet them person-to-person, or they will seek their care elsewhere.

Psychiatry is not toxic, necessitating the replacement of virtually all drugs and other biomedical therapies with psychotherapy, empathy, and love, as proposed by Peter Breggin.[5] The drugs we prescribe today are by and large safe and efficacious. Some drugs are undoubtedly overprescribed. Some people are treated with biological therapies who would be better treated by other therapies. Even so, we are not poisoning our patients. Pharmacotherapy, in and of itself, is not the problem with psychiatry. The way we use pharmacotherapy however, as I discuss next, might reflect the problem with psychiatry.

Psychiatry is not practicing false science, as Colin Ross and Alvin Pam accuse in their book *Pseudoscience in Biological Psychiatry*.[6] The neurobiology of psychiatric disorders is being advanced daily. We are truly unraveling the mysteries of mental illness. I have no doubt that the genetic revolution will pay significant dividends to psychiatry. New and improved biological therapies coupled with enhanced means of matching therapies with patients can only improve the care we deliver to our patients. Trade-offs will be necessary, for the cost of new therapies will eat into an overall expenditure for health care that cannot continue to increase unchecked. Psychiatry, however, is not unique among the medical specialties in confronting tough choices as we seek to provide not only effective but cost-effective care. So what is the problem?

The problem with psychiatry today, in my view, is that psychiatrists have lost their sociological imagination and concern.[7] This problem is of such consequence that I believe psychiatry is once again facing an intrinsic crisis (some would say psychiatry is perpetually facing a crisis). Yet psychiatrists do not feel this intrinsic crisis. The current problems with psychiatry have been almost totally projected outward onto managed care, cuts in federal and state support of mental health services, federal cutbacks in research and training dollars, and a lack of respect from our medical colleagues and our patients. Each of these external challenges to our specialty is very real. Even so, psychiatry is numbed to the intrinsic problem, similar to the problem Aldous Huxley described with *soma* in *Brave New World*.[1] The problem with soma, put simply, was that it numbed Huxley's fictional society to its social problems. We have become numbed to the social context from which mental illness (especially depression) emerges, and we have become numbed to those social forces that shape our specialty. The loss of this sociological imagination is my greatest concern for psychiatry in the 21st century.

Why are we numbed to the social forces around us? We practice in our hospital wards and clinics, rarely stepping outside these walls in our practice. The small worlds in which we individually live might be, for a time, relatively protected from the larger social forces at work. In addition, we shield ourselves from society's problems by soothing our natural responses to those problems. Huxley wrote about this type of shielding in *Brave New World*.[1] Unlike George Orwell's dystopian novel *Nineteen Eighty-Four*,[8] the characters in *Brave New World* are mostly happy and content. Soma facilitated their content. Soma presented a problem, however. We can learn a critical lesson from the problem with soma.

A CASE IN POINT

What is the problem with aspirin? Aspirin is one of the most frequently prescribed and purchased over-the-counter drugs. We are prescribed aspirin and we buy aspirin because aspirin relieves pain and lowers uncomfortable fevers. Aspirin is not without side effects, such as stomach distress and even gastrointestinal bleeding. Nevertheless, we have found aspirin (and its cousins) useful for maintaining our function. For example, if I experience a pain in my knee, I quite likely will take a couple of aspirin. After a few days, when the pain is better, I stop taking the aspirin.

Even though I take aspirin for the pain in my knee, I do not ascribe my knee pain to aspirin deficiency. I experience knee pain because I jog too many miles on a knee that I have been told has only so many "lifetime miles," sort of like an automobile tire. Even in the best of circumstances, I cannot expect a tire to last forever. If I abuse the tire, then its life is certainly shortened and I might experience a blowout or puncture at any time. This is exactly what an orthopedic surgeon told me about 20 years ago. I had begun training to run a marathon, and I kept experiencing knee pain about every 2 weeks. The surgeon said, "Dan, you have only so many jogging miles in that knee. If you keep jogging 30 miles a week on that knee, you are not going to be able to walk on it at the age of 65. In addition, you are never going to run a marathon. The structure of your knee just doesn't permit you to run that distance. If you want to avoid knee pain, I have a simple answer. Cut down on how much you run. You can take aspirin and it will help in the short run but it will not give you one more mile of running on that knee." That explanation made sense to me. I stopped training and now jog about 12 miles a week. I rarely experience knee problems. When I do, the aspirin really helps.

If I take aspirin for my knee, what is the problem? The problem is not that aspirin cannot relieve my knee pain (I do get relief from the aspirin). The problem is not the side effects (though I must watch for adverse effects). The problem is that I cover the pain and might ignore the cause of my knee problems by taking aspirin. The problem with my knee is not aspirin deficiency. I have mechanical problems (I was born with them) that prevent me from running marathons. My knee pain, however, is not directly due to the mechanical problems. Most of the time I experience no knee pain. If I stress my knee with too much running, I am going to experience knee pain. If I cover that pain with aspirin and neglect to cut back on my jogging, I face serious problems with my knee in the future.

A major problem with taking aspirin is that I can be lulled into complacency about damage I am doing to my body because I do not feel the pain. A big problem with Prozac is that I feel less depressed by taking the medication but no longer wish to explore the causes of the depression in the first place. If I feel better, I am less inclined to admit stress experienced in the workplace or problems in my marriage. We too often reason that symptom relief is enough. This short-term, downstream approach to knee pain and depression does not make sense in the long run. There is every reason to look for the origin of pain and of depression, even if the discomfort is temporarily relieved. Otherwise the pain or depression will eventually break through the medication. We must attempt to attack problems at their source.

Brave New World

In *Brave New World*, Aldous Huxley described a dysfunctional society in which its members had been numbed to that dysfunction.[1] When other methods to shield society's members to its problems failed, soma was used to blunt the pain. People were happy; they got what they wanted, and they never wanted what they could not get. If anything should go wrong, there was soma. There was a problem with soma, however. The following summary of one exchange reveals the problem one character experienced with soma.

Bernard Marx looked glum (pp. 30–45).[1] And people were beginning to notice. He did not like the fad sport of the day, Obstacle Golf. He was advised to take a holiday from reality. The answer? Soma. A magical drug that brought euphoria, pain relief, and pleasant hallucinations. Or, as another described it, "All the advantages of Christianity and alcohol; none of their defects" (p. 36).[1] Bernard could expect instant relief from his gloom and discomfort. Yet he was not happy, and he resisted soma.

Benito Hoover noticed. "'But I say ... you do look glum! What you need is a gramme of soma.' He took a phial out of his pocket and offered the drug to Bernard. 'One cubic centimetre cures ten gloomy. ...' Bernard turned and rushed away. Benito stared after him in disbelief. 'What can be the matter with the fellow?' What could be wrong with soma?" (p. 40)[1]

Though Bernard never fully appreciated the dysfunction of this dystopian society, another character, the Savage, did. Freedom had been abolished. The natural checks and balances in a society that arise from discontent among the disadvantaged elements, checks and balances that advance a society, had been eliminated. If a member of society, such as Bernard or the Savage, asked, "What is wrong with this picture?" the question was turned back on them: "What is wrong with you?"

What Was the Problem with Soma?

In contrast to the tense and oppressive atmosphere of George Orwell's *Nineteen Eighty-Four*, Huxley's *Brave New World* was bland. That blandness was more suffocating, though less terrifying, than the oppressive tyranny of *Nineteen Eighty-Four*. To maintain stability in society, officials had to condition and control intelligence and imagination. The highs and lows of emotion had to be controlled as well. The social and behavioral conditioning took the edge off most aspects of the society and the feelings of its inhabitants. If residual feelings of discomfort persisted, there was soma.

Huxley took a cue from Bertrand Russell when he created the fictional drug soma.[9] In *Brave New World*, the Director made certain that people were happy. Life lasts only as long as it is pleasant. Russell was very much in favor of a society that placed pleasure first.[10] He suggested, half seriously and half facetiously, the need for a new drug for our emerging new society with the euphoric qualities of alcohol but no tendency to create hangovers. For Russell, however, imagination and individuality were better than drugs to accomplish this purpose. Happiness was less a matter of pleasure than of experiencing one's own vitality. He sought a state in which the conflict between freedom and happiness dissolved.

Huxley, in *Brave New World Revisited*, commented on the need for the new drug in this tightly controlled fictionalized society:

There was no whiskey, no tobacco. Whenever anyone felt depressed or below par, he would swallow a tablet or two of a chemical compound called soma. The original soma, from which I took the name of this hypothetical drug, was an unknown plant used by the ancient Aryan invaders to India in one of the most solemn of their religious rites. The ... juice from the plant was drunk by the priests and nobles. ... The drinkers were blessed in many ways ... their bodies were strengthened, their hearts were filled with courage, joy and enthusiasm, their minds were enlightened and in the immediate experience of eternal life they received the assurance of their immortality. [Ancient soma, however, was a dangerous drug.] The soma of BNW [Brave New World] has none of the dangers. In small doses it brought a sense of bliss, in larger doses it made you see visions and, if you took three tablets, you would sink in a few minutes into refreshing sleep (all with no physiological or mental cost). BNW folks could take holidays from their black moods or from the familiar annoyances of everyday life. (p. 132)[11]

For Huxley, the soma habit was not a private vice but rather a political institution. Even as it promised pursuit of happiness and freedom from concerns, it was at the same time one of the most powerful instruments of rule in the dictator's armory. Providing soma was an insurance against personal maladjustment to the society, social unrest, and the spread of subversive ideas. Religion was not an opium of the people, but opium (soma) was the religion of the people.

Prior to the development of our modern armamentarium, Huxley envisioned that psychotropic drugs were moving toward temporarily altering the chemistry of the brain and the associated state of the mind without doing any permanent damage to the organism as a whole, specifically referencing Miltown and Thorazine.[11] He even believed that the antidepressants would become the most promising of these drugs. Huxley was not totally against psychotropic drugs. Rather he recognized the potential dangers and the potential benefits:

Pharmacology, biochemistry and neurology are on the march, and we can be quite certain that, in the course of the next few years, new and better chemical methods for increasing suggestibility and lowering psychological resistance will be discovered. Like everything else, these discoveries may be used well or badly. They may help the psychiatrist in his battle against mental illness, or they may help the dictator in his battle against freedom. More probably

... they will both enslave and make free, heal and at the same time destroy. (p. 94)[11]

More recently, Walker Percy, in *The Thanatos Syndrome*, expressed some of the same concerns.[12] A small group of people in Louisiana plotted to spike the drinking water with "heavy sodium," for the drug was found to improve morality, calm distress, and reduce the incidence of AIDS, along with many other benefits. The protagonist of the story, a psychiatrist who was a recovering alcoholic, discovered not only the plot but also the moral conflict. Should such a benefit be denied the populace? He personally had witnessed the temporary benefits and permanent problems associated with excessive alcohol use. Given that experience he was suspicious of this new wonder drug. He found in his investigations that the people who had been influenced by the sodium lost their sense of self and purpose. They were living and acting as the "living dead." The drug cured many specific ills but robbed the people of their humanity. The problem with heavy sodium was that it numbed people to real societal problems (in Percy's novel, the real overlooked problem was child abuse).

What Is the Problem with Psychiatry Today?

The problem with soma was not the drug. The problem was the attitude of the controllers of society toward the drug and the attitude of the participants in society toward the drug. As I have noted previously, many have critiqued modern psychiatry because of its overuse of medications, describing a conspiracy between the pharmaceutical industry and modern psychiatrists.[5, 13, 14] These critiques warrant some attention. Psychiatry has experienced nearly 15 lean years economically. The major practical gains in the field (as well as critical financial support) have come from the pharmaceutical industry. Psychiatry and industry are tightly intertwined, though I doubt that the two have conspired in devious ways. Regardless, such critiques beg the issue. Other than pointing fingers toward economic greed, the critics rarely ask the question, "Why is this happening now?" Supporters of biological psychiatry, in turn, rarely consider factors, other than advances in our understanding of the brain, that contribute to the hegemony of our current diagnostic system and the preeminence of medications in our treatment armamentarium.

One problem with psychiatry is that we inordinately feel compelled to name everything we see. Practical reasons abound for such naming. Specifically, we cannot expect to be reimbursed by third-party payers for treating emotional suffering if we do not give it a specific name, a name accepted as designating a specific disease.

In addition, we sound and act much more like physicians if we can name the ailments we treat, as does the surgeon when he or she names an infarcted bowel. Of course, the nuances and complications involved in an infarcted bowel vary with each patient, and the diagnosis usually does not provide a true picture of the problem. Nevertheless, psychiatrists are prone to naming, slicing emotional suffering into as many categories as possible (as we witness in the exploding number of diagnostic categories in the *Diagnostic and Statistical Manual of Mental Disorders* [*DSM*]).[15]

Psychiatry should be more sanguine about the science of establishing psychiatric diagnoses. The science of psychiatric nomenclature is profoundly social, social all the way down because there is no actual bedrock of nature on which to draw our diagnostic distinctions, apart from our consensus on the matter. Such is the nature of operational definitions, as I describe in chapter 2. Our current nomenclature is the product of the practices of our psychiatric research communities, and this product is primarily pragmatic to the society of psychiatrists and their patients.

So what does diagnosis do? At a minimum there are three parties involved in the practice of diagnosis. First, there is a specific patient to whom the diagnosis is applied. Second, there is the mental health professional who assigns the diagnosis. Finally, there is the society in which the process of assigning a diagnosis is embedded. Applying a diagnosis solves several social problems. It can justify an intervention such as hospitalization and therefore place the patient in a setting where treatment can be optimized. The social problem can also be corrected because the person is removed from society. If the person is dangerous to self or others, or both, then assigning a diagnosis can provide safety for the person and society. For the person, it entitles health and social services available in a hospital. For the practitioner the diagnosis alleviates confusion about the behavior. Specific diagnoses also make research easier to conduct and support.

Diagnoses provide an implicit explanation of the behavior, such as a chemical imbalance. By medicalizing the behavior, the person is entitled to the sick role, a positive feature, in part, for it removes personal blame. At times, however, diagnoses can unduly absolve people from personal responsibility. The relegation of people to the sick role by means of diagnoses highlights the social function of diagnoses, both for the practitioner and the person who is diagnosed.

Persons called attention to yet another conceptual pitfall in the process of assigning diagnoses that too often is not recognized.[16] She noted the ubiquity of what she termed "diagnostic category designs" (p. 1253). Diagnostic category designs simply compare samples of patients from one diagnostic category with samples from another category (including controls). For example, a population of individuals with major depression can be compared with a population of healthy controls. Populations who meet criteria for these categories can be readily identified. They can be readily compared. One can test average group differences and perform requisite statistical tests. This design, however, typically leads researchers away from studying specific problem behaviors or symptoms that in the first place led them to place an individual in one or another diagnostic category. For example, the frequency, distribution, and determinants of suicidal thoughts might be ignored. The diagnosis, in effect, trumps the symptoms.

Psychiatrists should not attempt to name everything. In our investigative studies, we should abandon the assumption that there is a specific, widespread disease "major depression" that captures the vast majority of people experiencing disabling depressive symptoms. We should also abandon the assumption that there are multiple, easily identifiable categories of depression into which we can fit all of our patients. Rather we must take an honest, empirical view of our data regarding depressive symptoms.

If we look honestly and carefully, I believe we will find patients, perhaps composing no more than 1% of the population, who suffer from a severe depression and for whom the biological diathesis so overwhelms psychological and social factors that they will experience recurrent severe depressive episodes that easily fit the criteria of major depression regardless of the social context. These patients will respond to biological intervention (if they respond at all) and will not respond to other interventions unless combined with biological intervention during their most severe episodes. Psychological therapies (such as cognitive-behavioral therapy) will assist them in adjusting to their illness and the precipitants of illness episodes. Social interventions, as yet to be discovered, could reduce the stress that could precipitate an episode. Yet these people will periodically experience episodes that can be controlled or prevented only with biological interventions regardless of the psychosocial interventions prescribed. Almost all of these people will seek professional help from some medical or mental health professional.

Empirical studies, I believe, will also reveal people in the community (perhaps composing no more than 1% to 3%) who meet all the criteria for major depression and for whom the stress side of the stress-diathesis model will predominate. Stress-inducing situations, such as a tragic loss, a dysfunctional work environment, or ongoing problems in the neighborhood (such as fear for safety), fuel their depressive symptoms and they will not ultimately benefit from (though they might be temporarily relieved) biological interventions. Even psychotherapy will be of little benefit for these people if it does not assist them in extricating themselves from their stressful social environment. Changing their attitude or their perceptions of the situation will be of little or no long-term benefit unless their changed perceptions in turn change their social milieu. These people might or might not seek mental health services. If they do and if the services cannot assist them in removing the social stressors, they will drop out of therapy or they will be among the chronic treatment failures that populate every psychiatric practice.

Honest empirical studies will also reveal, I believe, many people in the community (10% or more) who meet every symptom criterion for major depression at some time in their lives yet they are functioning adequately. Perhaps an additional 10% will meet criteria for minor depression at some point in their lives and likewise function adequately. These people might continue to exhibit depressive symptoms or the symptoms might remit. Regardless, they will not usually seek psychiatric help (though they are quite likely to be taking an antidepressant medication if prescribed) and by most of our measures they will function in our society. The cause of their depressive symptoms will be primarily psychological and social. Biologic interventions will lead to subjective relief of symptoms at times, yet the mechanisms by which symptom relief occurs might not be clear. For example, these people might be among those who experience a significant response to placebo as well.[17–19]

Only a minority of these people will accept psychosocial interventions, for they have found ways to cope with their mood or the situation in which they find themselves. For some, their dysphoric mood does not appear abnormal to them. Stanley Jacobson described such older adults who psychiatrists might be too hasty to label as diseased:

> The authors … want to apply their medical interpretations and their pharmacological treatment across the board, beyond the so-called clinically depressed … to those who are unhappy without apparent reason, the theory being that "these conditions [i.e., minor depressions] negatively affect quality of life and are associated with increased risk of comorbid medical illness and clinical depression." … [On the other hand], a depressive reaction to life experience is one thing, and vulnerability to a diagnosable disease called depression is another … [consider] depression as a personality trait, a tendency to experience feelings which varies in strength from person to person. The disposition is not pathological but a normally distributed, stable personality trait that neither increases nor declines with age. (p. 50)[20]

We will also find people in the community who are mildly dysphoric for no apparent psychosocial reason. They generally function reasonably well, yet the quality of their lives is not good. The cause of their dysphoric mood is biological, though they might never meet criteria for major depression. They might respond to antidepressant medications, and they might even respond beyond what could normally be expected. Peter Kramer in *Listening to Prozac* described these people in some detail:

> *I have seen patient after patient become ... "better than well." Prozac seemed to give social confidence to the habitually timid, to make the sensitive brash, to lend the introvert the social skills of a salesman. Prozac was transformative for patients in a way an inspirational minister or high-pressured group therapy can be—it made them want to talk about their experience. ... They had learned something about themselves from Prozac. ... I call this phenomenon "listening to Prozac." (p. xv)[21]*

Perhaps we could continue ad infinitum describing different expressions of depression, their probable causes, and their responses to treatment. Yet few of these descriptions lend themselves easily to being named. In other words, they can be portrayed but they cannot be categorized. The boundaries across these groups are fuzzy, and they can, over the course of their lives, move from one fuzzy grouping to another.[22] We attempt to fit these people into existing criteria, or we modify and even develop new names for syndromes to accommodate these variants. Such force fitting, however, stifles the objective study of the range of depressive symptoms and their nuances.

Psychiatry cannot abandon its diagnostic system, but it can constrain it. For many reasons, practicing psychiatrists must categorize the patients they treat. Even so, psychiatrists must refrain from adding one diagnosis after another to the nomenclature. Minor or subsyndromal depression provides an excellent example to watch as the *DSM–V* is developed. Criteria for making the diagnosis are currently found in the appendix of the *DSM–IV*.[15] Will the diagnosis make it into the *DSM–V* as a full participant? Probably. Yet the *DSM–IV* operational diagnosis for minor depression is one among many.[23–27]

Few data have emerged to favor one operational diagnosis of minor depression over another, though many investigators recognize the importance of further study of depressive symptoms that can lead to disability yet do not meet criteria for major depression or dysthymic disorder.[24, 28] If possible, the *DSM–V* authors should accumulate and analyze data from multiple sources to establish that a collection of symptom criteria actually hold together such that a diagnosis of minor depression is warranted. The late Sam Guze, one of the pioneers of the remedicalization of psychiatry and author of the diagnostic categories that were the foundation of DSM–III,[29] once told me that he believed we had reasonable data to justify no more than about 17 psychiatric diagnoses, not the hundreds found in the DSM–IV. I suspect he would not be in favor of adding yet another such diagnosis without sound empirical evidence.

In addition, the assignment of a diagnostic category must not constrain the nuances of emotional suffering for the practicing clinician. For years, those trained in psychiatry were taught to focus on the formulation of the psychiatric dis-ease in our patients. In this narrative, we described the symptoms and their context, including precipitants of symptoms and predisposing factors, such as childhood experiences that shape adult behavior. As diagnosis has become more central, the formulation has faded to the background in the assessment of the psychiatric patient. This fading has, I believe, adversely influenced the care of patients by psychiatrists. When we lose our flexibility, we lose our depth perception of the suffering that we witness.

Our nomenclature should not shape the empirical investigations of research-ers. We should view these diagnostic categories as hypotheses that continually must be tested. We must search for new statistical methods for analyzing our data to test these methods. Cluster and factor analytic procedures applied through time can inform our current understanding of depression and its vicissitudes.[30] A focus on specific symptoms (such as sleep disturbance) or small clusters of symptoms (such as the melancholic symptoms of depression) with the use of cluster and factor ana-lytic studies should assist investigators to focus on manageable spectra for future studies. Our propensity for splitting has in part lead to our fascination with comor-bidity. *Psychiatrists do not have to fit everything into a procrustean bed and then explain overlap with comorbidity.*

Another critical problem with modern psychiatry today is that psychiatrists have become excessively concerned with individual risk and are not concerned about the social production of disease. *Psychiatry should reintroduce a basic social science into the study of depression.* This basic social science must take advantage of the advances in the social sciences during the past 30 years, advances especially in understanding dysfunctional social networks (whether family, neighborhood, or workplace). Just as we train promising psychiatric investigators jointly in the neuro-sciences and clinical psychiatry, we should be training additional young investiga-tors jointly in the social sciences and clinical psychiatry. Many colleagues from other disciplines could work with psychiatrists and broaden our horizons, such as anthropologists, sociologists, social psychologists, and social workers. The same justification for placing clinician investigators in molecular biology laboratories applies to placing clinician investigators in the laboratory of families and communities.

If a revised basic social science is born, psychiatry must refrain from too visible a role in the public square. Rather psychiatry should be at the vanguard of discovering the data that will inform and then motivate policy makers and the public. For example, psychiatry might identify specific stressors in the workplace, such as excessive hours worked per week coupled with a sense of little control over one's work, and then demonstrate a clear and compelling association between this stressor and the onset of clinically important depression.

The emergence of a new social psychiatry impels not a conflict with the basic neurosciences but rather a complement. Psychiatrists (and the public) must not abandon the search for the psychobiological diathesis of severe and even mild depressive symptoms. Extreme allegiance to either the biological or the social origins of emotional suffering provides fertile ground for the emergence of reactions within and without psychiatry that can be destructive to our patients and our professions. *A new social psychiatry must not spawn a new antipsychiatry movement.*

As I have described throughout this book, the general public, as much as any group, demands that its dis-ease be named. We seek specific names and specific cures. Much discomfort, however, escapes clear categorization. Even the medications we use are not specific. The so-called antidepressants have been shown to be efficacious for the treatment of panic, anxiety, sleep problems, obsessive thoughts, and compulsive acts. They can be better labeled as a "tonic," tonic in a good sense.[13] Not only can the use of the medications be effectively expanded, though with caution, but we can also learn something of underlying pathophysiological mechanisms that cut across our current diagnostic categories based on the response to these medications. If these medications are found to have multiple uses and yet work by relatively specific mechanisms, then we should be thankful for these uses.

Psychiatrists should be more sanguine regarding the nature of human nature and avoid the modern-day myth that happiness is the natural state of our species. Psychiatrists do not have to explain all emotional suffering as psychiatric disorder! The need to diagnose and treat specific disorders, which dominates clinical medicine (and psychiatry) currently, should not unduly shape our explorations of emotional suffering in the community. In fact, indiscriminant interventions might not only numb society to its ills but also render some effective treatments ineffective over time. The history of the use of antibiotics is informative. Appropriate use of antibiotics has saved millions of lives. Yet indiscriminant use has lead to resistant bacteria and the potential for new epidemics of infectious diseases. Appropriate use of antidepressants has relieved the suffering of millions over the years and saved many lives (of this I am certain). We do not know, however, the influence of even more widespread use of antidepressants over long periods of time. Medicine is practiced best when it is practiced cautiously. If a depressed mood is not severe and appropriate to the context of the mood, watchful waiting and support on the part of the mental health professional or primary care physician might be the best course.

Finally, we must never take lightly the reality of emotional suffering among the depressed. The construct of major depression arose precisely because people were experiencing clinically significant depressive symptoms. A fatalistic attitude by psychiatrists and other mental health professionals would be extremely damaging. Returning to a parallel situation to which I alluded previously, the current rapid rise in obesity is not something that physicians should simply accept. Rather, we must explore the causes, ranging from the biomedical to the psychosocial. Where we can intervene with biomedical solutions that are safe and effective (and to the extent that these interventions show proof of long-term and short-term benefit), we must do so. When factors within the physical and social environment are identified that are outside the realm of the physician's direct influence, the physician has the responsibility to alert the public in service of the public's health. Over time, the public has been accepting of recommendations from the medical community, ranging from widespread vaccinations for infectious diseases through institution of safety devices that reduce injury and death, such as seat belts, to education of the public regarding the health hazards of cigarette smoking. In like manner, when we identify clear links between the social environment and depression through our investigations, we must alert the public of these risks for depression.

Notes

Chapter 1

1. Lewontin R, Rose S, Kanin L. *Not in Our Genes.* New York: Pantheon; 1984:1.
2. Klerman G. The current age of youthful melancholia: Evidence for increase in depression among adolescents and young adults. *British Journal of Psychiatry.* 1988;152:4–14.
3. Weissman M, Bruce M, Leaf P, Florio L, Holzer III C. Affective disorders. In: Regier DA, Robins LN, eds. *Psychiatric Disorders in America.* New York: Free Press; 1991:53–80.
4. Blazer DG, Kessler RC, McGonagle KA, Swartz MS. The prevalence and distribution of major depression in the National Comorbidity Survey. *American Journal of Psychiatry.* 1994;151:979–986.
5. Broadhead W, Blazer D, George L, Tse C. Depression, disability days and days lost from work: A prospective epidemiologic survey. *Journal of the American Medical Association.* 1990;264:2524–2528.
6. World Health Organization. *World Health Report 2001: Mental Health, New Understanding, New Hope.* Geneva: World Health Organization; 2001.
7. Wells K, Sturm R, Sherbourne C, Meredith L. *Caring for Depression.* Cambridge, MA: Harvard University Press; 1996.
8. Frank E, Spanier C. Interpersonal psychotherapy for depression: overview, clinical efficacy, and future directions. *Clinical Psychology—Science & Practice.* 1995;d2:349–365.
9. Auden W. *Collected Longer Poems.* New York: Random House; 2002.
10. Spitzer R, Endicott J, Robins E. Research diagnostic criteria: rationale and reliability. *Archives of General Psychiatry.* 1978;35:773–782.
11. American Psychiatric Association. *Diagnostic and Statistical Manual of Mental Disorders.* 3rd ed. Washington, DC: Author; 1980.
12. Feighner J, Robins E, Guze S, Woodruff R, Winokur G, Munoz R. Diagnostic criteria for use in psychiatric research. *Archives of General Psychiatry.* 1972;26:57–63.
13. American Psychiatric Association. *Diagnostic and Statistical Manual of Mental Disorders.* 2nd ed. Washington, DC: Author; 1968.
14. Berkman L, Kawachi I. *Social Epidemiology.* New York: Oxford University Press; 2000.
15. Kleinman A, Good B. Introduction: Culture and depression. In: Kleinman A, Good B, eds. *Culture and Depression: Studies in the Anthropology and Cross-Cultural Psychiatry of Affect and Disorder.* Berkeley: University of California Press; 1985:1–32.
16. Aneshensel C, Phelan J, eds. *Handbook of the Sociology of Mental Health.* New York: Plenum; 1999.
17. Krupinski J. Social psychiatry and sociology of mental health: A view on their past and future relevance. *Australian and New Zealand Journal of Psychiatry.* 1992;26:91–97.

18. Caplan G, Grunebaum H. Perspectives on primary prevention. *Archives of General Psychiatry.* 1967;17:331–346, 344.
19. Guze S. Comments on Blashfield's article. *Schizophrenia Bulletin.* 1982;8:6–7, 7.
20. Valenstein E. *Blaming the Brain.* New York: Free Press; 1998.
21. Engel G. The clinical application of the biopsychosocial model. *American Journal of Psychiatry.* 1980;137:535–544.
22. Diez-Roux A. Bringing context back into epidemiology: variables and fallacies in multilevel analysis. *American Journal of Public Health.* 1998;88:216–222.
23. Mercer S, Green L, Rosenthal A, Husten C, Khan L, Dietz W. Possible lessons from the tobacco experience for obesity control. *American Journal of Clinical Nutrition.* 2003;77:1073S–1082S.
24. Jeffery R, French S. Epidemic of obesity in the United States: are fast foods and television viewing contributing? *American Journal of Public Health.* 1998;88:277–280.
25. Kleinman A, Kleinman J. Somatization: The interconnections in Chinese society among culture, depressive experiences, and the meanings of pain. In: Kleinman A, Good B, eds. *Culture and Depression: Studies in the Anthropology and Cross-Cultural Psychiatry of Affect and Disorder.* Berkeley: California University Press; 1985:429–490.
26. Schulz K. Did antidepressants depress Japan? *New York Times Magazine*; August 22, 2004:39.
27. Blazer D, Swartz M, Woodbury M, Manton K, Hughes D, George L. Depressive symptoms and depressive diagnoses in a community population. *Archives of General Psychiatry.* 1988;45:1078–1084.
28. Nesse R. Is depression an adaptation? *Archives of General Psychiatry.* 2000;57:14–20.
29. Horwitz A. *Creating Mental Illness.* Chicago: University of Chicago Press; 2002.
30. *What Is Depression.* Chicago: Depression and Bipolar Support Alliance; 2002. Available at: www.dbsalliance.org/info/depression.html. Accessed September 24, 2004.
31. Healy D. *The Antidepressant Era.* Boston: Harvard University Press; 1997.
32. Schor J. *The Overworked American.* New York: Basic Books; 1992.
33. Kessler R, Berglund P, Demler O, et al. The epidemiology of major depressive disorder: Results from the National Comorbidity Survey Replication (NCS-R). *Journal of the American Medical Association.* 2003;289:3095–3105.
34. Huxley A. *Brave New World.* New York: Harper & Row; 1932.
35. Huxley A. *Brave New World Revisited.* New York: Harper & Brothers; 1958.

Chapter 2

1. Burton R. *The Anatomy of Melancholy*, ed. Floyd Dell and Paul Jordan-Smith. 1st ed. New York: Tudor; 1948.
2. Styron W. *Darkness Visible: A Memoir of Madness.* 1st ed. New York: Random House; 1990.
3. Kraepelin E. *Manic Depressive Insanity and Paranoia.* Edinburgh: E & S Livingstone; 1921.
4. Blazer DG, Kessler RC, McGonagle KA, Swartz MS. The prevalence and distribution of major depression in the National Comorbidity Survey. *American Journal of Psychiatry.* 1994; 151:979–986.
5. Hybels C, Blazer D, Pieper C. Toward a threshold for subthreshold depression: An analysis of correlates of depression by severity of symptoms using data from an elderly community survey. *Gerontologist.* 2001;41:357–365.
6. Hagnell O, Lanke J, Rorsman B. Are we entering an age of melancholy? Depressive illness in a prospective epidemiologic study over 25 years: The Lundby Study. *Psychological Medicine.* 1982;12:279–289.
7. Klerman GL, Lavori PW, Rice J, et al. Birth-cohort trends in rates of major depressive disorder among relatives of patients with affective disorder. *Archives of General Psychiatry.* 1985; 42(7):689–693.

8. Manley M. Psychiatric interview, history, and mental status examination. In: Sadock B, Sadock V, eds. *Kaplan and Sadock's Comprehensive Textbook of Psychiatry*. Vol. I. Seventh Edition. Philadelphia: Lippincott Williams & Wilkins; 2000:652–665.

9. Diez-Roux A. Bringing context back into epidemiology: Variables and fallacies in multilevel analysis. *American Journal of Public Health*. 1998;88:216–222.

10. Torrey E. *The Mind Game: Witchdoctors and Psychiatrists*. New York: Emerson Hall; 1972.

11. Regier DA, Myers JK, Kramer M, et al. The NIMH Epidemiologic Catchment Area Program: historical context, major objectives, and study population characteristics. *Archives of General Psychiatry*. 1984;41:934–941.

12. Kessler R, McGonagle K, Zhao S, et al. Lifetime and 12-month prevalence of DSM–III–R psychiatric disorders in the United States: results from the National Comorbidity Survey. *Archives of General Psychiatry*. 1994;51(1):8–19.

13. Breggin P. *Toxic Psychiatry*. New York: St. Martin's Press; 1991.

14. Healy D. *The Antidepressant Era*. Boston: Harvard University Press; 1997.

15. Valenstein E. *Blaming the Brain*. New York: Free Press; 1998.

16. Olfson M, Marcus S, Pincus H, Zito J, Thompson M, Zarin D. Antidepressant prescribing practices of outpatient psychiatrists. *Archives of General Psychiatry*. 1998;55:310–316.

17. Kramer P. Your Zoloft might prevent a heart attack. *New York Times*. June 22, 2003.

18. Kleinman A. *Rethinking Psychiatry: From Cultural Category to Personal Experience*. New York: Free Press; 1988.

19. Kleinman A, Good B. Introduction: Culture and depression. In: Kleinman A, Good B, eds. *Culture and Depression: Studies in the Anthropology and Cross-Cultural Psychiatry of Affect and Disorder*. Berkeley: University of California Press; 1985:1–32.

20. Kleinman A, Kleinman J. Somatization: The interconnections in Chinese society among culture, depressive experiences, and the meanings of pain. In: Kleinman A, Good B, eds. *Culture and Depression: Studies in the Anthropology and Cross-Cultural Psychiatry of Affect and Disorder*. Berkeley: California University Press; 1985:429–490.

21. Rosenberg C. Introduction: Framing disease; Illness, society and history. In: Rosenberg C, Golden J, eds. *Framing Disease, Studies in Cultural History*. New Brunswick, NJ: Rutgers University Press; 1988:xiii–xxvi.

22. Taussig M. *The Devil and Community Fetishism in South America*. Chapel Hill: University of North Carolina Press; 1980.

23. Menninger K. *Whatever Became of Sin?* New York: Bantam; 1973.

24. Spitzer R, Endicott J, Robins E. Research diagnostic criteria: rationale and reliability. *Archives of General Psychiatry*. 1978;35:773–782.

25. American Psychiatric Association. *Diagnostic and Statistical Manual of Mental Disorders*. 3rd ed. Washington, DC: Author; 1980.

26. Gutheil E. Reactive depressions. In: Arieti S, ed. *American Handbook of Psychiatry*. Vol. 1. New York: Basic Books; 1959:345–352.

27. Boland R, Keller M. Diagnostic classification of mood disorders: historical context and implications for neurobiology. In: Charney D, Nestler E, Bunney B, eds. *Neurobiology of Mental Illness*. New York: Oxford University Press; 1999:291–298.

28. Feighner J, Robins E, Guze S, Woodruff R, Winokur G, Munoz R. Diagnostic criteria for use in psychiatric research. *Archives of General Psychiatry*. 1972;26:57–63.

29. American Psychiatric Association. *Diagnostic and Statistical Manual of Mental Disorders*. 4th ed., text revision. Washington, DC: Author; 2000.

30. Broadhead W, Blazer D, George L, Tse C. Depression, disability days and days lost from work: A prospective epidemiologic survey. *Journal of the American Medical Association*. 1990;264:2524–2528.

31. Judd L, Rapaport M, Paulus M, Brown J. Subsyndromal symptomatic depression: A new mood disorder? *Journal of Clinical Psychiatry*. 1994;55(4, Suppl.):18–28.

32. Judd L, Akiskal H. *Delineating the Longitudinal Structure of Depressive Illness: beyond Thresholds and Subtypes*. Nuremberg, Germany: German College of Neuropsychopharmacology; October 1999.

33. Pincus H, Zarin D, Tanielian T, et al. Psychiatric patients and treatment in 1997: findings from the American Psychiatric Practice Research Network. *Archives of General Psychiatry.* 1999;56:441–449.

34. Berndt E, Bir A, Busch S, Frank R, Normand S. The medical treatment of depression, 1991–1996: productive inefficiency, expected outcome variations, and price indexes. *Journal of Health Economics.* 2002;21:373–396.

35. Boyd R. Confirmation, semantics, and the interpretation of scientific theories. In: Boyd R, Gasper P, Trout J, eds. *The Philosophy of Science.* Cambridge, MA: MIT Press; 1991:3–36.

36. Locke J. *An Essay Concerning Human Understanding.* Oxford: Oxford University Press; 1689/1975.

37. Bridgman P. *The Logic of Modern Physics.* New York: Macmillan; 1927.

38. American Psychiatric Association. *Diagnostic and Statistical Manual of Mental Disorders.* 3rd, revised ed. Washington, DC: Author; 1987.

39. Parker G, Hadzi-Pavlovic D. *Melancholia: A Disorder of Movement and Mood.* New York: Cambridge University Press; 1996.

40. Parker G. Classifying depression: should paradigms lost be regained? *American Journal of Psychiatry.* 2000;157:1195–1203.

41. Strauss J, Gabriel K, Kokes R. Do psychiatric patients fit their diagnoses? Patterns of symptomatology as described with a biplot. *Journal of Nervous and Mental Diseases.* 1981;167:105–113.

42. Blazer D, Swartz M, Woodbury M, Manton K, Hughes D, George L. Depressive symptoms and depressive diagnoses in a community population. *Archives of General Psychiatry.* 1988;45:1078–1084.

43. Blazer D, Kessler R, Swartz M. Treatment outcome of persons diagnosed with major depression in a community sample; 1995.

44. World Health Organization. *Composite International Diagnostic Interview.* Geneva: World Health Organization; 1993.

45. Beutler L, Malik M. Diagnosis and treatment guidelines: the example of depression. In: Beutler L, Malik M, eds. *Rethinking DSM: A Psychological Perspective.* Washington, DC: American Psychological Association; 2002:251–278.

46. Ruesch J. *Therapeutic Communication.* New York: Norton; 1973.

47. Sims A. *Symptoms in the Mind: An Introduction to Descriptive Psychopathology.* London: Bailliere Tindall; 1988.

48. Roy-Byrne P, Dagadakis C, Unutzer J, Ries R. Evidence for limited validity of the revised Global Assessment of Functioning scale. *Psychiatric Services.* 1996;47:864–866.

49. Tucker G. Putting *DSM–IV* in perspective. *American Journal of Psychiatry.* 1998;155:159–161.

50. Norton J. Buy American: Choosing psychiatry residents. *Academic Psychiatry.* 2001;25:181–183.

51. Moran M. Pendulum swings back to specialty training. *Pschiatric News.* 2003;38(8):1, 24–25.

52. Klerman G, Vaillant G, Spitzer R, Michels R. A debate on *DSM–III. American Journal of Psychiatry.* 1984;141:539–553.

53. Luhrmann T. *Of Two Minds: The Growing Disorder in American Psychiatry.* New York: Knopf; 2000.

54. Kendell R, Jablensky A. Distinguishing between the validity and utility of psychiatric diagnoses. *American Journal of Psychiatry.* 2003;160:4–12.

55. American Psychiatric Association. *Diagnostic and Statistical Manual of Mental Disorders.* 4th ed. Washington, DC: Author; 1994.

56. Robins E, Guze S. Establishment of diagnostic validity in psychiatric illness: Its application to schizophrenia. *American Journal of Psychiatry.* 1970;126:983–987.

57. American Psychiatric Association. Practice guidelines for major depressive disorder in adults. *American Journal of Psychiatry.* 1993;150(4 Suppl.):1–26.

58. Medicare proposal could be dangerous. *Psychiatric News;* August 20, 1999.

59. Whybrow P, Akiskal H, McKinney W. *Mood Disorders: Toward a New Psychobiology.* New York: Plenum; 1984.
60. Kupfer D. Research in affective disorders comes of age. *American Journal of Psychiatry.* 1999;156:165–167.
61. Krishnan K, Goli V, Ellinwood E, Blazer D, Nemeroff C. Leukoencephalopathy in patients diagnosed as major depressive. *Biological Psychiatry.* 1988;23:519–522.
62. Andreasen N. *The Broken Brain: The Biological Revolution in Psychiatry.* New York: Harper & Row; 1984.
63. Moss-Morris R. The role of illness cognitions and coping in the aetiology and maintenance of the chronic fatigue syndrome. In: Petrie K, Weinman J, eds. *Perceptions of Health & Illness.* Amsterdam: Harwood Academic;1999:411–439.
64. Wessley S, Butler S, Chalder T, David A. The cognitive behavioral management of the postviral fatigue syndrome. In: Jenkins R, Mowbrey J, eds. *Postviral Fatigue Syndrome.* Chichester: John Wiley & Sons;1991:305–334.
65. Burns D. *Feeling Good.* New York: New American Library; 1980.
66. Beck A. Cognitive model of depression. *Journal of Cognitive Psychotherapy.* 1987;1:2–27.
67. Klerman GL, Weissman MM, Rounsaville BJ, Chevron ES. *Interpersonal Psychotherapy of Depression.* New York: Basic Books; 1984.
68. Callahan C, Nienaber N, Hendrie H, Tierney W. Depression of elderly outpatients: primary care physicians' attitudes and practice patterns. *Journal of General Internal Medicine.* 1992;7:26–31.
69. Shapiro A, Shapiro E. *The Powerful Placebo: From Ancient Priest to Modern Physician.* Baltimore: Johns Hopkins University Press; 1997.

Chapter 3

1. Shorter E. *A History of Psychiatry: From the Era of the Asylum to the Age of Prozac.* New York: John Wiley & Sons; 1997.
2. Jackson SW. *Melancholia and Depression: From Hippocratic Times to Modern Times.* 1st ed. New Haven, CT: Yale University Press; 1986.
3. Lunbeck E. *The Psychiatric Persuasion: Knowledge, Gender, and Power in Modern America.* Princeton, NJ: Princeton University Press; 1994.
4. Andreasen N. *The Broken Brain: The Biological Revolution in Psychiatry.* New York: Harper & Row; 1984.
5. Adams F, ed. *The Extant Works of Aretaeus, the Cappadocian.* London: Sydenham Society; 1865.
6. Burton R. *The Anatomy of Melancholy,* ed. Floyd Dell and Paul Jordan-Smith. 1st ed. New York: Tudor; 1948.
7. Fox R. *The Tangled Chain: The Structure of Disorder in the Anatomy of Melancholy.* Berkeley: University of California Press; 1976.
8. Bate WJ. *Samuel Johnson.* New York: Harcourt Brace Jovanovich; 1977.
9. Hill G. *Johnsonian Miscellanies.* Oxford: Clarendon; 1897.
10. Akiskal H. Mood disorders: Introduction and overview. In: Sadock B, Sadock V, eds. *Comprehensive Textbook of Psychiatry.* Vol. 1. Philadelphia: Lippincott Williams & Wilkins; 2000:1284–1298.
11. Rubin J. *Religious Melancholy and the Protestant Experience in America.* New York: Oxford University Press; 1994.
12. Bowker J. *Problems of Suffering in the Religious World.* Cambridge: Cambridge University Press; 1970.
13. Alexander F, Selesnick S. *The History of Psychiatry.* New York: New American Library; 1966.
14. Blazer D. *Freud vs. God: How Psychiatry Lost Its Soul and Christianity Lost Its Mind.* Downers Grove, IL: InterVarsity Press; 1998.

15. Wuthnow R. *The Restructuring of American Religion, Society and Faith Since World War II.* Princeton, NJ: Princeton University Press; 1988.
16. Bloom H. *The American Religion: The Emergence of the Post-Christian Nation.* New York: Simon and Schuster; 1992.
17. Eaton J, Weil R. *Culture and Mental Disorders.* New York: Free Press; 1976.
18. Schwab JJ, Schwab ME. *Sociocultural Roots of Mental Illness: An Epidemiologic Survey.* New York: Plenum Medical; 1978.
19. Maudsley H. *The Physiology and Pathology of the Mind.* London: Macmillan; 1867.
20. Defendorf A. *Clinical Psychiatry: A Text-book for Students and Physicians, from 6th German Edition of Kraepelin's "Lehrbuch der Psychiatrie."* New York: Macmillan; 1902.
21. James W. *The Varieties of Religious Experience* (Original edition 1902). Cambridge, MA: Harvard University Press; 1982.
22. Campbell R. *Psychiatric Dictionary.* 7th ed. New York: Oxford University Press; 1996.
23. Healy D. *The Antidepressant Era.* Boston: Harvard University Press; 1997.
24. American Psychiatric Association. *Diagnostic and Statistical Manual of Mental Disorders.* 3rd ed. Washington, DC: Author; 1980.
25. Winters E. *The Collected Papers of Adolf Meyer.* Baltimore: Johns Hopkins Press; 1951.
26. Zilboorg G. *A History of Medical Psychology.* New York: Norton; 1941.
27. Bibring E. The mechanism of depression. In: Grenacre P, ed. *Affective Disorders.* New York: International Universities Press; 1953.
28. Parker G. Classifying depression: should paradigms lost be regained? *American Journal of Psychiatry.* 2000;157:1195–1203.
29. Gillespie R. The clinical differentiation of types of depression. *Guy's Hospital Reports.* 1929;79:306–344.
30. Lewis A. "Endogenous" and "exogenous": A useful dichotomony. *Psychological Medicine.* 1971;1:191–196.
31. Bleuler E. *Textbook of Psychiatry.* New York: Macmillan; 1924.
32. Boyce P, Hadzi-Pavlovic D. Issues in classification, I: some historical aspects. In: Parker G, Hadzi-Pavlovic D, eds. *Melancholia: A Disorder of Movement and Mood.* New York: Cambridge University Press; 1996:9–19.
33. Lewis A. Melancholia: a clinical survey of depressive states. *Journal of Mental Science.* 1934;80:1–43.
34. Robins E, Guze S. Classification of affective disorders: The primary-secondary, the endogenous-reactive, and the neurotic-psychotic concepts. In: Wiliams T, Katz M, Shelds J, eds. *Recent Advances in the Psychobiology of Depressive Illness.* Washington, DC: U.S. Government Printing Office; 1972:283–293.
35. Mendels J. *Concepts of Depression.* New York: John Wiley & Sons; 1970.
36. Mendels J, Cochrane C. The nosology of depression: The endogenous-reactive concept. *American Journal of Psychiatry.* 1968;124(Suppl.):1–11.
37. Kandel E. A new intellectual framework for psychiatry. *American Journal of Psychiatry.* 1998;155:457–469.
38. Kramer P. *Listening to Prozac.* New York: Penguin; 1997.
39. Shorter E. *From Paralysis to Fatigue: A History of Psychosomatic Illness in the Modern Era.* New York: Free Press; 1992.
40. Rogow A. *The Psychiatrists.* New York: Putnam; 1970.
41. Sargant W. *The Unquiet Mind.* London: Heinemann; 1967.
42. Norden M. *Beyond Prozac.* New York: Regan Books [HarperCollins]; 1995.
43. Breggin P. *Toxic Psychiatry.* New York: St. Martin's Press; 1991.
44. Ross C, Pam A. *Pseudoscience in Biological Psychiatry.* New York: John Wiley & Sons; 1995.

Chapter 4

1. Rennie T. Social psychiatry—A definition. *International Journal of Social Psychiatry.* 1955;1–10.

2. Foucault M. *Madness and Civilization: A History of Insanity in the Age of Reason*. New York: Random House; 1961.
3. Leff J. Principles of social psychiatry. In: Bhugra D, Leff J, eds. *Principles of Social Psychiatry*. Oxford: Blackwell Scientific;1993:3–11.
4. Klerman GL. The scope of social and community psychiatry. In: Michels R, ed. *Psychiatry*. Vol. 3. 1990 ed. Philadelphia: J.B. Lippincott;1995:1–14.
5. Bachrach L. American experience in social psychiatry. In: Bhugra D, Leff J, eds. *Principles of Social Psychiatry*. Oxford: Blackwell Scientific;1993:534–548.
6. Leighton A, Murphy J. Cross-cultural psychiatry. In: Murphy J, Leighton A, eds. *Approaches to Cross-cultural Psychiatry*. New York: Cornell University Press; 1965:3–20.
7. Jones F. Military psychiatry since World War II. In: Menninger R, Nemiah J, eds. *American Psychiatry After World War II (1944–1994)*. Washington, DC: American Psychiatric Press; 2000:3–36.
8. Joint Commission on Mental Illness and Health. *Action for Mental Health*. New York: Author; 1961.
9. Schwab J, Warheit G, McGinnis N. Current perspectives on social psychiatry. *Psychosomatics*. 1970;11:18–23.
10. Kupinski J. Social psychiatry and sociology of mental health: a review on their past and future relevance. *Australian and New Zeland Journal of Psychiatry*. 1992;26:91–97.
11. Freud S. Civilization and its discontents (1930). In: Strachy J, ed. *Standard Edition*. Vol. 21. London: Hogarth; 1961:57–145.
12. Grusky O, Pollner M, eds. *The Sociology of Mental Illness: Basic Studies*. New York: Holt, Rinehart and Winston; 1981.
13. Freud S. *Mourning and Melancholia*. Vol. 14. London: Hogarth Press; 1917.
14. Durkheim E. *Suicide: A Study in Sociology*. New York: Free Press; 1951.
15. Havens L. Main currents of psychiatric development. *International Journal of Psychiatry*. 1960;5:288–292.
16. Percy W. The coming crisis in psychiatry. In: Percy W, ed. *Signposts in a Strange Land*. New York: Farrar, Straus & Giroux; 1991:251–262. (Originally published in 1957)
17. Dunham H. The epidemiological study of mental illness: Its value for needs assessment. In: Bell R, Sundel M, Aponte J, Murrell S, eds. *Assessing Health and Human Service Needs: Concepts, Methods and Applications*. New York: Science Press; 1978.
18. Schwab JJ, Schwab ME. *Sociocultural Roots of Mental Illness: An Epidemiologic Survey*. New York: Plenum Medical; 1978.
19. Priebe S, Finzen A. On the different connotations of social psychiatry. *Social Psychiatry and Psychiatric Epidemiology*. 2002;37:47–49.
20. Illberg G. Soziale Psychiatrie. *Monatszeitschrift fur sociale Medizin*. 1904;1:321–398.
21. Fischer M. Die Soziale Psychiatrie im Rahmen der Sozialen Hygiene und Allgemeneinin Wohkfahrtpflege. *Allgemeine Zeitschrift fur Psychiatrie*. 1919;75:529–548.
22. Sartorius N. Future directions: a global view. In: Henderson A, Burrows G, eds. *Handbook of Social Psychiatry*. Amsterdam: Elsevier; 1988:341–346.
23. Aneshensel C, Phelan J, eds. *Handbook of the Sociology of Mental Health*. New York: Plenum; 1999.
24. Southard E. Contributions from the psychopathic hospital, Boston, Massachusetts: Introductory note. In: *Boston Psychopathic Hospital Collected Contributions. No. 1*. Boston: Boston Psychopathic Hospital; 1913:1–26.
25. Lunbeck E. *The Psychiatric Persuasion: Knowledge, Gender, and Power in Modern America*. Princeton, NJ: Princeton University Press; 1994.
26. Southard E. Alienists and psychiatrists: notes on divisions and nomenclature of mental hygiene. *Mental Hygiene*. 1917;1:567–571.
27. Luhrmann T. *Of Two Minds: The Growing Disorder in American Psychiatry*. New York: Knopf; 2000.
28. Southard E. Psychological wants of psychiatrists: A psychopathic hospital point of view. Paper presented at: annual meeting, American Psychological Association, 1917.

29. Shorter E. A *History of Psychiatry: From the Era of the Asylum to the Age of Prozac*. New York: John Wiley & Sons; 1997.
30. Leighton AH. *My Name Is Legion: Foundations for a Theory of Man in Relation to Culture*. Vol. 1. 1st ed. New York: Basic Books; 1959.
31. Langner T, Michael S. *Life Stress and Mental Health: The Midtown Manhattan Study*. New York: Free Press; 1963.
32. Faris R, Dunham H. *Mental Disorders in Urban Areas*. Chicago: University of Chicago Press; 1939.
33. Hollingshead A, Redlich F. *Social Class and Mental Illness*. New York: John Wiley; 1958.
34. Leighton A, Clausen J, Wilson R. *Explorations in Social Psychiatry*. New York: Basic Books; 1957.
35. Evans F. *Harry Stack Sullivan*. London: Routledge; 1996.
36. Havens L. *Approaches to the Mind: Movement of the Psychiatric Schools from Sects Toward Science*. Boston: Little, Brown; 1973.
37. Lief A, ed. *The Commonsense Psychiatry of Dr. Adolf Meyer*. New York: McGraw-Hill; 1948.
38. Cantril H. *Tensions that Cause War*. Urbana: University of Illinois Press; 1950.
39. Sullivan H. *Schizophrenia as a Human Process*. New York: Norton; 1962.
40. Devereaux G. *Reality and Dream: Psychotherapy of a Plains Indian*. New York: International Universities Press; 1951.
41. La Barre W. *The Human Animal*. Chicago: University of Chicago Press; 1954.
42. Murphy J. Social causes: the independent variables. In: Kaplan B, Wilson R, Leighton A, eds. *Further Explorations in Social Psychiatry*. New York: Basic Books; 1976:386–406.
43. Leighton A. Editor's notebook: Social psychiatry and the concept of cause. *American Journal of Psychiatry*. 1965;122:929–930.
44. Selye H. Stress and psychiatry. *American Journal of Psychiatry*. 1956;113:423–428.
45. MacMahon B, Pugh T. *Epidemiology: Principles and Methods*. Boston: Little, Brown; 1970.
46. Mora G. Recent American psychiatric developments (since 1939). In: Arieti S, ed. *American Handbook of Psychiatry*. Vol. 1. New York: Basic Books; 1959: 18–57.
47. Engel G, Schamle A. Conservation-withdrawal: a primary regulatory process for organismic homeostasis. In: Porter R, Night J, eds. *Physiology, Emotion, and Psychosomatic Illness*. Amsterdam: Associated Scientific Publishers; 1972: 57–85.
48. Rado S. *Psychoanalysis of Behavior*. New York: Grune & Stratton; 1962.
49. Wiener N. *Cybernetics, or Control and Communication in the Animal and the Machine*. Cambridge, MA: MIT Press; 1948.
50. Bertalanffy L. *Problems of Life*. New York: Wiley; 1952.
51. Alexander F, Selesnick S. *The History of Psychiatry*. New York: New American Library; 1966.
52. Menninger K. *The Vital Balance*. New York: Viking Press; 1963.
53. Kolb L, Frazier S, Sirovatka P. The National Institute of Mental Health: Its influence on psychiatry and the nation's mental health. In: Menninger R, Nemiah J, eds. *American Psychiatry After World War II*. Washington, DC: American Psychiatric Press; 2000:207–231.
54. Kiev A, ed. *Social Psychiatry*. No. I. New York: Science House; 1969.
55. Rabkin R. *Inner and Outer Space: Introduction to a Theory of Social Psychiatry*. New York: Norton; 1970.
56. Masserman J, Schwab J, eds. *Social Psychiatry*. No. 1. New York: Grune and Stratton; 1974.
57. Arthur R. Social psychiatry: an overview. *American Journal of Psychiatry*. 1973;130:841–849.
58. Ruesch J. Social psychiatry: an overview. *Archives of General Psychiatry*. 1965;12:501–509.
59. Mohl P, Weiner M. Other psychodynamic schools. In: Sadock B, Sadock V, eds. *Comprehensive Textbook of Psychiatry*. Vol. 1. Philadelphia: Lippincott Williams & Wilkins; 2000:615–638.
60. Waggoner R. The presidential address: cultural dissonance and psychiatry. *American Journal of Psychiatry*. 1970;127:1–8.
61. Dorner K. Einleitung. In: Dorner K, Plog U, eds. *Socialpsychiatrie*. Luchterhand: Neuwied; 1972:7–20.
62. Lewis A. *The State of Psychiatry*. London: Routledge & Kegan Paul; 1967.

63. Committee on Social Issues. *The Social Responsibility of Psychiatrists: A Statement of Orientation*. New York: Group for the Advancement of Psychiatry; 1950.
64. Torrey E. *The Death of Psychiatry*. Radnor, PA: Clinton; 1974.
65. Linn L. The fourth psychiatric revolution. *American Journal of Psychiatry*. 1968;124:1043–1048.
66. Leighton A. *Caring for Mentally Ill People: Psychological and Social Barriers in Historical Context*. Cambridge: Cambridge University Press; 1982.
67. Kaplan BHW, Robert N, Leighton, Alexander H., eds. *Further Explorations in Social Psychiatry*. 1st ed. New York: Basic Books; 1976.
68. Greenblatt M. The evolution of state mental hospital models of treatment. In: Kaplan B, Wilson R, Leighton A, eds. *Further Explorations in Social Psychiatry*. New York: Basic Books; 1976:29–44.
69. Caplan G. *Principles of Preventive Psychiatry*. New York: Basic Books; 1964.
70. Schwartz D. Community mental health in 1972: an assessment. In: Barton H, Belak L, eds. *Community Mental Health*. Vol. II. New York: Grune & Stratton; 1972.
71. Meyer A. Where should we attack the problem of prevention of mental defect and mental disease? Paper presented at: National Conference of Charities and Correction, 1915; Baltimore, MD.
72. Grob G. *The Mad Among Us: A History of the Care of America's Mentally Ill*. New York: Free Press; 1994.
73. President's Commission on Mental Health. *Report to the President*. Washington, DC: U.S. Government Printing Office; 1978.
74. Fleck S. Social psychiatry—An overview. *Social Psychiatry and Psychiatric Epidemiology*. 1990; 25: 48–55.
75. Jones M. *The Therapeutic Community: A New Treatment Method in Psychiatry*. New York: Basic Books; 1953.
76. Bloom B. *Community Mental Health: A Historical and Critical Analysis*. Morristown, NJ: General Learning Press; 1973.

Chapter 5

1. Elpers J. Public psychiatry. In: Sadock B, Sadock V, eds. *Comprehensive Textbook of Psychiatry*. Philadelphia: Lippincott Williams & Wilkins; 2000:3185–3199.
2. Berkman L, Kawachi I. *Social Epidemiology*. New York: Oxford University Press; 2000.
3. Bloom S, Moss J, Belville R, Freidenberg J, Indyk D, Speedling EJ. Community medicine: its contribution to the social science of medicine. *Mount Sinai Medical Journal*. 1992;59:461–468.
4. Shorter E. *From Paralysis to Fatigue: A History of Psychosomatic Illness in the Modern Era*. New York: Free Press; 1992.
5. Hales R, Yudofsky S, eds. *Textbook of Clinical Psychiatry*. 4th ed. Washington, DC: American Psychiatric Publishing; 2003.
6. Hales R, Yudofsky S, Talbott J, eds. *Textbook of Clinical Psychiatry*. 3rd ed. Washington, DC: American Psychiatric Publishing; 1999.
7. Lamb H. Public psychiatry and prevention. In: Hales R, Yudofsky S, Talbott J, eds. *Textbook of Clinical Psychiatr*. 3rd ed. Washington, DC: American Psychiatric Publishing; 1999:1535–1556.
8. Pincus H, David W, McQueen L. "Subthreshold" mental disorders: A review and synthesis of studies of minor depression and other "brand names." *British Journal of Psychiatry*. 1998;170:288–296.
9. Judd L, Rapaport M, Paulus M, Brown J. Subsyndromal symptomatic depression: A new mood disorder? *Journal of Clinical Psychiatry*. 1994;55(4, Suppl.):18–28.
10. Beekman A, Geerlings S, Deeg D, et al. The natural history of late-life depression. *Archives of General Psychiatry*. 2002;59:605–611.

11. Pincus H, Henderson B, Blackwood D, Dial T. Trends in research in two general psychiatric journals in 1969–1990: research on research. *American Journal of Psychiatry.* 1993;150:135–142.
12. Moncrieff J, Crawford M. British psychiatry in the 20th century—Observations from a psychiatric journal. *Social Science & Medicine.* 2001;53:349–356.
13. Bhugra D, Leff J, eds. *Principles of Social Psychiatry.* Oxford: Blackwell Scientific; 1993.
14. Henderson AS, Burrows GD, eds. *Handbook of Social Psychiatry.* Amsterdam: Elsevier; 1988.
15. Regier DA, Myers JK, Kramer M, et al. The NIMH Epidemiologic Catchment Area Program: historical context, major objectives, and study population characteristics. *Archives of General Psychiatry.* 1984;41:934–941.
16. Kessler R, McGonagle K, Zhao S, et al. Lifetime and 12-month prevalence of *DSM–III–R* psychiatric disorders in the United States: results from the National Comorbidity Survey. *Archives of General Psychiatry.* 1994;51(1):8–19.
17. Sartorius N. Future directions: a global view. In: Henderson A, Burrows G, eds. *Handbook of Social Psychiatry.* Amsterdam: Elsevier; 1988:341–346.
18. Opler M. *Culture and Social Psychiatry.* New York: Atherton Press; 1967.
19. Tseng W-S. *Handbook of Cultural Psychiatry.* New York: Academic Press; 2001.
20. Arthur R. Social psychiatry: an overview. *American Journal of Psychiatry.* 1973;130:841–849.
21. Srole L, Langer T, Michael S, Opler M, Rennie T. *Mental Health in the Metropolis.* New York: McGraw-Hill; 1962.
22. Leighton AH. *My Name Is Legion: Foundations for a Theory of Man in Relation to Culture.* Vol. 1. 1st ed. New York: Basic Books; 1959.
23. Gaw A. *Concise Guide to Cross-Cultural Psychiatry.* Washington, DC: American Psychiatric Press; 2001.
24. Griffith E, Gonzalez C, Blue H. Introduction to cultural psychiatry. In: Hales R, Yudofsky S, eds. *Textbook of Clinical Psychiatry.* Washington, DC: American Psychiatric Publishing; 2003:1551–1584.
25. Manson S, Walker R, Kivlahan D. Psychiatric assessment and treatment of American Indians and Alaska Natives. *Hospital and Community Psychiatry.* 1987;38:165–173.
26. Shore J. American Indian suicide: fact and fantasy. *Psychiatry.* 1975;38:86–91.
27. Sadock B, Sadock V, eds. *Kaplan & Sadock's Comprehensive Textbook of Psychiatry.* 7th ed. Philadelphia: Lippincott Williams & Wilkins; 2000.
28. Becker A, Kleinman A. Anthropology and psychiatry. In: Sadock B, Sadock V, eds. *Kaplan & Sadock's Comprehensive Textbook of Psychiatry.* Vol. 1. Philadelphia: Lippincott Williams & Wilkins; 2000:463–476.
29. Kleinman A. *Rethinking Psychiatry: From Cultural Category to Personal Experience.* New York: Free Press; 1988.
30. American Psychiatric Association. *Diagnostic and Statistical Manual of Mental Disorders.* 4th ed. Washington, DC: Author; 1994.
31. Kessler R. Sociology and psychiatry. In: Sadock B, Sadock V, eds. *Kaplan & Sadock's Comprehensive Textbook of Psychiatry.* Vol. 1. Philadelphia: Lippincott Williams & Wilkins; 2000:476–484.
32. Faris R, Dunham HW. *Mental Disorders in Urban Areas.* Chicago: University of Chicago Press; 1939.
33. Dunham H. Community psychiatry: The newest therapeutic bandwagon. *Archives of General Psychiatry.* 1965;12:303–313.
34. Grob G. *The Mad Among Us: A History of the Care of America's Mentally Ill.* New York: Free Press; 1994.
35. Flaherty J, Astrachan B. Social psychiatry. In: Weissman S, Sabshin M, Eist H, eds. *Psychiatry in the New Millennium.* Washington, DC: American Psychiatric Press; 1999:39–55.
36. Krupinski J. Confronting theory with data: the case of suicide, drug abuse and mental illness in Australia. *Australian and New Zealand Journal of Sociology.* 1972;12:91–100.
37. Hollingshead A, Redlich F. *Social Class and Mental Illness.* New York: John Wiley; 1958.

38. Krupinski J. Social psychiatry and sociology of mental health: A view on their past and future relevance. *Australian and New Zealand Journal of Psychiatry.* 1992;26:91–97.
39. Goldberg E, Morrison S. Schizophrenia and social class. *British Journal of Psychiatry.* 1963;109:1184–1189.
40. Blazer D, Crowell B, George L, Landerman R. Urban-rural differences in depressive disorders: does age make a difference? In: Barrett JE, Rose RM,, eds. *Mental Disorders in the Community: Progress and Challenge.* New York: Guilford Press; 1986:233–255.
41. Kolv L, Bernard V, Dohrenwend B. *Urban Challenges to Psychiatry.* Boston: Little, Brown; 1969.
42. Goldhamer H, Marshall A. *Psychosis and Civilization: Two Studies in the Frequency of Mental Disease.* Glencoe, IL: Free Press; 1953.
43. Leighton D, Harding J, Macklin D, Macmillan A, Leighton A. *The Character of Danger.* New York: Basic Books; 1963.
44. Sabshin M. Turning points in twentieth-century American psychiatry. *American Journal of Psychiatry.* 1990;147:1267–1274.
45. Stein L, Test M. Alternative to mental hospital treatment—Conceptual model treatment program, and clinical evaluation. *Archives of General Psychiatry.* 1980;37:392–397.
46. Eisenberg L. Preventing mental, neurological and psychosocial disorders. *World Health Forum.* 1987;8:245–253.
47. Grinker R. Psychiatry rides wide in all directions. *Archives of General Psychiatry.* 1964;10:228–235.
48. Klerman G. The psychiatric patient's right to effective treatment: Implications of Osheroff vs. Chestnut Lodge. *American Journal of Psychiatry.* 1990;147:409–418.
49. Redlich F. Cross-cultural psychiatry. Discussion. Paper presented at: IV. World Congress of Psychiatry, 1966.
50. Eisenberg L. Mindlessness and brainlessness in psychiatry. *British Journal of Psychiatry.* 1986;148:497–508.
51. Conrad P. A mirage of genes. *Sociology of Health & Illness.* 1999;21:228–241.
52. Dubos R. *Mirage of Health.* New York: Harper & Row; 1959.
53. Klerman G. Affective disorders. In: Nicholi A, ed. *Harvard Guide to Modern Psychiatry.* Cambridge, MA: Belknap Press;1978:253–281.
54. Nelkin D, Lindee M. *The DNA Mystique: the Gene as a Cultural Icon.* New York: WH Freeman; 1995.
55. Kolb L, Frazier S, Sirovatka P. The National Institute of Mental Health: Its influence on psychiatry and the nation's mental health. In: Menninger R, Nemiah J, eds. *American Psychiatry After World War II.* Washington, DC: American Psychiatric Press; 2000:207–231.
56. Regier D, Hirschfeld R, Goodwin F, Burke J, Lazar L, Judd L. The NIMH Depression Awareness, Recognition, and Treatment program: structure, aims, and scientific basis. *American Journal of Psychiatry.* 1988;145:1351–1357.
57. Judd L. NIMH during the tenure of Director Lewis L. Judd, M.D. (1987–1990): the decade of the brain and the four national research plans. *American Journal of Psychiatry.* 1998;155(9 Suppl.):25–31.
58. National Institute of Mental Health. *The Strategic Plan for Mood Disorders Research.* Bethesda, MD: Author; July 9, 2002.
59. Joint Commission on Mental Illness and Health. *Action for Mental Health.* New York: Author; 1961.
60. Modlin H. Comment to Walter E. Barton: GAP Papers, Archives of Psychiatry, New York–Cornell Medical Center; 1966.
61. Fleck S. Social psychiatry—An overview. *Social Psychiatry and Psychiatric Epidemiology.* 1990;25:48–55.
62. Koegel P. *Homelessness in America.* New York: Oryx Press; 1996.
63. Kirk S, Therrien M. Community mental health myths and the fate of former hospitalized patients. *Psychiatry.* 1975;38:209–217.
64. Foucault M. *Madness and Civilization: A History of Insanity in the Age of Reason.* New York: Random House; 1961.

65. Shorter E. *A History of Psychiatry: From the Era of the Asylum to the Age of Prozac.* New York: John Wiley & Sons; 1997.
66. Horwitz A. *Creating Mental Illness.* Chicago: University of Chicago Press; 2002.
67. Scheff T. *Being Mentally Ill: A Sociological Theory.* Chicago: Aldine; 1966.
68. Szasz T. *The Myth of Mental Illness.* New York: Harper & Row; 1974.
69. Porter R, Micale M. Introduction: Reflections on psychiatry and its histories. In: Micale M, Porter R, eds. *Discovering the History of Psychiatry.* New York: Oxford University Press; 1994:3–38.
70. Torrey E. *The Death of Psychiatry.* Radnor, PA: Clinton; 1974.
71. Healy D. *The Antidepressant Era.* Boston: Harvard University Press; 1997.
72. Kuhn R. The treatment of depressive states with G22355 (imipramine) hydrochloride. *American Journal of Psychiatry.* 1958;115:459–464.

Chapter 6

1. Wells K, Stewart A, Hays R. The functioning and well-being of patients with chronic conditions: results from the Medical Outcomes Study. *Journal of the American Medical Association.* 1989;262:914–919.
2. Seligman K. Help for depression lacking, studies find: 14 million Americans suffer major episode annually. *San Francisco Chronicle.* June 17, 2003, 2003:A1, A17.
3. Kessler R, Berglund P, Demler O, et al. The epidemiology of major depressive disorder: Results from the National Comorbidity Survey Replication (NCS–R). *Journal of the American Medical Association.* 2003;289:3095–3105.
4. Leighton AH. *My Name Is Legion: Foundations for a Theory of Man in Relation to Culture.* Vol. 1. 1st ed. New York: Basic Books; 1959.
5. Leighton D, Harding J, Macklin D, Macmillan A, Leighton A. *The Character of Danger.* New York: Basic Books; 1963.
6. Langner T, Michael S. *Life Stress and Mental Health: The Midtown Manhattan Study.* New York: Free Press; 1963.
7. Srole L, Langer T, Michael S, Opler M, Rennie T. *Mental Health in the Metropolis.* New York: McGraw-Hill; 1962.
8. Schwab JJ, Schwab ME. *Sociocultural Roots of Mental Illness: An Epidemiologic Survey.* New York: Plenum Medical; 1978.
9. Regier DA, Myers JK, Kramer M, et al. The NIMH Epidemiologic Catchment Area program: historical context, major objectives, and study population characteristics. *Archives of General Psychiatry.* 1984;41:934–941.
10. Regier DA, Robins LN, eds. *Psychiatric Disorders in America.* New York: Free Press; 1991.
11. Kessler R, McGonagle K, Zhao S, et al. Lifetime and 12-month prevalence of *DSM–III–R* psychiatric disorders in the United States: results from the National Comorbidity Survey. *Archives of General Psychiatry.* 1994;51(1):8–19.
12. Faris R, Dunham H. *Mental Disorders in Urban Areas.* Chicago: University of Chicago Press; 1939.
13. Eaton J, Weil R. *Culture and Mental Disorders.* New York: Free Press; 1976.
14. Hollingshead A, Redlich F. *Social Class and Mental Illness.* New York: John Wiley; 1958.
15. Dohrenwend B, Dohrenwend B. *Social Status and Psychological Disorder: A Causal Inquiry.* New York: John Wiley; 1969.
16. Blazer D, Burchett B, Service C, George L. The association of age and depression among the elderly: An epidemiologic exploration. *Journal of Gerontology: Medical Sciences.* 1991;46:M210–M215.
17. Canino GL, Bird HR, Shrout PE, et al. The prevalence of specific psychiatric disorders in Puerto Rico. *Archives of General Psychiatry.* 1987;44:727–735.
18. Leighton A, Lambo T, Hughes C. *Psychiatric Disorders among the Yoruba.* Ithaca, NY: Cornell University Press; 1963.

19. Hughes C, Tremblay M, Rapaport R, Leighton A. *People of Cove and Woodlot*. New York: Basic Books; 1960.
20. Murphy J. The Stirling County study. In: Weissman M, Myers J, Ross C, eds. *Community Surveys of Psychiatric Disorders*. New Brunswick, NJ: Rutgers University Press; 1986:133–153.
21. MacMillan A. The *Health Opinion Survey*: Technique for estimating prevalence of psycho-neurotic and related types of disorder in communities. *Psychological Reports*. 1957;3:325–339.
22. Stouffer S. *The American Soldier*. Vol. II, IV. Princeton, NJ: Princeton University Press; 1949.
23. Leighton A. Conceptual perspectives. In: Kaplan B, Wilson R, Leighton A, eds. *Further Explorations in Social Psychiatry*. New York: Basic Books; 1976:14–23.
24. American Psychiatric Association. *Diagnostic and Statistical Manual of Mental Disorders*. Washington, DC: Author; 1952.
25. Regier D, Boyd J, Burke J, et al. One-month prevalence of mental disorders in the United States. Based on five Epidemiologic Catchment Area sites. *Archives of General Psychiatry*. 1988;45:977–986.
26. Leighton A. Poverty and social change. *Scientific American*. 1965;212:21–27.
27. Rennie T. Social psychiatry—A definition. *International Journal of Social Psychiatry*. 1955;1:10.
28. Srole L, Fischer A. The Midtown Manhattan Longitudinal Study vs "The Mental Paradise Lost" doctrine. *Archives of General Psychiatry*. 1980;37:209–221.
29. Selye H. *General Theory of Adaptation*. Rev. ed. New York: McGraw-Hill; 1976.
30. Srole L, Fischer A. The Midtown Manhattan Longitudinal Study: Aging, generations, and genders. In: Weissman M, Myers J, Ross C, eds. *Community Surveys of Psychiatric Disorders*. New Brunswick, NJ: Rutgers University Press; 1986:77–108.
31. American Psychiatric Association. *Diagnostic and Statistical Manual of Mental Disorders*. 3rd ed. Washington, DC: Author; 1980.
32. Star S. The screening of psychoneurotics in the army: technical development of tests. In: Stouffer S, Guttman L, Suchman E, Lazarsfeld P, Star S, Clausen J, eds. *Measurement and Prediction*. Princeton, NJ: Princeton University Press; 1950:486–547.
33. Link B, Dohrenwend B. Formulation of hypotheses about the true relevance of demoraliza-tion in the United States. In: Dohrenwend B, Dohrenwend B, Gould M, Link B, Neuge-bauer R, Wensch-Hitzig R, eds. *Mental Illness in the United States: Epidemiological Estimates*. New York: Praeger; 1980:114–132.
34. Kessler R. The categorical versus dimensional assessment controversy in the sociology of mental illness. *Journal of Health and Social Behavior*. 2002;43:171–188.
35. Horwitz A. *Creating Mental Illness*. Chicago: University of Chicago Press; 2002.
36. Langner T. A twenty-two item screening score of psychiatric symptoms indicating impair-ment. *Journal of Health and Human Behavior*. 1962;3:269–287.
37. Foucault M. *Madness and Civilization: A History of Insanity in the Age of Reason*. New York: Random House; 1961.
38. Szasz T. *The Myth of Mental Illness*. New York: Harper & Row; 1974.
39. Frank J. *Persuasion and Healing*. Baltimore: Johns Hopkins University Press; 1973.
40. Robins L, Helzer J, Croughan J. *Diagnostic Interview Schedule*: its history, characteristics and validity. *Archives of General Psychiatry*. 1981;38:381–389.
41. Radloff L. The CES–D scale: A self-report depression scale for research in the general pop-ulation. *Applied Psychological Measures*. 1977;1:385–401.
42. Callahan C, Nienaber N, Hendrie H, Tierney W. Depression of elderly outpatients: pri-mary care physicians' attitudes and practice patterns. *Journal of General Internal Medicine*. 1992;7:26–31.
43. Beck AT. *Depression*. New York: Hoeber Medical Division, Harper & Row; 1967.
44. Wells K, Sturm R, Sherbourne C, Meredith L. *Caring for Depression*. Cambridge, MA: Harvard University Press; 1996.

45. President's Commission on Mental Health. *Report to the President.* Washington, DC: U.S. Government Printing Office; 1978.
46. Regier D, Narrow W, Rae D, Manderscheid R, Locke B, Goodwin F. The de facto U.S. mental and addictive disorders service system: Epidemiologic Catchment Area Prospective 1-year prevalence rates of disorders and services. *Archives of General Psychiatry.* 1993;50:85–94.
47. Eaton W, Kramer M, Anthony J, Dryman A, Shapiro S, Locke B. The incidence of specific DIS/DSM–III mental disorders: Data from the NIMH epidemiologic catchment area program. *Acta Psychiatrica Scandinavica.* 1989;79:109–125.
48. Narrow W, Rae D, Robins L, Regier D. Revised prevalence estimates of mental disorders in the United States: Using a clinical significance criterion to reconcile 2 surveys' estimates. *Archives of General Psychiatry.* 2002;59:115–123.
49. American Psychiatric Association. *Diagnostic and Statistical Manual of Mental Disorders.* 4th ed., text revision. Washington, DC: Author; 2000.
50. Broadhead W, Blazer D, George L, Tse C. Depression, disability days and days lost from work: A prospective epidemiologic survey. *Journal of the American Medical Association.* 1990;264:2524–2528.
51. Judd L, Rapaport M, Paulus M, Brown J. Subsyndromal symptomatic depression: A new mood disorder? *Journal of Clinical Psychiatry.* 1994;55(4, Suppl.):18–28.
52. Keller M, Shapiro R, Lavori P, Wolfe N. Recovery in major depressive disorder: analyses with the life table. *Archives of General Psychiatry.* 1982;39:905–910.
53. Judd L, Akiskal H. Delineating the longitudinal structure of depressive illness: Beyond thresholds and subtypes. *Pharmacopsychiatry.* 2000;33:307.
54. Jacobson S. Overselling depression to old folks. *Atlantic Monthly.* 1995:46–51.
55. Goodwin D, Guze S. *Psychiatric Diagnosis.* 2nd ed. New York: Oxford University Press; 1979.
56. 56.Pincus H, Tanielin S, Marcus S, et al. Prescribing trends in psychotropic medications: primary care, psychiatry, and other medical specialties. *Journal of the American Medical Association.* 1998;279:526–531.
57. Hirschfeld R, Keller M, Panico S. The National Depressive and Manic Depressive Association consensus statement on the undertreatment of depression. *Journal of the American Medical Association.* 1997;277:333–340.
58. American Psychiatric Association. *Diagnostic and Statistical Manual of Mental Disorders.* 3rd, revised ed. Washington, DC: Author; 1987.
59. World Health Organization. Mental Health and Behavioral Disorders (including disorders of psychological development). In: *International Classification of Diseases—10th Revision.* Geneva: Author; 1991.
60. World Health Organization. *Composite International Diagnostic Interview.* Geneva: Author; 1993.
61. Blazer DG, Kessler RC, McGonagle KA, Swartz MS. The prevalence and distribution of major depression in the National Comorbidity Survey. *American Journal of Psychiatry.* 1994;151:979–986.
62. Kessler R, Zhao S, Katz S, et al. Past-year use of outpatient services for psychiatric problems in the National Comorbidity Survey. *American Journal of Psychiatry.* 1999;156:115–123.
63. Kessler R, Nelson C, McGonagle K, Edlund M, Frank R, Leaf P. The epidemiology of co-occurring addictive and mental disorders: Implications for prevention and service utilization. *American Journal of Orthopsychiatry.* 1996;66:17–31.
64. Kessler R, Zhao S. Overview of descriptive epidemiology of mental disorders. In: Aneshensel C, Phelan J, eds. *Handbook of the Sociology of Mental Health.* New York: Kluwer Academic/Plenum; 1999:127–150.
65. Zimmerman M, McDermut W, Mattia J. Frequency of anxiety disorder in psychiatric outpatients with major depressive disorder. *American Journal of Psychiatry.* 2000;157:1337–1340.

66. Sanderson W, Beck A, Beck J. Syndrome comorbidity in patients with major depression or dysthymia: prevalence and temporal relationships. *American Journal of Psychiatry.* 1990;147:1025–1028.

67. Kendler K. Major depression and generalized anxiety disorder. Same genes, (partly) different environments—Revisited. *British Journal of Psychiatry.* 1996;(30, Suppl.):68–75.

68. Kendell R. The stability of psychiatric diagnoses. *British Journal of Psychiatry.* 1974;124:352–356.

69. Healy D. *The Antidepressant Era.* Boston: Harvard University Press; 1997.

70. Zimmerman M, Mattia J, Posternak M. Are subjects in pharmacological treatment trials of depression representative of patients in routine clinical practice? *American Journal of Psychiatry.* 2002;159:469–473.

71. Hagnell O, Lanke J, Rorsman B. Are we entering an age of melancholy? Depressive illness in a prospective epidemiologic study over 25 years: The Lundby Study. *Psychological Medicine.* 1982;12:279–289.

72. Lavori PW, Klerman GL, Keller MB, Reich T, Rice J, Endicott J. Age-period-cohort analysis of secular trends in onset of major depression: findings in siblings of patients with major affective disorder. *Journal of Psychiatric Research.* 1987;21:23–35.

73. Weissman M, Bruce M, Leaf P, Florio L, Holzer III C. Affective disorders. In: Regier DA, Robins LN, eds. *Psychiatric Disorders in America.* New York: Free Press; 1991:53–80.

74. Wickramaratne M, Weissman M, Leaf P, Holford T. Age, period and cohort effects on the risk of major depression: results from five United States communities. *Journal of Clinical Epidemiology.* 1989;42:333–343.

75. Blazer D. Is depression more frequent in late life? An honest look at the evidence. *American Journal of Geriatric Psychiatry.* 1994;2:193–199.

76. Klerman GL, Lavori PW, Rice J, et al. Birth-cohort trends in rates of major depressive disorder among relatives of patients with affective disorder. *Archives of General Psychiatry.* 1985;42(7):689–693.

77. Klerman G. The current age of youthful melancholia. Evidence for increase in depression among adolescents and young adults. *British Journal of Psychiatry.* 1988;152:4–14.

78. Kessler R, McGonagle K, Nelson C, Hughes M, Swartz M, Blazer D. Sex and depression in the National Comorbidity Survey II: cohort effects. *Journal of Affective Disorders.* 1994;30:15–26.

79. Klerman G, Leon A, Wickramaratne P, et al. The role of drug and alcohol abuse in recent increases in depression in the US. *Psychological Medicine.* 1996; 6:343–351.

80. Giuffra L, Risch N. Diminished recall and the cohort effect of major depression: a simulation study. *Psychological Medicine.* 1994;24:375–383.

81. Hasin D, Link B. Age and recognition of depression: inplications for a cohort effect in major depression. *Psychological Medicine.* 1988;18:683–688.

82. Twenge J, Nolen-Hoeksema S. Age, gender, race, socioeconomic status, and birth cohort differences on the children's depression inventory: a meta-analysis. *Journal of Abnormal Psychology.* 2002;111:578–588.

83. Stassen HH, Ragaz M, Reich T. Age-of-onset or age-cohort changes in the lifetime occurrence of depression? *Psychiatric Genetics.* 1997;7(1):27–34.

84. U.S. Department of Health and Human Services. *Mental Health: A Report of the Surgeon General.* Rockville, MD: U.S. Department of Human Services, Substance Abuse and Mental Health Services Administration, Center for Mental Health Services, National Institutes of Health, National Institute of Mental Health; 1999.

85. Black D, Winokur G. Suicide and psychiatric diagnosis. In: Blumenthal S, Kupfer D, eds. *Suicide Over the Life Cycle: Risk Factors, Assessment, and Treatment of Suicidal Patients.* Washington, DC: American Psychiatric Press; 1990:135–153.

86. Goldsmith S, Pellmar T, Kleinman A, Bunney W, eds. *Reducing Suicide: A National Perspective.* Washington, DC: National Academies Press; 2002.

87. Blazer D, Hybels C, Simonsick E, Hanlon J. Marked differences in antidepressant use by race in an elderly community sample: 1986–1996. *American Journal of Psychiatry.* 2000;157:1089–1094.

88. van Praag H. Why has the antidepressant era not shown a significant drop in suicide rates? *Crisis.* 2002;23:77–82.
89. Gunnell D, Middleton N, Whitley E, Dorling D, Frankel S. Influence of cohort effects on patterns of suicide in England and Wales, 1950–1999. *British Journal of Psychiatry.* 2003;182:164–170.
90. Carlsten A, Waern M, Ekedahl A, Ranstam J. Antidepressant medication and suicide in Sweden. *Pharmacoepidemiology and Drug Safety.* 2001;10:525–530.
91. Whitley E, Gunnell D, Dorling D, Davey Smith G. Ecological study of social fragmentation, poverty, and suicide. *British Medical Journal.* 1999;319:1034–1037.
92. Mathur V, Freeman D. A theoretical model of adolescent suicide and some evidence from U.S. data. *Health Economics.* 2002;11:695–708.
93. Singh G, Siahpush M. Increasing rural-urban gradients in U.S. suicide mortality 1970–1997. *American Journal of Public Health.* 2002;92:1161–1167.
94. Wakefield J. The concept of mental disorder: On the boundary between biological facts and social values. *American Psychologist.* 1992;47:373–388.
95. Shorter E. *From Paralysis to Fatigue: A History of Psychosomatic Illness in the Modern Era.* New York: Free Press; 1992.

Chapter 7

1. Babington A. *Shell-Shock: A History of the Changing Attitudes to War Neurosis.* London: Leo Cooper; 1997.
2. Jones F. Military psychiatry since World War II. In: Menninger R, Nemiah J, eds. *American Psychiatry After World War II (1944–1994).* Washington, DC: American Psychiatric Press; 2000:3–36.
3. Da Costa J. On irritable heart: A clinical study of a form of functional cardiac disorder and its consequences. *American Journal of Medical Science.* 1871;61:17–52.
4. Hyams C, Wignall S, Roswell R. War syndromes and their evaluation: From the US Civil War to the Persian Gulf. *Annals of Internal Medicine.* 1996;125:398–405.
5. Calhoun J. Nostalgia as a disease of field experience. *Medical and Surgical Reporter.* 1864;11:130–132.
6. Shorter E. *From Paralysis to Fatigue: A History of Psychosomatic Illness in the Modern Era.* New York: Free Press; 1992.
7. Beard G. Neurasthenia, or nervous exhaustion. *British Medical Society Journal.* 1869;80:217–221.
8. Lewis T. Report on neuro-circulatory asthenia and its management. *Military Surgeon.* 1918;42:409–426.
9. Graves R. *Good-bye to All That: An Autobiography.* New York: Bantam; 1987.
10. Fussell P. *The Great War and Modern Memory.* London: Oxford University Press; 2000.
11. Menninger W. *Psychiatry in a Troubled World.* New York: Macmillan; 1948.
12. Glass A. Lessons learned. In: Glass A, ed. *Medical Department, United States Army, Neuropsychiatry in World War II, Vol. 2: Overseas Theaters.* Washington, DC: U.S. Government Printing Office;1973:989–1027.
13. Grinker R, Spiegel J. *War Neuroses.* Philadelphia: Lippincott; 1945.
14. Beebe G, Appel J. *Variations in Psychological Tolerance to Ground Combat in World War II.* Washington, DC: National Academy of Science; 1958.
15. American Psychiatric Association. *Diagnostic and Statistical Manual of Mental Disorders.* Washington, DC: Author; 1952.
16. Office of the Surgeon General ASF. Nomenclature of psychiatric disorders and reactions. *Journal of Clinical Psychology.* 1946;2:289–296.
17. American Psychiatric Association. *Diagnostic and Statistical Manual of Mental Disorders.* 2nd ed. Washington, DC: Author; 1968.
18. Grob G. *The Mad Among Us: A History of the Care of America's Mentally Ill.* New York: Free Press; 1994.

19. Appel J, Beebe G. Preventive psychiatry: An epidemiologic approach. *Journal of the American Medical Association.* 1946;131:1469–1475.
20. Lee K, Vaillant G, Torrey W, Elder G. A 50-year prospective study of the psychological sequelae of World War II combat. *American Journal of Psychiatry.* 1995;152:516–522.
21. Star S. The screening of psychoneurotics in the army: Technical development of tests. In: Stouffer S, Guttman L, Suchman E, Lazarsfeld P, Star S, Clausen J, eds. *Measurement and Prediction.* Princeton, NJ: Princeton University Press;1950:486–547.
22. Marren J. Psychiatric problems in troops in Korea during and following combat. *Military Medicine.* 1956;7:715–726.
23. Leighton AH. *My Name Is Legion: Foundations for a Theory of Man in Relation to Culture.* Vol. 1. 1st ed. New York: Basic Books; 1959.
24. Binneveld H. *From Shell Shock to Combat Stress.* Amsterdam: Amsterdam University Press; 1997.
25. Jones F, Johnson A. Medical and psychiatric treatment policy and practice in Vietnam. *Journal of Social Issues.* 1975;31:49–65.
26. American Psychiatric Association. *Diagnostic and Statistical Manual of Mental Disorders.* 3rd ed. Washington, DC: Author; 1980.
27. Martin J, Cline W. Mental health lessons from the Persian Gulf War. In: Martin J, Sparacino L, Belenky G, eds. *The Gulf War and Mental Health.* Westport, CT: Praeger; 1996:161–178.
28. Doebbeling B, Clarke W, Watson D, et al. Is there a Persian Gulf War syndrome? Evidence from a large population-based survey of veterans and nondeployed controls. *American Journal of Medicine.* 2000;108:695–704.
29. Presidential Advisory Committee on Gulf War Veteran's Illnesses. Final report. Washington, DC: U.S. Government Printing Office; 1996.
30. Sutker P, Uddo M, Brailey K, Allain A, Errera P. Psychological symptoms and psychiatric diagnoses in Operation Desert Storm troops serving graves registration duty. *Journal of Trauma and Stress.* 1994;7:159–171.
31. Haley R. Is there a Gulf War syndrome? Searching for syndromes by factor analysis of symptoms. *Journal of the American Medical Association.* 1997;277:215–222.
32. Haley R, Hom J, Roland P. Evaluation of neurologic function in Gulf War veterans: A blinded case-control study. *Journal of the American Medical Association.* 1997;277:223–230.
33. Haley R. Re: "Factor analysis of self-report symptoms: Does it identify a Gulf War Syndrome?" *American Journal of Epidemiology.* 2000;152:1204–1205.
34. Haley R. Is Gulf War Syndrome due to stress? *American Journal of Epidemiology.* 1997;146:695–703.
35. Ismail K, Kent K, Brugha T, et al. The mental health of UK Gulf war veterans: Phase 2 of a two phase cohort study. *British Medical Journal.* 2002;325:576–582.
36. Bruce M, Seeman T, Merrill S, Blazer D. The impact of depressive symptomotology on physical disability: MacArthur studies of successful aging. *American Journal of Public Health.* 1994;84:1796–1799.
37. Gray G, Reed R, Kaiser K, Smith T, Gastanaga V. Self-reported symptoms and medical conditions among 11,868 Gulf War–era veterans. *American Journal of Epidemiology.* 2002;155:1033–1044.
38. Miles A. *The Mentally Ill in Contemporary Society: A Sociological Introduction.* Oxford: Martin Robinson; 1981.
39. American Psychiatric Association. *Diagnostic and Statistical Manual of Mental Disorders.* 4th ed. Washington, DC: Author; 1994.
40. Rosenberg C. Introduction: Framing disease; Illness, society and history. In: Rosenberg C, Golden J, eds. *Framing Disease, Studies in Cultural History.* New Brunswick, NJ: Rutgers University Press; 1988:xiii–xxvi.
41. Afari N, Buchwald D. Chronic fatigue syndrome: A review. *American Journal of Psychiatry.* 2003;160:221–236.
42. Kleinman A. *Rethinking Psychiatry: From Cultural Category to Personal Experience.* New York: Free Press; 1988.

43. Antonovsky A. *Health, Stress, and Coping*. San Francisco: Jossey-Bass; 1979.
44. Shacter S, Singer J. Cognitive, social and physiological determinants and emotional states. *Psychological Review*. 1962;69:379–399.
45. Cacioppa J, Petty R. *Social Psychophysiology*. New York: Guilford; 1983.
46. Torrey E. *The Mind Game: Witchdoctors and Psychiatrists*. New York: Emerson Hall; 1972.
47. Oates J. I'm not OK, You're not OK [book review]. *New York Times*; June 24, 2001.
48. Solomon A. *The Noonday Demon*. New York: Scribner; 2001.
49. Showalter E. *Hystories: Hysterical Epidemics and Modern Culture*. New York: Columbia University Press; 1998.

Chapter 8

1. Yeates W. Selected poetry. In: Jeffares N, ed. *Selected Poetry*. London: Macmillan; 1965.
2. Mills C. *The Sociological Imagination*. New York: Oxford University Press; 1959.
3. Giddens A. *The Consequences of Modernity*. Stanford, CA: Stanford University Press; 1990.
4. Lyon D. *Postmodernity*. Minneapolis: University of Minnesota Press; 1994.
5. Gergen K. *The Saturated Self: Dilemmas of Identity in Contemporary Life*. New York: Basic Books; 1991.
6. Middleton JR, Walsh BJ. *Truth Is Stranger Than It Used to Be: Biblical Faith in a Post Modern Age*. 1st ed. Downers Grove, IL: InverVarsity Press; 1995.
7. Flax J. *Thinking Fragments: Psychoanalysis, Feminism and Postmodernism in the Contemporary World*. Berkeley: University of California Press; 1990.
8. Berger P. *The Sacred Canopy: Elements of a Sociological Theory of Religion*. Garden City, NY: Doubleday; 1967.
9. Geertz C. *The Interpretation of Cultures*. New York: Basic Books; 1973.
10. Langer S. *Philosophy in a New Key*. Cambridge, MA: Harvard University Press; 1960.
11. Nesse R. Is depression an adaptation? *Archives of General Psychiatry*. 2000;57:14–20.
12. Gitlin T. *Media Unlimited*. New York: Henry Holt; 2002.
13. Riesman D. *The Lonely Crowd*. New Haven, CT: Yale University Press; 1950.
14. Yalom I. *Existential Psychotherapy*. New York: Basic Books; 1980.
15. Bugental J. *The Search for Authenticity*. New York: Holt, Rinehart & Winston; 1965.
16. Hippocrates. On airs, waters and places, circa 400 BCE. *Medical Classics*. 1939;119:19.
17. Alexander F, Selesnick S. *The History of Psychiatry*. New York: New American Library; 1966.
18. Freud S. *Civilization and Its Discontents* (1930). In: Strachy J, ed. *Standard Edition*. Vol. 21. London: Hogarth Press; 1961:57–145.
19. Freud S. An autobiographical study. In: Strachey J, ed. *The Standard Edition of the Complete Psychological Works of Sigmund Freud*. Vol. 20. London: Hogarth Press; 1959.
20. Lief A, ed. *The Commonsense Psychiatry of Dr. Adolf Meyer*. New York: McGraw-Hill; 1948.
21. Harvey D. *The Condition of Postmodernity*. Cambridge, MA: Blackwell; 1990.
22. Lyotard J-F. *The Postmodern Condition: A Report on Knowledge*. Vol. 10. Minneapolis: University of Minnesota Press; 1984.
23. Haldane E, Ross G, eds. *The Philosophical Works of Descartes*. Cambridge: Cambridge University Press; 1968.
24. Reese W. *Dictionary of Philosophy and Religion: Eastern and Western Thought*. Atlantic Highlands, NJ: Humanities Press; 1980.
25. Reichenbach H. *The Rise of Scientific Philosophy*. Berkeley: University of California Press; 1963.
26. Dewey J. *Reconstruction in Philosophy*. New York: Henry Holt; 1929.
27. Adams H. *Education Adams*. New York: Houghton Mifflin; 1973.
28. Erikson E. *Identity, Youth and Crisis*. New York: Norton; 1968.
29. Erikson E. *Childhood and Society*. 2nd ed. New York: Basic Books; 1963.
30. Hemingway E. *Old Man and the Sea*. New York: Scribner; 1999.
31. Freud S. *The Interpretation of Dreams*. London: Hogarth Press; 1900.

32. Jung C. Concerning the archetypes, with special reference to the anima concept. In: Read H, Stein L, Riviere D, eds. *Collected Works of C.G. Jung*. Vol. 9. Princeton, NJ: Princeton University Press; 1954:3–41.

33. Roback A. Is psychoanalysis a Jewish movement? *B'nai B'rith Magazine*. 1926;40:198–199, 201, 238–239.

34. American Psychiatric Association. *Diagnostic and Statistical Manual of Mental Disorders*. 4th ed, text revision. Washington, DC: Author; 2000.

35. Fancher R. *Cultures of Healing: Correcting the Image of American Mental Health Care*. New York: W.H. Freeman; 1995.

36. Burns D. *Feeling Good*. New York: New American Library; 1980.

37. Churchland P. *The Engine of Reason, the Seat of the Soul*. Cambridge, MA: MIT Press; 1995.

38. American Psychiatric Association. Practice guidelines for major depressive disorder in adults. *American Journal of Psychiatry*. 1993;150(Suppl. 4):1–26.

39. Durkheim E. *Suicide: A Study in Sociology*. New York: Free Press; 1951.

40. Kuhn T. *The Structure of Scientific Revolutions*. Chicago: University of Chicago Press; 1962.

41. Feyerabend P. *Against Method*. London: Verso; 1975.

42. Horgen J. *The End of Science*. New York: Broadway Books; 1996.

43. Lawrence B, Denny F. *Defenders of God: The Fundamentalist Revolt Against the Modern Age*. Columbia: University of South Carolina Press; 1995.

44. Hofstadter R. *Anti-intellectualism in American Life*. New York: Vintage; 1962.

45. Bullock A, Stallybrass O, eds. *The Fontana Dictionary of Modern Thought*. London: Fontana Books; 1977.

46. Rodrigues C, Garrat C. *Introducing Modernism*. Duxford, Cambridge: Icon Press; 2001.

47. Joyce J. *Ulysses*. New York: Knopf; 1961.

48. Conrad J. *Heart of Darkness*. New York: Charles Tuttle; 1997.

49. Lyon D. *Jesus in Disneyland: Religion in Postmodern Times*. Cambridge, UK: Polity; 2000.

50. Bauman Z. *Intimations of Postmodernity*. New York: Routledge; 1992.

51. Sheline Y, Mintun M, Moerlein S, Snyder A. Greater loss of 5-HT(2A) receptors in midlife than in late life. *American Journal of Psychiatry*. 2002;159:430–435.

52. Sperling R, Bates J, Cocchiarella A, Schacter D, Rosen B, Albert M. Encoding novel face-name associations: A functional MRI study. *Human Brain Mapping*. 2001;14:129–139.

53. Kevles B. *Naked to the Bone: Medical Imaging in the Twentieth Century*. New Brunswick, NJ: Rutgers University Press; 1997.

54. Gunderman R, Kirk S. *One Hundred Years of Roentgen Rays: Radiology and the Changing Image of Man*. Chicago: Department of Radiology, University of Chicago.

55. Jamison K. *An Unquiet Mind: A Memoir of Moods and Madness*. New York: Knopf; 1995.

56. President of the United States PP. *Project on the Decade of the Brain*. 1990.

57. Kutchins HK, Kirk S. *Making Us Crazy. DSM: The Psychiatric Bible and The Creation of Mental Disorder*. London: Constable; 1999.

58. Beahrs J. The cultural impact of psychiatry: The question of regressive effects. In: Meninger R, Nemiah J, eds. *American Psychiatry After World War II (1944–1994)*. Washington, DC: American Psychiatric Press; 2000:321–342.

59. Moyers B, ed. *The World of Ideas*. New York: Doubleday; 1989.

60. Menninger K. *Whatever Became of Sin?* New York: Bantam; 1973.

61. Mead L. *Beyond Entitlement: The Obligations of Citizenship*. New York: Free Press; 1986.

62. Bloom A. *The Closing of the American Mind*. New York: Touchtone; 1987.

63. Jaspers K. *General Psychopathology (Seventh Edition, 1959)*. Manchester: Manchester University Press; 1963.

64. Hutcheon L. *The Politics of Postmodernism*. London: Routledge; 1989.

65. Laing RD. *The Politics of Experience*. New York: Ballantine Books; 1967.

66. Lundin R. *The Culture of Interpretation: Christian Faith and the Postmodern World*. 1st ed. Grand Rapids, MI: William B. Eerdmans; 1993.

67. Blackburn S. *The Oxford Dictionary of Philosophy.* 1st ed. Oxford: Oxford University Press; 1994.
68. Bauman Z. *Liquid Modernity.* Cambridge, MA: Polity; 2000.
69. Fish S. *There's No Such Thing as Free Speech: And It's a Good Thing Too.* New York: Oxford University Press; 1994.
70. D'Sousa D. *Illiberal Education: The Politics of Race and Sex on Campus.* New York: Free Press; 1991.
71. Rabinow P, ed. *The Foucault Reader.* Harmondsworth: Penguin; 1984.
72. Lasch C. *The Culture of Narcissism: American Life in an Age of Diminishing Expectations.* New York: Norton; 1979.
73. Delbanco A. *The Real American Dream: A Meditation on Hope.* Cambridge, MA: Harvard University Press; 1999.
74. Brown G, Harris T. *Social Origins of Depression: A Study of Psychiatric Disorder in Women.* New York: Free Press; 1978.
75. Flanagan O. *Consciousness Reconsidered.* Cambridge, MA: MIT Press; 1992.
76. Barratt BB. *Psychoanalysis and the Postmodern Impulse: Knowing and Being Since Freud's Psychology.* Baltimore: Johns Hopkins University Press; 1993.
77. MacIntyre A. *After Virtue.* 2nd ed. Notre Dame, IN: Notre Dame Press; 1984.
78. Thiselton AC. *Interpreting God and the Postmodern Self: On Meaning, Manipulation and Promise.* 1st ed. Grand Rapids, MI: William B. Eerdmans; 1995.
79. Spiegal H. Silver linings in the clouds of war: A five-decade retrospective. In: Menninger W, Nemiah J, eds. *American Psychiatry After World War II.* Washington, DC: American Psychiatric Press; 2000:52–72.
80. Solomon RC. *Continental Philosophy Since 1750: The Rise and Fall of the Self.* Vol. 7. Oxford: Oxford University Press; 1988.
81. Rogers C. *On Becoming a Person.* Boston: Houghton Mifflin; 1961.
82. Murphy J. Psychiatric labeling in cross-cultural perspective. *Science.* 1976;191:1019–1028.
83. Kleinman A, Kleinman J. Somatization: The interconnections in Chinese society among culture, depressive experiences, and the meanings of pain. In: Kleinman A, Good B, eds. *Culture and Depression: Studies in the Anthropology and Cross-Cultural Psychiatry of Affect and Disorder.* Berkeley: California University Press; 1985:429–490.
84. Kleinman A, Good B. Introduction: Culture and depression. In: Kleinman A, Good B, eds. *Culture and Depression: Studies in the Anthropology and Cross-Cultural Psychiatry of Affect and Disorder.* Berkeley: University of California Press; 1985:1–32.
85. Blazer D, Hybels C, Simonsick E, Hanlon J. Marked differences in antidepressant use by race in an elderly community sample: 1986–1996. *American Journal of Psychiatry.* 2000;157:1089–1094.
86. Ricoeur P. *Freud and Philosophy: An Essay on Interpretation.* New Haven, CT: Yale University Press; 1970.
87. Anderson WT. *Reality Isn't What It Used to Be: Theoretical Politics, Ready-to-Wear Religion, Global Myths, Primitive Chic and Other Wonders of the Postmodern World.* San Francisco: Harper & Row; 1990.
88. Blazer D. *Freud vs. God: How Psychiatry Lost Its Soul and Christianity Lost Its Mind.* Downers Grove, IL: InterVarsity Press; 1998.
89. Bruno G. "Ramble city": postmodernism and *Blade Runner. October.* 1987;41:61–74.
90. Beck A. Cognitive model of depression. *Journal of Cognitive Psychotherapy.* 1987;1:2–27.
91. Carter S. *The Culture of Disbelief.* New York: Basic Books; 1992.
92. Frankl V. *Man's Search for Meaning: An Introduction to Logotherapy.* Boston: Beacon Press; 1962.
93. Wulff D. *Psychology of Religion: Classic and Contemporary Views.* New York: John Wiley & Sons; 1991.
94. Moore T. *Care of the Soul.* New York: HarperCollins; 1992.
95. Koenig H. An 83-year-old woman with chronic illness and strong religious beliefs. *Journal of the American Medical Association.* 2002;288:487–493.

96. Edwards P, ed. *The Encyclopedia of Philosophy*. New York: Macmillan, and Free Press; 1967.
97. Karp D. *Speaking of Sadness*. New York: Oxford University Press; 1996.

Chapter 9

1. Singer BH, Ryff CD, eds. *New Horizons in Health: An Integrative Approach*. Washington, DC: National Academy Press; 2001.
2. Committee on Assuring the Health of the Public in the 21st Century. *The Future of the Public's Health in the 21st Century*. Washington, DC: National Academies Press; 2002.
3. Kleinman A. *Rethinking Psychiatry: From Cultural Category to Personal Experience*. New York: Free Press; 1988.
4. Gardner H. *The Mind's New Science: A History of the Cognitive Revolution*. New York: Basic Books; 1984.
5. Flannagan O. *The Science of Mind*. Cambridge, MA: MIT Press; 1991.
6. Lyon M. C. Wright Mills meets Prozac: the relevance of "social emotion" to the sociology of health and illness. In: James V, Gabe J, eds. *Health and the Sociology of Emotions*. Oxford: Blackwell; 1996.
7. Kramer P. *Listening to Prozac*. New York: Penguin; 1997.
8. Norden M. *Beyond Prozac*. New York: Regan Books (HarperCollins); 1995.
9. Sampson R, Raudenbush S, Earls F. Neighborhoods and violent crime: a multilevel study of collective efficacy. *Science*. 1997;277:918–924.
10. Berkman L, Kawachi I. *Social Epidemiology*. New York: Oxford University Press; 2000.
11. Faris R, Dunham H. *Mental Disorders in Urban Areas*. Chicago: University of Chicago Press; 1939.
12. Hollingshead A, Redlich F. *Social Class and Mental Illness*. New York: John Wiley; 1958.
13. Leighton AH. *My Name Is Legion: Foundations for a Theory of Man in Relation to Culture*. Vol. 1. 1st ed. New York: Basic Books; 1959.
14. Srole L, Langer T, Michael S, Opler M, Rennie T. *Mental Health in the Metropolis*. New York: McGraw-Hill; 1962.
15. Graham S. Social factors in relation to chronic illness. In: Freeman H, Levine S, Reeder L, eds. *Handbook of Medical Sociology*. New Jersey: Prentice Hall; 1963.
16. Cassel J. The contribution of the social environment to host resistance. *American Journal of Epidemiology*. 1976;104:107–123.
17. De Graaf J. Workweek woes. *New York Times*. April 12, 2003.
18. Spurgeon A, Harrington M, Cooper C. Health and safety problems associated with long working hours: a review of the current position. *Occupational and Environmental Medicine*. 1997;54:367–375.
19. Marmot M, Siegrist J, Theorell T, Feeney A. Health and the psychosocial environment at work. In: Marmot M, Wilkinson R, eds. *Social Determinants of Health*. Oxford: Oxford University Press; 1999.
20. Kohn M, Schooler C. Occupational experience and psychological functioning: An assessment of reciprocal effects. *American Sociological Review*. 1973;38:97–118.
21. Williams R, Barefoot J, Blumenthal J, et al. Psychosocial correlates of job strain in a sample of working women. *Archives of General Psychiatry*. 1997;54:543–548.
22. Depression. *Women's Health Weekly*. 2002: 12.
23. Druss B, Rosenheck R, Sledge W. Health and disability costs of depressive illness in a major U.S. corporation. *American Journal of Psychiatry*. 2000;157:1274–1278.
24. Stewart W, Ricci J, Chee E, Hahn S, Morganstein D. Cost of lost productive work time among US workers with depression. *Journal of the American Medical Association*. 2003;289:3135–3144.
25. Tennant C. Work-related stress and depressive disorders. *Journal of Psychosomatic Research*. 2001;51:697–704.

26. Kawakarmi N, Araki S, Kawashima M. Effects of perceived job stress on depressive symptoms in blue-collar workers of an electrical factory in Japan. *Scandinavian Journal of Work, Environment and Health.* 1992;18:195–200.
27. Melamed S, Luz J, Green M. Noise exposure, noise annoyance and their relation to psychological distress, accident and sickness absence among blue-collar workers—The Cordis Study. *Israel Journal of Medical Science.* 1992;28:629–635.
28. Stansfield S, Fuhrer R, Head J, Ferrier J, Shipley M. Work and psychiatric disorder in the Whitehall II study. *Journal of Psychosomatic Research.* 1997;43:73–81.
29. Stansfeld SA, Head J, Marmot MG. Explaining social class difference in depression and well-being. *Social Psychiatry & Psychiatric Epidemiology.* 1998;33(1):1–9.
30. Heinish D, Jex S. Negative affectivity and gender as moderators of the relationship between work-related stressors and depressed mood. *Work Stress.* 1997;11:46–57.
31. Cherry N. Stress, anxiety and work: a longitudinal study. *Journal of Occupational Psychology.* 1978;5:259–270.
32. Firth H, Britton P. "Burnout" absence and turnover amongst British nursing staff. *Journal of Occupational Psychology.* 1989;62:55–59.
33. Schaefer J, Moos R. Effects of work stressors and work climate on long-term care staff's job morale and functioning. *Research on Nursing Health.* 1996;19:63–73.
34. Savicki V, Colley E. Burnout in child protective service workers: a longitudinal study. *Journal of Organizational Behavior.* 1994;15:655–666.
35. Grzywacz J, Dooley D. "Good jobs" to "bad jobs": replicated evidence of an employment continuum from two large surveys. *Social Science and Medicine.* 2002;56:1749–1760.
36. Karasek R. Job demands, job decision latitude and mental strain: implications for job design. *Administrative Science Quarterly.* 1979;24:285–308.
37. Pelfrene E, Vlerick P, Mak R, Desmet P, Kornitzer M, De Backer G. Scale reliability and validity of the Karasek "Job Demand-Control-Support" model in the Belstress study. *Work and Stress.* 2001;15:297–313.
38. Griffin J, Fuhrer R, Stansfeld SA, Marmot M. The importance of low control at work and home on depression and anxiety: do these effects vary by gender and social class? *Social Science and Medicine.* 2002;54:783–798.
39. Price R, Choi J, Vinokur A. Links in the chain of adversity following job loss: How financial strain and loss of personal control lead to depression, impaired functioning and poor health. *Journal of Occupational Health Psychology.* 2002;7:302–312.
40. Dooley D, Catalano R. The epidemiology of economic stress. *American Journal of Community Psychology.* 1984;12:387–409.
41. Dew M, Bromet E, Penkower L. Mental health effects of job loss in women. *Psychological Medicine.* 1992;22:751–764.
42. Kasl S, Rodriguez E, Lasch K. The impact of unemployment on health and well-being. In: Dohrenwend B, ed. *Adversity, Stress and Psychopathology.* New York: Oxford University Press; 1998:111–131.
43. Kessler R, House J, Turner J. Unemployment and health in a community sample. *Journal of Health and Social Behavior.* 1987;28:51–59.
44. Gunnell D, Lopatatzidis A, Dorling D, Wehner H, Southall H, Frankel S. Suicide and unemployment in young people: Analysis of trends in England and Wales, 1921–1995. *British Journal of Psychiatry.* 1999;175:263–270.
45. Watson P, Andrews P. Toward a revised evolutionary adaptionist analysis of depression: The social navigation hypothesis. *Journal of Affective Disorders.* 2002;72:1–14.
46. Lewis A. Melancholia: A clinical survey of depressive states. *Journal of Mental Science.* 1934;80:1–43.
47. Price J, Sloman L, Gardner R, Gilbert P, Rohde P. The social competition hypothesis of depression. *British Journal of Psychiatry.* 1994;164:309–315.
48. Sheppard L, Teasdale J. Depressive thinking: changes in schematic mental models of self and world. *Psychological Medicine.* 1996;26:1043–1051.

49. Gannon K, Skowronski J, Betz A. Depressive diligence in social information-processing: Implications for order effects in impressions and for social memory. *Social Cognition.* 1994;12:263–280.
50. Sweeney P, Anderson K, Bailey S. Attributional style in depression: a meta-analytic review. *Journal of Personality and Social Psychology.* 1986;50:9745–9991.
51. Brown J. Evaluations of self and others: self-enhancement biases in social judgments. *Social Cognition.* 1986;4:353–376.
52. Yost J, Weary G. Depression and the correspondent inference bias: Evidence for more effortful cognitive processing. *Personality and Social Psychological Bulletin.* 1996;22:192–200.
53. MacIntyre S, Ellaway A. Ecological approaches: Rediscovering the role of the physical and social environment. In: Berkman L, Kawachi I, eds. *Social Epidemiology.* New York: Oxford University Press; 2000:332–348.
54. Diez-Roux A. Bringing context back into epidemiology: variables and fallacies in multilevel analysis. *American Journal of Public Health.* 1998;88:216–222.
55. Catalano R. Paradigm succession in the study of public health. In: Catalano R, ed. *Health, Behavior, and the Community.* New York: Pergamon; 1979:87–137.
56. Scheuch E. Social context and individual behavior. In: Dogan M, Rockkam S, eds. *Social Ecology.* Boston: MIT Press; 1969:135–155.
57. Koopman J, Lynch J. Individual causal models and population system models in epidemiology. *American Journal of Public Health.* 1999;89:1170–1174.
58. Kearns R. Place and health: towards a reformed medical geography. *Professional Geographer.* 1993;98:139–147.
59. Putman R. *Making Democracy Work: Civic Traditions in Modern Italy.* Princeton, NJ: Princeton University Press; 1993.
60. Putnam R. *Bowling Alone.* New York: Simon & Schuster; 2000.
61. Hanifan L. The rural school community center. *Annals of the American Academy of Political and Social Science.* 1916;67:130–138.
62. George L, Blazer D, Hughes D, Fowler N. Social support and the outcome of major depression. *British Journal of Psychiatry.* 1989;154:478–485.
63. Blazer D. Impact of late-life depression on the social network. *American Journal of Psychiatry.* 1983;140:162–166.
64. Wilkinson R. *Unhealthy Societies: From Inequality to Well-being.* London: Routledge; 1996.
65. Susser M. *Causal Thinking in the Health Sciences: Concepts and Strategies in Epidemiology.* New York: Oxford University Press; 1973.
66. Susser M. The logic in ecological: I; The logic of analysis. *American Journal of Public Health.* 1994; 84: 825–829.
67. Susser M. The logic in ecological: II; The logic in design. *American Journal of Public Health.* 1994;84:830–835.
68. Susser M, Susser E. Choosing a future for epidemiology: I; Eras and paradigms. *American Journal of Public Health.* 1996;86:668–673.
69. Susser M. Does risk factor epidemiology put epidemiology at risk? Peering into the near future. *Journal of Epidemiology and Community Health.* 1998;52:608–611.
70. Rose G. *The Strategy of Preventive Medicine.* Oxford: Oxford University Press; 1992.
71. Durkheim E. *Suicide: A Study in Sociology.* New York: Free Press; 1951.
72. Syme S. To prevent disease: the need for a new approach. In: Blane D, Brunner E, Wilkinson R, eds. *Health and Social Organization.* London: Routledge; 1996:477–480.
73. Schwartz S. The fallacy of the ecological fallacy: the potential misuse of a concept and the consequences. *American Journal of Public Health.* 1994;84:819–824.
74. Riley M. *Sociological Research 1: A Case Approach.* New York: Harcourt Brace; 1963.
75. Scheuch E. Social context and individual behavior. In: Dogan M, Rokkan S, eds. *Quantitative Ecological Analysis in the Social Sciences.* Cambridge, MA: MIT Press; 1969.
76. Ross C, Reynolds J, Geis K. The contingent meaning of neighborhood stability for residents' psychological well-being. *American Sociological Review.* 2000;65:581–597.

77. Silver E, Mulvay E, Swanson J. Neighborhood structural characteristics and mental disorder: Faris and Dunham revisited. *Social Science and Medicine.* 2002;55:1457–1470.
78. Whitley E, Gunnell D, Dorling D, Davey Smith G. Ecological study of social fragmentation, poverty, and suicide. *British Medical Journal.* 1999;319:1034–1037.
79. Wilson WJ. *When Work Disappears: The World of the New Urban Poor.* New York: Vintage Books; 1996.
80. Blazer D, Hughes D, George L. Age and impaired subjective support: predictors of depressive symptoms at one-year follow-up. *Journal of Nervous and Mental Diseases.* 1992;180:172–178.
81. Turner R, Wheaton B, Lloyd D. The epidemiology of social stress. *American Sociological Review.* 1995;60:104–125.
82. Bryk A, Raudenbush S. *Hierarchical Linear Models: Applications and Data Analysis Methods.* Newbury Park, CA: Sage; 1992.

Chapter 10

1. James W. *Psychology: The Briefer Course.* New York: Harper & Row; 1892.
2. Lutz C. Depression and the translation of emotional worlds. In: Kleinman A, Good B, eds. *Culture and Depression: Studies in the Anthropology and Cross-Cultural Psychiatry of Affect and Disorder.* Berkeley: University of California Press; 1985.
3. Wilson E. *Consilience: The Unity of Knowledge.* New York: Knopf; 1998.
4. Akiskal H, McKinney W. Overview of recent research in depression: integration of ten conceptual models into a comprehensive clinical frame. *Archives of General Psychiatry.* 1975;32:285–305.
5. Williams S. Reason, emotion and embodiment: is "mental" health a contradiction of terms? In: Bushfield J, ed. *Rethinking the Sociology of Mental Health.* London: Blackwell; 2001:17–38.
6. Weiner H. Notes on an evolutionary medicine. *Psychosomatic Medicine.* 1998;60:510–520.
7. Nesse R. Is depression an adaptation? *Archives of General Psychiatry.* 2000;57:14–20.
8. Good B, Delvecchio-Good M-J. The meaning of symptoms: A cultural hermeneutic model for clinical practice. In: Eisenberg L, Kleinman A, eds. *The Relevance of Social Science to Medicine.* Boston: Reidel; 1981.
9. Rowe D. Do people make environments or do environments make people? *Annals of the New York Academy of Science.* 2001;935:62–74.
10. Scheff T. *Being Mentally Ill: A Sociological Theory.* Chicago: Aldine; 1966.
11. Hamer D. Rethinking behavior genetics. *Science.* 2002;298:71–72.
12. Caspi A, Sugden K, Moffitt T, et al. Influence of life stress on depression: moderation by a polymorphism in the 5-HTT gene. *Science.* 2003;301:386–389.
13. Ehlers C, Frank E, Kupfer D. Social zeitgebers and biological rhythms. *Archives of General Psychiatry.* 1988;45:948–952.
14. McEwen B. Protective and damaging effects of stress mediators. *New England Journal of Medicine.* 1998;338:171–179.
15. McEwen B, Lasley E. *The End of Stress as We Know It.* Washington, DC: Joseph Henry Press; 2002.
16. Carroll B, Feinberg M, Greden J. A specific laboratory test for the diagnosis of melancholia. *Archives of General Psychiatry.* 1981;38:15–22.
17. Reynolds C, Busse D, Kupfer D, Hoch C, Houch P. Rapid eye movements, and sleep-deprivation as a probe in elderly subjects. *Archives of General Psychiatry.* 1990;47:1128–1136.
18. Sims A. *Symptoms in the Mind: An Introduction to Descriptive Psychopathology.* London: Bailliere Tindall; 1988.
19. Tompkins S. Affect as amplification: Some modifications in theory. In: Plutchik R, Kellerman H, eds. *Emotion: Theory, Research, and Experience.* New York: Academic Press; 1980.
20. Russell J. A circumplex model of affect. *Journal of Personality and Social Psychology.* 1980;39:1161–1178.

21. Lawler E, Thye S. Bringing emotion into social exchange theory. *Annual Review of Sociology.* 1999;25:217–244.
22. Oatley K, Johnson-Laird P. Toward a cognitive theory of emotion. *Cognition and Emotion.* 1987;1:29–50.
23. Darwin C. *The Expression of Emotions in Man and Animals.* New York: Appleton Press; 1896.
24. de Sousa R. *The Rationality of Emotion.* Cambridge, MA: MIT Press; 1995.
25. James W. What is an emotion? *Mind.* 1884;19:188–204.
26. Lyon M. C. Wright Mills meets Prozac: the relevance of "social emotion" to the sociology of health and illness. In: James V, Gabe J, eds. *Health and the Sociology of Emotions.* Oxford: Blackwell; 1996.
27. Damasio A, Grosset P. *Descartes' Error: Emotion, Reason, and the Human Brain.* New York: HarperCollins; 1995.
28. Bowlby J. *Attachment and Loss. Volume 3 (Loss: Sadness and Depression).* London: Penguin; 1980.
29. Sartre J. *Sketch for a Theory of the Emotions.* London: Methuen; 1971 (1939).
30. Flanagan O. *Consciousness Reconsidered.* Cambridge, MA: MIT Press; 1992.
31. Marsella A. Thoughts on cross-cultural studies on the epidemiology of depression. *Culture, Medicine and Psychiatry.* 1978;2:343–357.
32. Holsboer F. Neuroendocrinology of mood disorders. In: Bloom F, Kupfer D, eds. *Psychopharmacology: The Fourth Generation of Progress.* New York: Raven Press; 1995:957–979.
33. Sheline Y, Wany P, Gado M, Csernansky J, Vannier M. Hippocampal atrophy in recurrent major depression. *Proceedings of the National Academy of Sciences.* 1996;93:3908–3913.
34. Wehr T. Chronobiology. In: Sadock B, Sadock V, eds. *Comprehensive Textbook of Psychiatry.* Vol. 1. Philadelphia: Lippincott Williams and Wilkins; 2000:133–142.
35. Minors D, Waterhouse J. Circadian rhythms in general. *Occupational Medicine.* 1990;5:165–182.
36. Wehr T, Rosenthal N. Seasonality and affective illness. *American Journal of Psychiatry.* 1989;146:829–836.
37. McGrath J, Kelly J. *Time and Human Interaction: Toward a Social Psychology of Time.* New York: Guilford; 1986.
38. Wehr T. Effects of sleep and wakefulness on depression and mania. In: Montplaisir J, Godbout R, eds. *Sleep and Biological Rhythms.* London: Oxford University Press; 1990.
39. Larsen R, Kasimatis M. Individual differences in entrainment of mood to the weekly calendar. *Journal of Personality and Social Psychology.* 1990;58:164–171.
40. Reid S, Towell A, Golding J. Seasonality, social zeitgebers and mood variability in entrainment of mood: Implications for seasonal affective disorders. *Journal of Affective Disorders.* 2000;59:47–54.
41. Larsen R. The stability of mood variability: A spectral analytic approach to daily mood assessments. *Journal of Personality and Social Psychology.* 1987;52:1195–1204.
42. Eysenck H, Eysenck M. *Personality and Individual Differences.* New York: Plenum; 1985.
43. Wever R. Order and disorder in human circadian rhythmicity: Possible relations to mental disorders. In: Kupfer D, Monk T, Barchas J, eds. *Biological Rhythms and Mental Disorders.* New York: Guilford; 1988.
44. Brown L, Reynolds C, Monk T, et al. Social rhythm stability following late-life spousal bereavement: associations with depression and sleep impairment. *Psychiatry Research.* 1996;62:161–169.
45. Monk T, Kpufer D, Frank E, Ritenour A. The *Social Rhythm Metric* (SRM): Measuring daily social rhythms over 12 years. *Psychiatry Research.* 1991;36:195–207.
46. Cartwright R. Rapid eye movement sleep characteristics during and after mood-disturbing events. *Archives of General Psychiatry.* 1983;40:197–201.
47. Feather N, Bond J. Time structure and purposeful activity among employed and unemployed university graduates. *Journal of Occupational Psychology.* 1983;56:241–254.

48. Prigerson H, Reynolds C, Machen A, Kupfer D. Stressful life events, social rhythms, and depressive symptoms among the elderly: An examination of hypothesized linkages. *Psychiatry Research.* 1992;51:33–49.

49. Aschoff J, Hoffman K, Pohl H, Wever R. Re-entrainment of circadian rhythms after phase-shifts of the zeitgeber. *Chronobiologia.* 1975;2:23–78.

50. Szuba M, Yager A, Guze B, Allen E, Baxter L. Disruption of social circadian rhythms in major depression: a preliminary report. *Psychiatry Research.* 1992;42:221–230.

51. Sapolsky R. Depression, antidepressants, and the shrinking hippocampus. *Proceedings of the National Academy of Sciences.* 2001;98:12320–12323.

52. Hybels C, Pieper C, Blazer D. Gender differences in the relationship between subthreshold depression and mortality in a community sample of older adults. *American Journal of Geriatric Psychiatry.* 2002;10:283–291.

53. Darwin F, ed. *The Life and Letters of Charles Darwin.* University Press of the Pacific; 2001.

54. Blazer DG, Kessler RC, McGonagle KA, Swartz MS. The prevalence and distribution of major depression in the National Comorbidity Survey. *American Journal of Psychiatry.* 1994;151:979–986.

55. Kendler K, Gardner C. Boundaries of major depression: an evaluation of *DSM–IV* criteria. *American Journal of Psychiatry.* 1998;155:172–177.

56. Judd L, Akiskal H. *Delineating the Longitudinal Structure of Depressive Illness: Beyond Thresholds and Subtypes.* Nuremberg, Germany: German College of Neuropsychopharmacology; October 1999.

57. Coyne J, Kessler R, Tal M, Turnbull J. Living with a depressed person. *Journal of Consulting and Clinical Psychology.* 1987;55:347–352.

58. Lewis A. Melancholia: a clinical survey of depressive states. *Journal of Mental Science.* 1934;80:1–43.

59. Klerman G. Depression and adaptation. In: Friedman R, Katz M, eds. *The Psychology of Depression.* Washington, DC: V.H. Winston & Sons; 1974:127–156.

60. Engel G, Schamle A. Conservation-withdrawal: a primary regulatory process for organismic homeostasis. In: Porter R, Night J, eds. *Physiology, Emotion, and Psychosomatic Illness.* Amsterdam: Associated Scientific Publishers; 1972:57–85.

61. Price J. The dominance hierarchy and the evolution of mental illness. *Lancet.* 1967;2:243–246.

62. Sloman L, Price J, Gilbert P, Gardner R. Adaptive function of depression: psychotherapeutic implications. *American Journal of Psychotherapy.* 1994;48:401–416.

63. Singh-Manoux A, Adler N, Marmot M. Subjective social status: its determinants and its association with measures of ill-health in the Whitehall II study. *Social Science and Medicine.* 2003;56:1321–1333.

64. Holsboer F. Animal models of mood disorders. In: Charney D, Nestler E, Bunney B, eds. *Neurobiology of Mental Illness.* New York: Oxford University Press; 1999:317–332.

65. Willner P, Muscat R, Papp M. Chronic mild stress-induced anhedonia: a realistic animal model of depression. *Neuroscience and Biobehavioral Review.* 1992;16:525–534.

66. Hofer M. Relationships as regulators: a psychobiologic perspective on bereavement. *Psychosomatic Medicine.* 1984;46:183–197.

67. McKinney W, Bunney W. Animal model of depression: I. Review of evidence: implications for research. *Archives of General Psychiatry.* 1969;21:240–248.

68. Bibring E. The mechanism of depression. In: Grenacre P, ed. *Affective Disorders.* New York: International Universities Press; 1953.

69. Hamburg D. Coping behavior in life-threatening circumstances. *Psychotherapeutic Psychosomatics.* 1974;23:13–25.

70. Hyland M. Control theory interpretation of psychological mechanisms of depression: comparison and integration of several theories. *Psychological Bulletin.* 1987;102:109–121.

71. Monroe S, Simons A. Diathesis-stress research: implications for the depressive disorders. *Psychological Bulletin.* 1991;110:406–425.

72. Brown GW, Craig TKJ, Harris TO. Depression: Distress or disease? Some epidemiological considerations. *British Journal of Psychiatry.* 1985;147:612–622.

73. Eaton J, Weil R. *Culture and Mental Disorders*. New York: Free Press; 1976.
74. Kahnemann D, Deiner E, Schwarz N. *Well-being: Foundations of Hedonic Psychology*. New York: Russell Sage Foundation; 1999.
75. Cross-National Collaborative Group. The changing rate of major depression. *Journal of the American Medical Association*. 1992;268:3098–3105.
76. Seligman MEP. Learned helplessness. *Annual Review of Medicine*. 1972;23:407.

Chapter 11

1. Huxley A. *Brave New World*. New York: Harper & Row; 1932.
2. Horwitz A. *Creating Mental Illness*. Chicago: University of Chicago Press; 2002.
3. Hobson J, Leonard J. *Out of Its Mind: Psychiatry in Crisis; A Call for Reform*. New York: Perseus Publishing; 2001.
4. Blazer D. *Freud vs. God: How Psychiatry Lost Its Soul and Christianity Lost Its Mind*. Downers Grove, IL: InterVarsity Press; 1998.
5. Breggin P. *Toxic Psychiatry*. New York: St. Martin's; 1991.
6. Ross C, Pam A. *Pseudoscience in Biological Psychiatry*. New York: John Wiley & Sons; 1995.
7. Mills C. *The Sociological Imagination*. New York: Oxford University Press; 1959.
8. Orwell G. *Nineteen Eighty-Four*. Oxford: Clarendon; 1948.
9. Ryan A. *Bertrand Russell: A Political Life*. New York: Oxford University Press; 1988.
10. Russell B. *The Scientific Outlook*. New York: Norton; 1931.
11. Huxley A. *Brave New World Revisited*. New York: Harper & Brothers; 1958.
12. Percy W. *The Thanatos Syndrome*. New York: Farrar, Straus & Giroux; 1987.
13. Healy D. *The Antidepressant Era*. Boston: Harvard University Press; 1997.
14. Valenstein E. *Blaming the Brain*. New York: Free Press; 1998.
15. American Psychiatric Association. *Diagnostic and Statistical Manual of Mental Disorders*. 4th ed., text revision. Washington, DC: Author; 2000.
16. Persons J. The advantages of studying psychological phenomenon rather than psychiatric diagnoses. *American Psychologist*. 1986;41:1252–1260.
17. Shapiro A, Shapiro E. *The Powerful Placebo: From Ancient Priest to Modern Physician*. Baltimore: Johns Hopkins University Press; 1997.
18. Quitkin F. Placebos, drug effects, and study design: a clinician's guide. *American Journal of Psychiatry*. 1999;156:829–836.
19. Leuchter A, Cook I, Witte E, Morgan M, Abrams M. Changes in brain function of depressed subjects during treatment with placebo. *American Journal of Psychiatry*. 2002; 159:122–129.
20. Jacobson S. Overselling depression to old folks. *Atlantic Monthly*. 1995:46–51.
21. Kramer P. *Listening to Prozac*. New York: Penguin; 1997.
22. Strauss J, Gabriel K, Kokes R. Do psychiatric patients fit their diagnoses? Patterns of symptomatology as described with a biplot. *Journal of Nervous and Mental Diseases*. 1981;167:105–113.
23. Judd L, Rapaport M, Paulus M, Brown J. Subsyndromal symptomatic depression: A new mood disorder? *Journal of Clinical Psychiatry*. 1994;55(4, Suppl.):18–28.
24. Broadhead W, Blazer D, George L, Tse C. Depression, disability days and days lost from work: A prospective epidemiologic survey. *Journal of the American Medical Association*. 1990;264:2524–2528.
25. Beekman A, Deeg D, van Tilberg T, Smit J, Hooijer C, van Tilberg W. Major and minor depression in later life: A study of prevalence and risk factors. *Journal of Affective Disorders*. 1995;36:65–75.
26. Snaith R. The concepts of mild depression. *British Journal of Psychiatry*. 1987;150:387–393.
27. *ICD-10 Classification of Mental and Behavioural Disorders: Diagnostic Criteria for Research*. Geneva: World Health Organization; 1993.

28. Judd LL, Akiskal HS, Paulus MP. The role and clinical significance of subsyndromal depressive symptoms (SSD) in unipolar major depressive disorder. *Journal of Affective Disorders.* 1997;45(1–2):5–17.
29. Goodwin D, Guze S. *Psychiatric Diagnosis.* 2nd ed. New York: Oxford University Press; 1979.
30. Blazer D, Woodbury M, Hughes D, et al. A statistical analysis of the classification of depression in a mixed community and clinical sample. *Journal of Affective Disorders.* 1989;16:11–20.

Index

A

Acute combat stress reaction, 123
Adaptation
    depression as, 195, 196
    psychotherapeutic interventions
        emphasizing, 165
Affect, 187
Affective reaction, 49
Affluence, as predictor of depression, 163
Age effects, 114–115
Age of anxiety, 3
Alcohol abuse, comorbidity with
    depression, 112
Alienation
    and attachment to subcultures, 156
    in Civil War, 120
    in postmodern psyche, 151
Allostatic load, 16–17, 183, 184, 193–198,
    197
Altruistic suicide, 62, 85
Ambulatory psychotherapy, 71
American imperialism, revival of, 136
American Psychiatric Association, 5
Anatomy of Melancholy, 42, 44
Animal models, 196
Anomic suicide, 62, 85
Antibiotics use, history of, 211
Antidepressant Era, The, 55
Antidepressant medications, 10
    appropriate *vs.* inappropriate use of,
        211–212
    coverage by health insurance, 36
    effectiveness of, 24, 53
    Huxley's predictions on, 204
    overprescription of, 200
    role of, 52–54
    widespread use of, 17

Antipsychiatry movement, 12, 91–93
    future avoidance of, 211
Anxiety, in 21st century, 136
Artaeus of Cappadocia, 41
Aspirin, as metaphor for medication
    overuse, 201–202
Assertiveness community training program,
    86
Attribution of symptoms, 131–133
Authority, postmodern abolishment of, 157
Autonomous depression, 50–51
Autonomy
    as hallmark of modernity, 141, 142
    isolation due to, 144

B

Beck Depression Inventory, 107
Bereavement, disruption of social rhythms
    by, 192–193
Beyond Prozac, 53, 165
Biblical examples, 44–46
Biliousness, 41
Binary model of depression, 50
Biological diathesis, 207
Biological psychiatry, 16, 87
    eclipse of social psychiatry by, 71
Biological reductionism, 47
Biological rhythms, emotion and, 190–193
Biological studies, hegemony of, 81
Biological vulnerability, 10
Biology, inseparable from social realm, 3
Biology *vs.* society debate, 181
Biomedical model
    of major depression, 23–25
    shift to, 89
Bipolar disorder, and happiness, 187
Black bile, 41

pharmacological *vs.* psychotherapeutic
    interventions, 165
Financial strain, as factor in depression,
    172
Fixed ideas, about illness, 130–131
Foucault, Michel, 91, 150
Framing, 15, 25
    and attribution of symptoms, 132–133
    of emotional response to social stress,
        132
Frequency of depression, historical,
    114–115
Freud, Sigmund, 68
    Civilization and its Discontents, 139
    view of civilization, 61–62
*Freud vs. God: How Psychiatry Lost Its Soul
    and Christianity Lost Its Mind*, 199
Functional autonomy, 165

G
Genes *vs.* environment debate, 181, 183
Genetic model, 88
    and Human Genome Project, 90
Genetic predisposition, 182
Geographical responsibility, 60
Germ theory of disease, 174
Germany, social psychiatry in, 64
Giants, disappearance from psychiatry, 143
Good-bye to All That: An Autobiography,
    122
Great Society program, 70
Gross stress reaction, 123
Group for Advancement of Psychiatry, 70
Gulf War syndrome, 7–8, 15, 117, 118,
    126–129
    biological causes of, 128–129
    case study, 118–119

H
Happiness, and bipolar disorder, 187
Health care workers, psychological morbidity
    among, 170–171
Health-related behavior, 43
Heart of Darkness, 145
Heavy sodium, as metaphor for medication
    overuse, 205
Heredity
    as base of manic-depressive illness, 48
    contribution to melancholy, 43
Hierarchical linear regression, 178
Hierarchy conflicts, 195
Homelessness, and deinstitutionalization,
    91
Homeostasis, and allostatic load, 193–194
Hope

loss as core symptom of depression,
    151–152
postmodern loss of, 150, 151
Hormonal cycling, 191
Humanization of services, 60
Humoral theory of medicine, 41–42
Huxley, Aldous, 17, 199–201, 202–203
Hypothalamic-pituitary-adrenal system, 194
    in animal model studies, 196
Hysterical epidemics, 133
Hysterical paralysis, 116, 132

I
Identity
    community no longer basis of, 142
    importance of personal and communal,
        145
    loss in postmodern psyche, 154–155
Ifaluk culture, emotions in, 189–190
Illiberal Education, 149
Illness behavior, 31
Illness categories, 165
Illness onset, social and cultural contributions
    to, 6
Immune system, allostatic links to brain
    and endocrine system, 194
Inadequate jobs, *vs.* unemployment, 171
Individual risk-factor approach
    dependence on community setting, 177
    limitations of, 176–177
    separating from neighborhood risk, 178
Infant mortality rates, and social cohesion,
    176
Institute of Medicine of the National
    Academies, 164
Insurance coverage
    for physical diseases, 55
    for treatment of depression, 36
Integrated communities, 103
International Classification of Disease, 111
Interpersonal psychotherapy, 66
Interventions
    community-wide, 6
    efficacy of, 37
    range limited by medicalization of
        depression, 35
Isolation
    stemming from autonomy, 144
    and suicide, 115

J
James, William, 47–48, 187–188
Japan, depression in contemporary, 9
Job, despair of, 45
Job control, 171–172, 173, 211